THE FELLĀHĪN OF UPPER EGYPT

ROPE-MAKING AT AKHMĪM

The man seated in the centre of the picture is twisting the split and softened strands into a thin cord. See p. 161.

THE FELLĀHĪN OF UPPER EGYPT

THEIR RELIGIOUS, SOCIAL AND INDUSTRIAL LIFE
WITH SPECIAL REFERENCE
TO SURVIVALS FROM ANCIENT TIMES

Winifred S. Blackman

With a Foreword by

R. R. MARETT

FRANK CASS & CO. LTD.
1968

Published by
FRANK CASS AND COMPANY LIMITED
67 Great Russell Street, London WC1
by arrangement with George G. Harrap & Co. Ltd.

First edition	1927
New impression	1968

Printed in Great Britain by
Thomas Nelson (Printers) Ltd., London and Edinburgh

TO

MY MANY EGYPTIAN FRIENDS

I DEDICATE THIS BOOK

FOREWORD

HERODOTUS, the father of anthropology, might have been surprised to learn that he was destined to number daughters as well as sons among his intellectual progeny. There can be no doubt, however, that Miss Blackman can justly claim to be reckoned in the direct line of his descendants. In Egypt, her chosen field of research, Herodotus gathered some of his most valuable material. His method too was like hers, namely, to take down the traditional lore of the folk as it came fresh and straight from their lips. The ideal collector of folklore must have a genius for hob-nobbing. From lettered priest to unlettered peasant, all classes of the population must be on gossiping terms with him. Of course, he does not plague them with set questions. Though he keeps a note-book handy he does not flourish it in their faces. He makes it his business not so much to talk as to listen. If the soul of the people is to be revealed they must be overheard as, all unconscious of the presence of the stranger, they fuss and chatter about the affairs of the hour—about the prices of the market and the state of the crops, about yesterday's funeral and to-morrow's wedding, about the donkey's sore back and the sore eyes of the baby. The secret, in short, is to observe unobserved. The folklorist should be capable of melting like a disembodied spirit into the atmosphere of the local life. Or, if he is to be noticeable at all, let it at least be in some character that is strictly consonant with his surroundings. Thus Miss Blackman might possibly have preferred to dispense altogether with her widespread reputation for healing power. Yet to go about trailing clouds of contagious virtue was at all events more in keeping with prevailing notions of normal behaviour than if they had happened, say, to be clouds of exotic scent.

Moreover, not only is anthropology the product of friendly relations, but it likewise produces them. I am thinking more especially of the great kindness which Miss Blackman experienced everywhere at the hands of the leading officials of Egypt. They were evidently in full sympathy with her scientific aims. Unfortunately, politics and even religion cannot always avoid conforming to lines of ethnic cleavage too closely to prove wholly effective instruments of mutual understanding. Science, on the other hand, is absolutely disinterested in spirit. Its discoveries are for the whole world to enjoy. There can be no rivalry between the nations as regards their respective shares in the creation of knowledge except in so far as it takes the form of honourable competition in the training of sound scholars. The time is doubtless coming when more Egyptians will come forward as investigators duly educated in the critical use of evidence; and they will be welcome.

After all, it is hard to say whether the Egyptians themselves or the rest of the world have more to gain from the study of the age-long history of Egypt and of the no less enduring individuality of its people. The country is self-contained enough, thanks to the geographical barriers that shut in the Nile Valley, to maintain a civilization answering to its own needs. Even physically the Egyptian type breeds true to itself. As often as racial intermixture occurs, the foreign strain would seem to become recessive to the point of extinction. On the other hand, Egypt is situated at the meeting-point of three continents. It presides over the junction of the Western and Eastern water-ways of the Old World. How far its influence has extended, whether by direct or by indirect propagation, at various critical periods of history is a problem, much discussed at the present moment, on which the most distant regions may be able to throw light. Any diffusion of culture, however, tends to fade out toward its circumference, and is only to be fully understood by intensive study at the centre. In the case of Egypt it is possible to grasp the complex nature of the centrifugal force thence set in motion all the more thoroughly because there is literary as well as material evidence at the disposal of the archæologist. Silent monuments, too, often form the only yield of the spade. Even pictures speak at best in riddles. Literature, however, when it came into existence in Egypt or in Mesopotamia could in some measure disclose that ethnic psychology which alone is the key to genuine history.

Nevertheless, the psychic life of a people is but partially and imperfectly reflected in its literature. Just as in the individual the unconscious part of the mind may be supremely determinative of the total character, so in a community the non-literary and largely inarticulate classes may do much by way of help or hindrance to shape its destiny. The people of Egypt, having retained their self-identity unimpaired during at least five millennia, a record which puts all other nations into the shade, can be studied now so as to frame a fair estimate of what, psychologically, they have always been. Miss Blackman's work having been mainly among the folk—that portion of the society whose hidden but none the less active impulses and beliefs govern the making of history as it were from below—she is contributing just what is needed to afford an adequate explanation of Egypt's civilizing activity as a spiritual movement.

A word in conclusion as to the usefulness of the woman anthropologist. She is sympathetic by nature. She is not politically suspect. She can get at the women, who as the educators of the rising generation exercise an immense influence on the formation of mental habits. In short, anthropology is as much a woman's job as a man's. It only remains to add that a woman who wishes to be useful in this way must follow Miss Blackman's example, and go through a suitable training before she enters the field.

R. R. MARETT

PREFACE

THIS book represents but a small portion of the work upon which I have been engaged in Egypt during the last six years. I have spent, on an average, six months annually in the country, living almost entirely among the *fellāḥīn*. I wish to make it quite clear to my readers that the customs and beliefs, and the general manner of life, described in this book represent those of the peasants only; by the upper classes they have, of course, long been discarded. These customs and beliefs are of great importance and interest in themselves, but the fact that most of them are very ancient makes it still more urgent that they should be adequately studied and recorded. Already my researches have thrown light on points hitherto obscure to students of ancient Egypt; hence this book may, I hope, be not only an addition to anthropological knowledge, but also a contribution to Egyptology.

It has been my aim to describe the life of the modern inhabitants of the Nile Valley in the simplest way, avoiding technical language, for my purpose in writing this book has been to interest the general public and present them with a readable and, at the same time, true description of the peasants of Egypt.

I want to emphasize the fact that though the contents of this book form but a tithe of the information I have collected, yet even so I am only at the beginning of my work. Many years of research still lie ahead of me, for the sources of information are very far from exhausted. When my work is more nearly complete my intention is to produce a large and strictly scientific volume on the beliefs and practices and the social and industrial life of the modern Egyptians.

I have endeavoured to be strictly accurate in all my statements. Every custom and belief here dealt with has been most carefully inquired into before I committed it to paper. Nevertheless, those who are experienced field-workers in anthropology know how easy it is to make mistakes and to misunderstand, even after careful investigation, the true inwardness of things. I therefore invite criticism, and I hope that, if I have misunderstood a point, my Egyptian friends will not hesitate to inform me. I am most anxious that educated Egyptians should recognize the importance of the anthropology and folklore of their country, and my earnest hope is that some of them will be persuaded to take up this study. They surely, if they received the proper training, would be best able to undertake anthropological research among their own people. Before very long I much hope that I may see a flourishing anthropological institute established in Cairo, forming a centre for all such research work, not only in Egypt itself, but in adjacent countries—for who knows how far the influence of ancient Egypt has extended? Some writers in England even postulate an almost world-wide diffusion of Egyptian culture!

I have said that I am only at the beginning of my work. I have not as yet touched Lower Egypt, and my idea is to include in my researches not only the whole of Egypt proper, but the Egyptian Oases and Lower Nubia. I must also undertake a far more intensive study of the provinces which I have already visited, carefully recording all local differences. This of course requires many more years of hard work.

The cult of Muslim sheikhs and Coptic saints is a subject in which I have particularly interested myself. I have not dealt with it here in detail, as I hope shortly to bring out a book dealing solely with the beliefs, ceremonies, and mythology connected with these venerated persons.

I am glad to have this opportunity of expressing my sincere thanks to the Trustees of the Percy Sladen Memorial Fund for the grants which they have made me during the last four years, and to the Royal Society and the Committee for Anthropology in Oxford for supplementary grants. I owe much also to the encouragement and kindly appreciation of my work which I have received from so many in the University and elsewhere, and to the support afforded me by the special committee appointed by the British Association to promote the furtherance of my researches. To the officials in Egypt and to the Egyptians generally I owe more than I can express. Without the assistance and facilities afforded me by the officials, and the friendliness I have encountered among all classes alike, it would have been quite impossible for me to have accomplished the work I have done. Some of the officials have personally assisted me in my investigations, and the way the peasants have welcomed me into their lives has enabled me to get into much closer touch with them than is possible for the ordinary foreigner. I can truly say that the kindness generally that I have received has made the years which I have spent in Egypt the happiest in my life. My desire is that I may be able to continue my work and leave behind me a true record of the many interesting and ancient customs of that most attractive country.

To my brother, Dr A. M. Blackman, I am indebted for all the ancient analogies. Not only so, but he has devoted hours to the careful perusal of my manuscript, and moreover has seen this book through the press and made all the indexes, thus enabling me to carry on uninterruptedly my researches in Egypt. If, therefore, the book achieves any success I feel that much of that success will be due to him.

To the Councils of the Royal Anthropological Institute and of the Folklore Society, to the Committee of the Egypt Exploration Society, to the publishers of *Discovery* (Messrs Benn), and to the editors of *The Manchester Guardian* and *The Evening News* I am indebted for permission to include in this book articles of mine that have already appeared in their various journals and papers.

To Professor J. L. Myres I must here express my sincere thanks for reading through all the proofs in collaboration with my brother; and to Mr E. S. Thomas, late of the Egyptian Ministry of Finance, and now Assistant in the Pitt-Rivers Museum in Oxford, thanks are due for supplying me with better translations of the Arabic charms, etc., than I had before.

All the photographs, I should state, have been taken by myself, with the exception of a few which were taken in 1920 by my friend Mr D. J. V. Forster, of Pembroke College, Oxford, at my request, on the occasions when he was present with me at the ceremonies which they illustrate.

I have purposely suppressed the names of people and villages in nearly every instance as I do not think it would be either desirable or fair (see p. 231) to publish them in a semi-popular book of this kind.

Finally, I should like to point out that with the spread of education the old customs and beliefs are already beginning to die out. It is thus most important that they should be recorded at once, before they suffer complete extinction. I hope, therefore, that my work may not be left unfinished for lack of financial support, and that this book may awaken sufficient interest in Egypt and in England to induce those who have the means and the power to support my researches for some years to come and to enable me to bring them to a successful conclusion.

WINIFRED S. BLACKMAN

CONTENTS

ILLUSTRATIONS

ILLUSTRATIONS

THE FELLĀḤĪN OF UPPER EGYPT

ILLUSTRATIONS

THE FELLĀḤĪN OF UPPER EGYPT

CHAPTER I

EGYPTIAN VILLAGES AND THEIR INHABITANTS

THE natural barriers of Egypt (Fig. 1) have enabled the inhabitants, particularly those of the upper country, to live in comparative isolation throughout the whole of their history. On the north side lies the sea, along the east and west sides stretch vast, almost waterless deserts, while to the south ingress by way of the Nile is impeded by a series of cataracts. Their geographical isolation has doubtless been responsible for the characteristic conservatism of the Egyptian peasants. This conservatism is particularly apparent in their religious and social customs and their commoner industries, which, as will be more especially seen in the final chapter, have remained almost, if not entirely, unchanged from Pharaonic times.

The vast solitudes of the deserts are terrifying to the country folk, most of whom, up to the present day, cannot be induced to traverse even the lower fringes of those wastes after sunset (see Fig. 2). Fear of hyenas, and, still more, fear of *ʿafārīt*,[1] forbids any man to venture beyond the cultivation at night. The ordinary peasant, unless he is obliged to remain in the fields either to protect his crops or to watch over his sheep and goats, returns to his village before sunset, remaining there until just before the dawn of the following day.

The deserts have proved themselves valuable defences against invasion, the peoples who conquered the country at different periods of its history having usually entered it from the north-east. These invaders do not seem to have left any very marked impression on the physical aspect of the Upper Egyptians at any rate; most of these still bear a striking facial resemblance to the ancient inhabitants of the land whom we see depicted on the walls of the temples and tomb-chapels and in the portrait-statues of the Old,

[1] See Chapter XIV.

Middle, and New Kingdoms. What really is beginning to affect the racial purity of the Egyptians is the presence among them of the descendants of negro slaves, who have been imported in large numbers by the Arabs in comparatively recent times. Many of them are now settled in certain of the villages, where they have

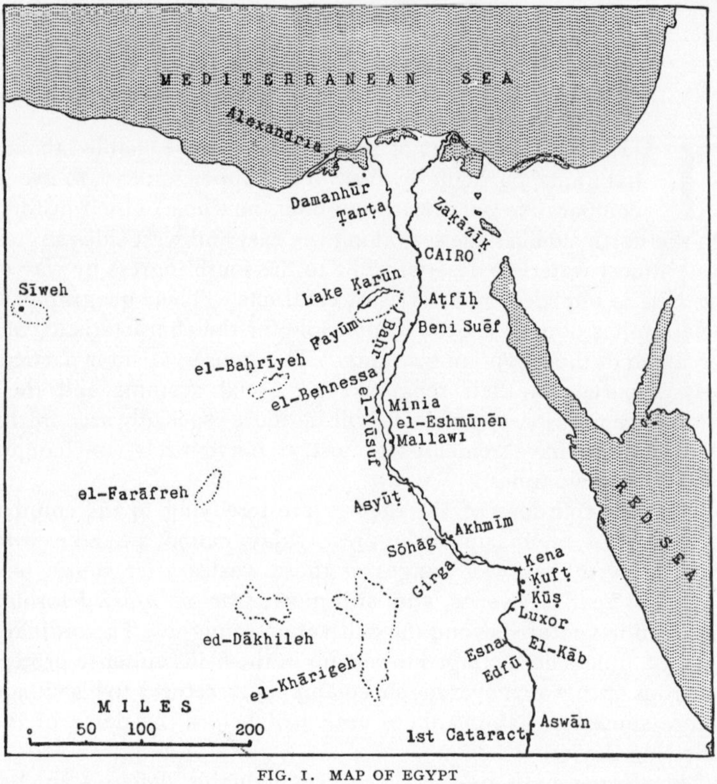

FIG. I. MAP OF EGYPT

married among themselves or with the *fellāḥīn*, the result being that the population of such villages is almost entirely composed of black, or half-black, people. So far as I have observed, this negroid element is particularly marked in the Fayūm and Beni Ṣuēf, and on the edge of the cultivation in Minia and Asyūṭ provinces, where large numbers of Arabs have been settled for several generations.

The influence of the deserts may be seen in Egyptian folk-tales, many of which tell of encounters there with *ʿafārīt* and other supernatural beings. Secret caves in "the mountain," as the people call the steep, sometimes almost precipitous ascent to the high-desert plateau, also enter into the adventures recounted by the village story-tellers; these 'caves' are, of course, the ancient rock-hewn tomb-chapels with which the outer face of "the mountain" is in some places honeycombed (see Fig. 3).

Egypt is a land of contrasts, the marked difference between the very fertile Nile Valley and the arid, waterless deserts on either

FIG. 2. EDGE OF THE HIGH-DESERT PLATEAU, THE LOWER DESERT, AND IN THE DISTANCE THE CULTIVATION

side of it striking the eye of every visitor to the country. These physical features are, I think, reflected in the character of the peasants, for it is a remarkable fact that the most divergent traits of character can be seen in a single individual. The Egyptian peasants, in spite of much poverty and sickness, and with few amusements to break the monotony of their lives, are as a whole a wonderfully cheerful and contented people. They are very quick of comprehension, of ready wit, dearly loving a joke, even if directed against themselves, usually blessed with a retentive memory, light-hearted, kindly, and very hospitable; they are also very hard-working. At the same time they are very emotional, highly strung, most inflammable, generally very ignorant, and nearly always conspicuously lacking in self-control.

Thus a man normally of a quiet, gentle, and peaceful disposition may on the spur of the moment commit some brutal murder. One year when I was staying in a small, out-of-the-way village in Upper Egypt a man killed a neighbour in a terrible way because he had stolen some onions from his (the murderer's) field. The moment after he had committed the crime he was weeping over the body of his victim !

One of the besetting sins of the Egyptian *fellāḥīn* is jealousy, which often becomes such a raging passion that a jealous man or

FIG. 3. THE FACE OF "THE MOUNTAIN" AND ENTRANCES TO ANCIENT TOMB-CHAPELS

woman is rendered capable of committing any violent crime. The women are liable to be jealous of one another's children, the wives about their husbands, the men of each other's prosperity or position, and so on to an endless degree. I do not wish to imply that jealousy is uncommon in other parts of the world, but I certainly think that it has a large share in the general make-up of the Egyptian character.

Again, the love of money tends to make them very avaricious, and is the cause of many serious troubles among them. On the other hand, they are capable of, and often actually perform, most generous actions, both in the giving of money and in the forgiveness of an injury. Quarrels between individuals, occasionally very violent ones, are common in the villages, but if a judicious peacemaker arrives in time a serious disturbance can usually be avoided.

The accounts given in subsequent chapters of blood-feuds, inter-village fights, and other crimes of violence should not, however, cause the reader to pass too harsh a judgment on the Egyptian peasants if he will but bear in mind that the violent contrasts in the physical features of the country are reflected in the psychology of the inhabitants collectively and individually.

The *fellāḥīn* form the bulk of the population of Egypt, and the

FIG. 4. A VILLAGE ON THE BANKS OF THE BAḤR EL-YŪSUF

larger number of them are Muslims. The Copts, who at one time were far more numerous than they are at the present day, are scattered about all over the country, though in a few towns and villages they may form the greater part of the population. The word ' Copt,' it must be borne in mind, does not denote a racial, but rather a religious, distinction.

The Beduins (Arabic *Bedu*, singular *Bedawī*), many of whom still lead a more or less nomadic desert life, and the Arabs, who have settled down as cultivators of the soil, also form a not inconsiderable portion of the population. Their facial features and certain styles of dress distinguish them from the native inhabitants. Nubians, Sudan negroes, Turks, Greeks, Syrians, and Jews are also to be found in large numbers, the four latter peoples chiefly in Lower Egypt, though they do not altogether confine themselves to the northern part of the country. Europeans of various nationalities have for many years past settled in Egypt, most of them being engaged in business connected with the production and sale of cotton, sugar, and the like.

The villages of Egypt (see Fig. 4), as seen from the railway-carriage or from points of vantage in the cultivation, present a most picturesque appearance. They are generally surrounded with palm-groves, often very extensive, while palm-trees also grow actually among the houses, affording a welcome shelter from the

FIG. 5. A PIGEON-HOUSE

heat. These palm-girt villages are dotted about all over the cultivation, the brilliant green of which presents a startling contrast to the immediately adjacent, and seemingly endless, desert. Sometimes a village encroaches right on to the edge of the desert, the upper slopes of which tower above it, forming a most romantic background. During the period of inundation the villages, which stand on a somewhat higher level than the surrounding cultivation, appear like palm-encircled islands in a vast inland sea, a geographical feature also remarked upon by Herodotus.[1]

Pigeon-houses (see Fig. 5) are prominent architectural features in a village. They are sometimes in the form of towers, with sloping, white-washed mud walls, surmounted by several layers of large pottery jars placed side by side in rows. Every jar has a hole in the base, for the ingress and egress of the pigeons. Some-

[1] ii, 97.

times the pigeon-houses are painted with simple white designs. This is done, so I was told in one or two villages, because the birds like it, and it draws them back to their own houses ! Pigeons are kept chiefly for the sake of the dung, which is considered to be a valuable fertilizer for the fields. Probably, however, more harm than good is done to the crops by the breeding of these birds, for they accumulate in large flocks when the corn is ripening, and are with difficulty dispersed by men and boys armed with slings and stones.

FIG. 6. A VILLAGE HOUSE OF THE BETTER SORT

The houses of the peasants, in many cases mere hovels, are made of crude bricks, sometimes covered over with mud plastering. In the better houses (see Fig. 6) there is generally a flight of steps leading to an upper story, where there may be a sitting-room (*mandareh*), furnished with benches (called *dikak*, singular *dikkeh*), which are covered with rugs and supplied with cushions. The room in which the foodstuffs are kept is also usually in this upper story. The flat roof (Fig. 7) is a pleasant place on which to sit and watch the life in the streets below ; it also serves as a hen-run, dog- and cat-run, a drying-ground, and is put to other utilitarian purposes. Here, for example, are stored huge bundles of sticks and dry maize-stalks (called *būṣ*), together with quantities of cakes of cow- and buffalo-dung, neatly stacked in rows, which are used with the sticks or *būṣ* as fuel. Here, too, are set up the household granaries.

The houses, especially the better-built ones, admirably suit the Egyptian climate. There is only one thing lacking to make them really pleasant places to live in, and that is greater cleanliness within the houses themselves and without in the streets. The salvation of the people lies in the fact that they lead essentially an outdoor life, the houses being regarded almost solely as places to sleep and cook in ; otherwise the mortality would be considerably higher than it is.

FIG. 7. VIEW OVER THE HOUSE-TOPS

I know how comfortable a well-kept house of the better kind can be, having lived in one for five months. This house stood on a high mound formed by the *débris* of earlier buildings ; for in Egypt, when a house has collapsed or has been pulled down, the mass of rubbish is not necessarily removed, but when it has been sufficiently levelled another house is erected on the top of it. The whole of the upper floor of this house was placed at my disposal, my apartments consisting of a small bedroom and a sitting-room. The latter had two unglazed but shuttered windows, from which I could look over the tops of the neighbouring houses and be a spectator of the varied life on the roofs. Outside the rooms was a partly covered passage, from which a glorious view of the sunsets could be obtained.

The villages are intersected by narrow lanes—in most cases they can hardly be dignified by the name of streets—progress along which is often impeded, sometimes almost entirely blocked, by piles of refuse and mud. In some of the larger villages there may be one or two broader streets, forming the chief thoroughfares (Fig. 8). At the side of one of the narrow lanes there may be an open space in which palm-trees grow (Fig. 9), and here the village weaver often arranges the warp for his cloth, the threads being attached to the trunks of two of the trees (Fig. 10). When this process is completed the warp is taken indoors and attached to the

FIG. 8. A VILLAGE STREET

loom, which usually stands in a somewhat dark room, with mud-coloured walls, and so small in size that it is impossible to obtain a satisfactory photograph.

Itinerant vendors ply their trades up and down these tortuous village lanes, uttering their characteristic cries. For example, the onion-seller advertises his wares by calling out, " Oh, onion, sweet as honey ! " The cries are usually intoned in a minor key, sounding to the uninitiated more like a plaintive chant than the proclamation of goods for sale. Another hawker may trade in coloured cotton cloths, printed with various designs to suit all tastes. He usually conveys his goods about on a small hand-cart. From such humble beginnings more than one fortune has been made, for the peasants are fond of hoarding their money, their daily living costing them but little. In time the small sums thus carefully put by amount to a considerable total, which may be profitably invested. Thanks to a lucky deal in cotton, or some other venture, the former humble itinerant vendor finds himself well on the way to becoming a man of substance.

The house-doors are often decorated with a china plate or saucer fixed into the masonry above the lintel, as a charm against the evil eye. A house may also be decorated with coloured line-drawings of camels, boats, trains, trees, and other objects, some hardly

FIG. 9. A VILLAGE STREET

identifiable. Such artistic efforts denote that one or more members of the family inhabiting the house have performed the pilgrimage to Mecca, the design representing the various objects seen by the pilgrim on his way to the sacred city.

The interiors of the villages are often very picturesque, in spite of the dirt and squalor usually found in them. The Arabs are far more particular in this respect, their villages and settlements being much cleaner in every way than those of the Egyptian peasants. This difference between the two races is so marked that I can almost always tell if a village is Arab or Egyptian directly I enter it.

A mosque is to be found in every village, and in many places there are three or four such buildings. Five times a day a *mueddin* chants the call to prayer from each mosque—from the minaret if there is one—and the resonant voices of these officiants may be heard far beyond the confines of the village.

An old graveyard often stands in the middle of a village, probably indicating the older boundary, the houses built beyond it having been erected later owing to the increasing population (see below, p. 72 and Fig. 32). A whitewashed building, crowned with

FIG. 10. WARP-THREADS ATTACHED TO PALM-TREES

a dome, stands, perhaps, on the highest point of the burial-ground, indicating the last resting-place of a sheikh, or holy man, or, at any rate, erected in his honour. Candles are usually lighted in the building on "the night of Friday"—*i.e.*, the night preceding the Friday—in commemoration of the sheikh. Such lights are, in most cases, the only illumination out of doors to guide the late wayfarer. These buildings, and there are often several in or around one village, are prominent architectural features, standing up with their whitewashed walls and domes above, and in glaring contrast to, the mud houses and hovels of the peasants.

Shops of different kinds are situated in the wider streets or lanes, with open fronts which can be closed with wooden shutters when the owners are away (Fig. 11). Through the open shop-fronts the tailors are to be seen making *galālīb* (long blouses; singular, *gallabīyeh*) for their customers, and in some villages one may watch the coppersmiths manufacturing bowls and jars. The vessels are hammered into shape over iron bars fixed in the ground. The iron bar is bent over at a right angle at the top, and flattened out so as to form a kind of anvil, on which the bowl or other vessel is beaten into shape.

FIG. 11. A VILLAGE STREET WITH SHOPS AND BUTCHERS' BOOTHS

Benches of bricks and mud (*maṣāṭib*, singular *maṣṭabeh*) are found outside some of the houses, and on them is usually to be seen a collection of children, fowls, goats, and even sheep, in happy promiscuity. Or perhaps a *maṣṭabeh* may be occupied solely by an old man, spinning wool, or holding a rosary in his hand and slowly passing the beads between his fingers and thumb (Fig. 12).

During harvest-time the swishing of the sticks as men and women beat the grain from the bundles of corn which they have received as wages for work in the fields,[1] resounds along the village streets.

The Yūsuf Canal (Figs. 4 and 13) flows past a village in which I have frequently resided, and there is a good deal of folklore connected with it. The water is believed to possess curative properties

[1] See Chapter X.

for sore eyes, fever, and other complaints. The canal, according to the peasants, was made in a miraculous way by the patriarch Joseph (Yūsuf). They relate that he started one day to walk from Deirūṭ, where the Baḥr el-Yūsuf (Canal of Joseph) diverges from the Ibrâhimīyeh Canal, and as he went he trailed his stick behind him. Water began to flow along the course marked by his stick until he came to the lake Ḳarūn, at the north-west side of Fayūm Province, and into this lake the numerous streams in which the Baḥr terminates disgorge themselves. Owing to this belief regarding the origin of the canal, its water is believed to contain much *baraḳeh* (blessing, healing virtues, good luck), and accordingly, on the day of *Shemm en-Nesīm*, which coincides with the Coptic Easter Monday, the men make a point of bathing in the canal, for on this occasion the water is believed to be endowed with *barakeh* to a special degree.

FIG. 12. A MAN WITH A ROSARY SITTING ON A MAṢṬABEH

The following is another tradition connected with the Baḥr el-Yūsuf.[1] It is a translation from an Arabic manuscript. "Joseph, to whom may Allah show mercy and grant peace, when he was Prime Minister of Egypt and high in favour with Raiyan, his

[1] Quoted by Sir R. H. Brown, K.C.M.G., R.E., in *The Fayûm and Lake Moeris* (London, 1892), pp. 22–24.

sovereign, after that he was more than a hundred years old, became an object of envy to the favourites of the King and the puissant seigneurs of the Court of Memphis, on account of the great power which he wielded and the affection entertained for him by his monarch. They accordingly thus addressed the King: 'Great King, Joseph is now very old; his knowledge has diminished; his beauty has faded; his judgment is unsound; his sagacity has failed.'

"The King said: 'Set him a task which shall serve as a test'

FIG. 13. A VIEW OF THE BAḤR EL-YŪSUF, WITH A SHĀDŪF AND WATER-WHEEL ON THE RIGHT

At that time el-Fayūm was called el-Hun, or 'the Marsh.' It served as a waste basin for the waters of Upper Egypt, which flowed in and out unrestrained. The courtiers, having taken council together what to propose to the King, gave this reply to Pharaoh: 'Lay the royal commands upon Joseph that he shall direct the water of the Nile from el-Hun and drain it, so as to give you a new province and an additional source of revenue.'

"The King assented, and, summoning Joseph to his presence, said: 'You know how dearly I love my daughter, and you see that the time has arrived in which I ought to carve an estate for her out of the crown lands, and give her a separate establishment, of which she would be the mistress. I have, however, no territory available for this purpose except the submerged land of el-Hun. It is in many respects favourably situated. It is a convenient distance from my capital. It is surrounded by desert. My daughter will thus be independent, and protected.'

" ' Quite true, great King,' responded Joseph, ' when would you wish it done? For accomplished it shall be by the aid of Allah, the all-powerful.'

" ' The sooner the better,' said the King.

" Then Allah inspired Joseph with a plan. He directed him to make three canals; one from Upper Egypt, a canal on the east, and a canal on the west. Joseph collected workmen and dug the canal of Menhi from Eshmunēn to el-Lahūn. Then he excavated the canal of el-Fayūm and the eastern canal, with another canal near it called Beni-Hamed to the west. In this way the water was drained from el-Hun; then he set an army of labourers at work. They cut down the tamarisks and bushes which grew there and carried them away. At the season when the Nile begins to rise the marsh had been converted into good cultivable land. The Nile rose; the water entered the mouth of the Menhi Canal and flowed down the Nile Valley to el-Lahūn; thence it turned towards el-Fayūm and entered that canal in such volume that it filled it, and converted the land into a region irrigated by the Nile.

" King Raiyan thereupon came to see his new province with the courtiers who had advised him to set Joseph this task. When they saw the result they greatly marvelled at the skill and inventive genius of Joseph, and exclaimed: ' We do not know which most to admire, the draining of the marsh and the destruction of the noxious plants, or the conversion of its surface into fertile and well-watered fields.'

" Then the King said to Joseph: ' How long did it take you to bring this district into the excellent state in which I find it?'

" ' Seventy days,' responded Joseph.

" Then Pharaoh turned to his courtiers and said: ' Apparently one could not have done it in a thousand days.'

" Thus the name was changed from el-Hun, or ' the Marsh,' to el-Fayūm, ' the land of a thousand days.' "

CHAPTER II

THE WOMEN AND CHILDREN

FOREIGNERS are often heard talking about "the poor oppressed Egyptian woman." She is spoken of as overworked and ill-treated, and her husband as a brute without feeling or thought for her. I would have my readers bear in mind that in this book I am dealing only with the *fellāḥīn* ; I have no intention of discussing or criticizing the aspirations for emancipation which are now finding voice among many Egyptian ladies of the upper classes. What I have to say here concerns the peasants only, among whom I have sojourned for several years. No one is more anxious than I am to see the status of Egyptian women raised, for until they are made fit to hold a higher position in their world there is, I think, little chance of the country taking a more exalted place among the nations of the earth.

The girls' education should be entirely practical to start with, and book-learning should come by slow degrees. They should be taught the best way of carrying out their domestic duties, which are, after all, very simple—how to cook their food in a cleanly way, to realize that hands should be carefully washed before handling food or mixing the flour and kneading the dough for bread, and that a *clean*, not a dirty, dress should be worn when they are engaged in any culinary operation. They should also be made to realize that if they would spend but half an hour to an hour every morning sweeping their mud floors and the ground outside their house-doors, and then burning the refuse, they would have both healthier and brighter homes and villages. At present they are without the most elementary knowledge of hygiene, and are unmethodical in the carrying out of most, if not all, their domestic duties. It is in matters such as these that the village girls need instruction first and foremost.

The somewhat inferior position that the peasant women occupy in village society compared with that of the men follows as a natural consequence of their greater ignorance.

Little girls have a perfectly free life until they reach marriageable age, when their freedom is somewhat more restricted. After marriage they are still more secluded, but the degree of seclusion varies, being rather stricter among the better-class peasants than among those of lower social status. Among the latter there may be considerable freedom of intercourse between the sexes. It must be remembered that there are quite definite social grades among the *fellāḥīn*, the lines of demarcation being very strongly em-

FIG. 14. A MOTHER WITH HER CHILDREN

phasized. For instance, in a family well known to me the women are not allowed to speak freely to the men, and, with the exception of the elderly mother, none of the females are allowed to enter a room in which male visitors may be seated, and even the mother does not appear unless there is something which renders her presence necessary. One of the women in this family is a widow of about thirty years of age, possibly a little older, and her brother objects to her even being seen walking in the streets of their village, except when she goes, accompanied by her mother, to get the water for household use or for some other necessary purpose. He told me that if he allowed her to be seen walking about in public places his family would at once lose their position, and they would be looked down upon as nobodies. To our Western ideas such restrictions are apt to be regarded as a form of tyranny, but it is not a fair judgment. Seclusion is partly a sign of respect among Egyptians, and indicates the value that the men put upon their womenfolk. Most of the women have unfortunately a difficult and dangerous temperament, which, until they have learnt self-control, and have been inspired with higher ideals, makes them anything but an elevating influence in village society.

Though theoretically they are supposed to be entirely in subjection to the male sex, in practice they can, and often do, maintain a very firm hold on their husbands. I have known many men who are in mortal terror of their wives. Indeed, I am often inclined to think that it is the poor oppressed Egyptian *man* who has a claim to my sympathy, and that the over-ruled, oppressed wife is somewhat of a myth.

More often than not a man marries a girl from his own village, the favourite marriage being with a daughter of his father's brother. On the smallest provocation, some imagined slight, for example, a girl will run off to her father's or brother's house, and remain there until her husband, from fear of mischief being made against him in the village by his wife's relations, is induced to agree to do whatever his wife demands of him. She may require him to buy her gold earrings, a nose-ring, an anklet, or fine clothes, and, though a poor man, he may feel obliged to purchase one or more of these articles for fear of what his wife may do. Many men have run into debt for such reasons.

A man of my acquaintance, who owns a certain amount of land and is by way of being one of the rather superior people of his village, divorced his wife a year or two ago. She was quite a decent woman, but, her relations being poor, she had no land of her own, and, moreover, her husband's brother had died, bequeathing his widow a *feddān* (acre) of land and a little money. My acquaintance had his eye on this land, which was family property, belonging originally to his father, and the only way he could obtain it was by marrying his brother's widow. He did not want to have two wives, for it is expensive to keep up such an establishment; also, monogamy is becoming much more common in Egypt, and to have more than one wife is looked upon as rather barbarous even among the peasants. The only thing to do was to get rid of his first wife.

The poor woman was in great distress, and begged me to intercede for her. I spoke to the man about it, but the *feddān* of land proved to be too much of a temptation to him, and he accordingly obtained his divorce.[1] For some time after this he was ashamed to meet me, and always got out of my way when he knew I was coming to the village. However, his divorced wife was lucky enough to get another husband fairly quickly, and, moreover, one who was in an even better position than her former partner, whom dire vengeance has overtaken in the person of his new wife (Fig. 15). This woman is inordinately jealous, and if her wretched husband is a few minutes later in returning home from his work than she thinks he ought to be she flies into a passion and imagines that he has gone to see his former wife, or, rather, "to look upon her," as she puts it. For this reason she has, on more than one occasion, left his house and gone to her brother's, where she has remained for two or three days before her husband could by any means persuade her to return to him.

FIG. 15. HUSBAND AND JEALOUS WIFE

One day when I was visiting this man's village I was informed that his wife had again left him and remained in her brother's house for six days, because the man had gone to sell some of his *dura* (maize) to a customer living in the street in which his divorced wife now resides with her new husband. The jealous woman had returned to her husband's house only the evening before my visit! Her brother had warmly espoused her cause and told his sister's husband that in future he was not so much as to cast a look in the direction of his former wife!

[1] I think he obtained his divorce on the ground of her childlessness—see Chapter VI.

I fancy that there was really no just cause for the woman's jealous suspicions. However, she has reduced her husband to a state of abject fear lest he may arouse her anger—though I did hear that on one occasion he had plucked up sufficient courage to exercise his 'rights' as a husband, and so had administered a whipping for some fault she had committed!

With regard to the division of labour among the sexes, the men certainly have the hardest and largest share, the most strenuous work in the fields being invariably done by them. The women and girls join their menfolk in the cultivation after the sun has risen, but their work is usually confined to the gathering of dry roots, tending the cattle, fetching the water for the household (Fig. 16), and so on. Of course, living is simple among the peasants, so that very strenuous work for the women is not necessary. Much, however, that might be done by them is neglected simply because they are without training in domestic duties and do not realize what important work lies to their hands.

It is, of course, very difficult for the peasants to be as clean as they should be. All the water has to be fetched by the women, often from some distance. No water is laid on in the villages, no bathrooms exist, and the houses lack the most ordinary domestic offices. Excuses must, therefore, be made for the Egyptian women, who have had none of the advantages of the poorest woman in England. The instinct of the Egyptian *fellāḥīn*, however, is to be clean, and the religion of Islām commands ablutions. A man will almost instinctively strip and bathe if he happens to be near a canal or the river, but this privilege is denied to the women, as modesty forbids their bathing in public.

One of the most crying needs in Egypt is that both girls and women should have instruction in the care and upbringing of children. The children undergo a great deal of unnecessary suffering during the early years of their infancy; not because their mothers are lacking in affection, for Egyptian women are, as a rule, devoted mothers, but because they are so hopelessly ignorant.

The results of such ignorance more often than not leave an indelible mark on the child, such as defective eyesight or even absolute blindness. To prevent or cure disease in their children the women will go to one magician after another and purchase from them amulets and written charms, not grudging for a moment the expenditure of what may be to them considerable sums of money.

FIG. 16. WOMEN CARRYING WATER-POTS ON THEIR HEADS

Numbers of these prophylactics may be seen hanging from the necks of the hapless infants.

The various primitive medicinal remedies, well known to, and used by, all village matrons, are of such a nature that one wonders how any child manages to survive at all. Most of the women have a deeply rooted objection to going to a doctor for advice, supposing one to be available in the neighbourhood ; and I have found it hard work to overcome this prejudice, even in the case of people who know me well and who have every confidence in me. It is encouraging to hear that the Egyptian Government has recently allocated a certain sum of money for the purpose of starting baby-welfare centres. If only these institutions can be got into good working order, and can be utilized for the purpose of training young girls in the proper care and management of children, it will be a big step in the right direction, will ensure a much stronger and healthier peasantry, and will put an end to a vast amount of unnecessary suffering. During the years I have lived among these people I have had hundreds of sick children of all ages brought to me, and it has been heartbreaking to realize, as having had no medical training I inevitably must, that I am quite incapable of dealing with the terrible diseases from which they are often suffering. As will be seen in some of the subsequent chapters, a great deal of this sickness is due to superstition—taboos against washing, for instance, being very strict.

Much good has, of course, been done by the dispensaries, which in the past were run by Englishwomen ; but they are naturally limited in number, and the mothers will often defer taking their children there for advice and medicine till it is almost too late, or, at any rate, till the child has become very ill indeed. I myself had the privilege of seeing something of what was accomplished by an English lady at one of these dispensaries during the first three or four years that I resided in Egypt. I can bear witness to the splendid work she did, and I know how much she was loved and respected by the hundreds of poor women who brought their children to her for treatment. I am sure, from what I have heard of similar institutions in other parts of the country, that the same good work has been done by many others in the different provinces. The number of these dispensaries is not great enough to meet the crying need, and those that do exist have to be supported by funds from the Government, for they receive practically no support, so far as I know, from private individuals. It is very different in England, where the hospitals for children and adults alike are supported by voluntary contributions. It is not that charity is lacking in Egypt—far from it; but for *organized* charity such as we have in England there is a crying need.

It is not altogether surprising, considering the state of ignorance in which they exist, that the mental outlook of most of the villagers is low. As far as the women are concerned, there is nothing to raise it. Sexual matters form the chief topic of their conversation, and this has a most degrading effect both on them and on their children, before whom they discuss the most private matters without the slightest reserve. Thus the children from their very early years hear subjects spoken of and joked about in a manner that is most revolting to educated people. What chance have the children in such circumstances of growing up into pure-minded men and women? I am told (for such conversation rarely takes place in my presence) that the women are far greater offenders in this respect than the men, who usually refrain from discussing their wives with outsiders. Whether this is true or not I am not in a position to say, but at any rate the children, and especially the girls, who are more constantly with their mothers than the boys, hear the most private sexual matters openly discussed, and in such a way as to poison their minds at the very outset of their lives. Marriage is, of course, the one and only aim in life among the girls, and the desire to get a husband is encouraged in every way by the mothers. It is quite a pitiful sight to see a little girl decked out in all the jewellery she can muster, dressed in a gaily coloured frock decorated with beads and jangles (Fig. 17), and with a veil drawn coquettishly across her face, standing about the village street, or outside the house, obviously on the look-out to attract some man. In all this they are aided and abetted by their mothers, who regard it as a compliment to themselves as well as to their daughters if the latter are sought after as wives at an early age. The Egyptian Government is endeavouring to prohibit the very early marriages which have been usual in the past, and there is now a law forbidding a girl to marry till she is sixteen and a boy till he is eighteen. However, in small, out-of-the-way villages the law has been disobeyed to my certain knowledge in more than one case. False ages were, I suppose, given to the *ḳāḍi*, as the man who draws up the marriage contracts is called; and he, in view of the fee he obtains for his business, probably refrained from examining the statement as to age made by the girl's parents.

The childbearing age lasts over a long period, for girls mature early, and it is a common thing in Egypt for a woman of fifty to give birth to a child. From an economic point of view it is probably an advantage that so many of the children die, for otherwise the country would soon become over-populated. What is so desirable is that those who do survive should be brought up in healthier surroundings, both moral and physical, and without the unnecessary suffering inflicted upon them by the ignorance of the mothers.

FIG. 17. YOUNG GIRL DRESSED UP TO ATTRACT A HUSBAND

In spite of the frequently indecent talk on sexual matters, there is a strict moral code, especially with regard to unmarried girls, the infringement of which often entails a terrible punishment. This seems somewhat unfair on the girls, considering the atmosphere in which they are brought up. If a girl has misconducted herself before marriage, and is discovered at marriage to be unchaste, the disgrace to her family is looked upon as such a terrible one that her own parents will often kill her, sometimes taking the unfortunate child—for she is hardly more than a child—into the desert, and there dispatching her, usually, I believe, by cutting her throat. Unfaithfulness in a wife may likewise be punished by death, sometimes death by drowning. If her paramour also is caught they may be thrown into the river or a canal together.

The moral standard is very much lower in some villages than others, and I have observed that villages of pure, or comparatively pure, Egyptian stock are more moral sexually, more honest, and less prone to crimes of violence than are those of mixed negro or Arab origin.

In any case, it is not fair to judge these peasants too harshly. Much cannot be expected of them in their present condition of ignorance, and I believe that until the women can be depended on to exercise a purer and higher influence on their society there is not much prospect of the moral tone of the village communities being raised.

In later years a woman, especially if she has sons, has an honourable position in the family. A man's love and respect for his mother is a marked characteristic among Egyptians, and even after marriage the mother retains the highest place in her son's love and respect. Some years ago I was told that if a man ill-treated his mother and did not show her the greatest honour and respect the whole village would consider him a reprobate. In the married son's household his mother reigns supreme, and the wife who does not show proper respect to her mother-in-law usually has no chance of finding favour with her husband. As an old friend of mine, a man who had always had the greatest veneration and love for his mother, once said to me, " My wife is good, and I am pleased with her, but she must remain there [pointing downward]. My mother is up there [pointing upward]. Did she not carry me here for nine months [pressing his hands on his stomach] ? Did she not endure pain to give me birth, and did she not feed me from her breast ? How could I not love her ? She is always first and above all with me. My wife may change and may lose her love for me. My mother is always the same ; her love for me cannot change."

I fear I may seem to have given a very unpleasant impression in many respects of the peasants of Egypt, but I have dwelt on the darker side of the picture at some length not because there is no brighter side, nor because I am lacking in appreciation of the many excellent qualities to be found in most of my village friends. It is because of my real affection for them, and because I very greatly desire to see their lives improved, especially from the moral standpoint, that I venture to speak openly on a subject in which I am much interested—*i.e.*, how to assure a more wholesome childhood and a higher mental training for the girls, so that they may be better and wiser wives and mothers.

I have every cause to speak of these people with affection, for their courtesy to me has been unbounded, and I have often marvelled at their patience and cheerfulness, even in the midst of poverty and great privations, which they bear with a courage that enforces respect. Their kindness to each other in times of trouble is most marked, and they will as a rule, however poor they may be, share their scanty fare with one whose position may be even worse than their own. This nobler side of their character shows what a fine people they might become were the women, the chief influence in any community, to receive a better training in childhood, a more suitable education, and to have held up before them a higher ideal of life.

CHAPTER III

PERSONAL DECORATION AND ORNAMENTS

LOVE of personal adornment seems to be instinctive in the human race, and it has probably existed in some form or another as an element in human character from the earliest times. The beautifying of the person may be achieved in a variety of ways, sometimes involving mutilation of the body. A study of the true inwardness of ornaments and personal decoration in general is most instructive, and may serve a useful purpose on occasions, as I hope to show later.

The simple jewellery of the modern Egyptian peasants, and their body-markings, such as tattooing, supply material for an interesting chapter in the study of these people.

The *fellāḥeh* (peasant woman) is by no means more backward than the average Englishwoman in her endeavours to make the most of whatever personal attractions she may possess, and, as I have stated, her demands for gold and silver ornaments may involve her unfortunate husband in considerable financial embarrassment.

The young girl, usually a mere child, who is on the look-out for a husband often wears a necklace of particular shape, made of gold coins. It is quite an attractive ornament, and also serves as an outward and visible sign of her wealth. A man when about to marry may present his bride with such a necklace, investing some of his money in it, for the women's jewellery is often regarded as a safe form of investment, which can easily be turned into ready cash should the necessity arise. Every girl has her ears and nose bored at a fairly early age, when she becomes the proud possessor of a pair of earrings (Fig. 18, bottom), as well as of a nose-ring (Fig. 18, in centre of necklace). These may be of gold or silver, or, in the case of the poorer people, even of brass. Anklets may be of silver-gilt, silver, or some white metal. Bracelets are usually much in request, and are made of glass of various colours (Fig. 18, extreme left and right), of small beads woven together to form a

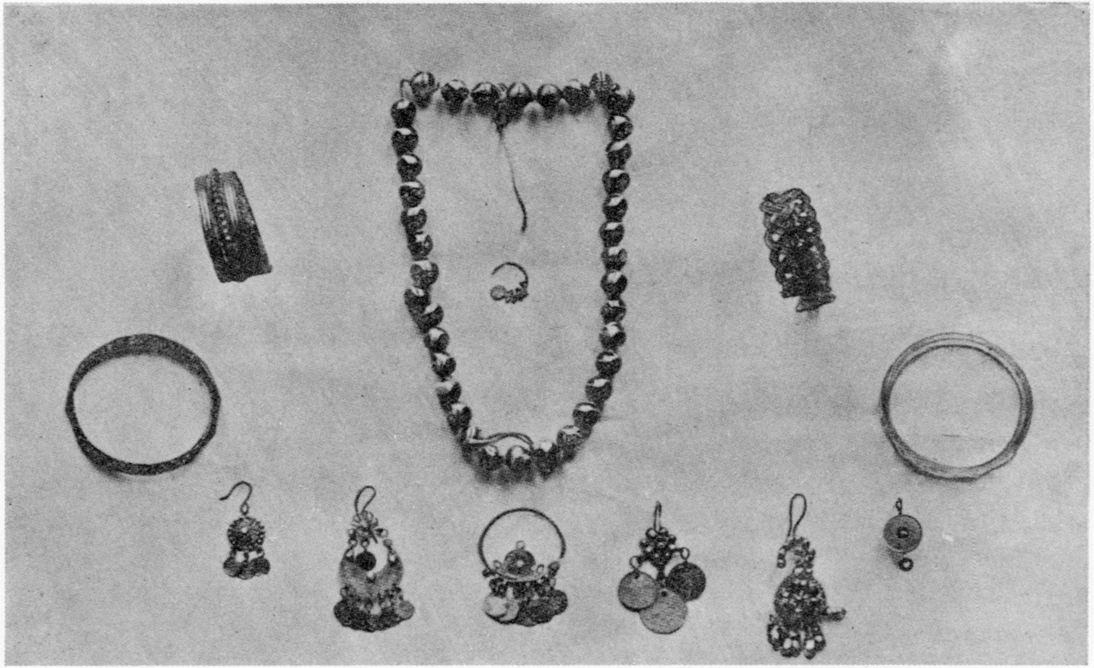

FIG. 18. WOMEN'S ORNAMENTS: NECKLACE, NOSE-RING, METAL BRACELETS, GLASS BANGLES, AND EARRINGS

solid round band, or of silver or gold. The ornaments of the less wealthy peasants are usually made of cheap materials, though some women may be lucky enough to possess one gold or silver bracelet.

In some parts of Egypt, at any rate, the unmarried girl is not supposed to wear many bracelets at once, and her ornaments generally are not so numerous or so massive as those of the married woman. However, when she is anxious to marry she will somewhat overload herself with jewellery, cheap or otherwise, and, not content with her ear- and nose-rings and her somewhat massive necklace, she often hangs gold, silver, or brass ornaments from the kerchief which she ties round her head, the latter ornaments being attached in such a way that they hang over her forehead.

FIG. 19. MOURNING NECKLACES OF DARK BLUE BEADS

In some parts of Egypt a girl on becoming a bride may don such a number of glass bracelets of various colours that they completely cover both arms from wrist to elbow! Silver or white metal bracelets of particular design may also now be worn by her. I was told in Asyūṭ Province that unmarried girls are never allowed to wear this type of bracelet, which is thus a means of indicating social status.

A red heart-shaped ornament, attached either to a silver chain or to a necklace of red beads, is worn by women suffering from sheikh-possession.[1] A necklace of light blue beads, or even a single bead of this colour, is often worn as a charm against the evil eye. It will thus be seen from these two examples—and there are many others—that ornaments may have a utilitarian as well as a decorative value.

[1] See Chapter XI.

When a woman's husband dies one of the first things she does is to take off all her jewellery—nose-ring, earrings, finger-rings, gold, silver, or brass bracelets—wearing instead a necklace of dark blue or black beads (Fig. 19) and sometimes blue or black earrings and bracelets. The nose-ring is discarded for good, unless she marries again.

Knowledge of this custom is sometimes very useful. I was calling on a certain Captain of Police one day and happened to arrive at the moment when he was investigating a case of murder. An old man had been waylaid not far from his village and killed, but all his fellow-villagers declared that they knew nothing whatever about it. The wife, a son by a former marriage, and some other relations had been locked up pending investigations. The wife, very negroid in type, as, indeed, were many of the people of her village, was, together with her stepson, undergoing examination when I arrived. The officer strongly suspected that the wife was implicated, and possibly the stepson also. The woman was much younger than her husband, who was, for a *fellāḥ*, a man of some substance. I watched the woman carefully while she was being questioned, and she certainly was far from prepossessing in appearance. On looking more closely I noticed that she was still wearing all her ornaments of gold and other materials, including her nose-ring. If she had really cared anything about her unfortunate husband she would have removed them immediately upon hearing that he was dead. I asked my friend the Captain of Police if he had noticed this, and then pointed out to him how many ornaments she was still wearing. He was delighted with this piece of evidence, which had quite escaped his notice, and which certainly went to confirm his suspicion. This incident shows that a knowledge of personal adornment, and of the customs associated with certain ornaments, may be quite useful to officials who are concerned with criminal investigation among the *fellāḥīn*.

Among the *fellāḥīn* it is usually the custom to pierce one ear of a young boy if he is an only son, and in this ear he wears a decorative ring (Fig. 20). When he gets older he discards the ring, but the perforation is always visible. No reason was given for this custom, but I suspect it is most likely a method of protection against the evil eye, and is possibly regarded as a means of disguising his sex.

Tattooing is another form of personal decoration. It is popular with both sexes among the peasants, and it may be resorted to for utilitarian as well as for decorative purposes. The operation of tattooing is a very painful one, and is performed by specialists in the art. Sometimes a woman tattoos women and girls, and a man men and boys, but there is no hard-and-fast rule about this (see Fig. 25). The street cry of the tattooer is "*Yā ṣabī taʿāla duḳḳ!*" ("O lad, come and be tattooed!"). A woman who desires to be tattooed will, on hearing a female tattooer utter her street cry, call out, "Come here, O damsel who tattoos!"

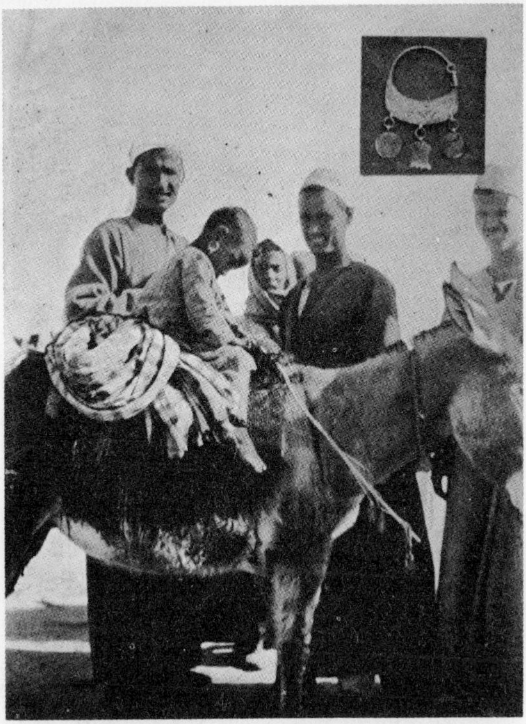

FIG. 20. CHILD (AN ONLY SON) WEARING SPECIAL EARRING—FOR WHICH SEE INSET

The implement used in tattooing consists of seven needles fixed into a short stick, which is bound round at the end and then plastered over to keep the needles firmly in position. Sometimes smaller needles, and only five in number, are used for tattooing children. Lamp-black is the pigment employed, and this is usually mixed with oil, though some people say that water is used. However, when I last witnessed the operation of tattooing oil was mixed with the lamp-black.

A tattooer often attends the village market, where he can be seen plying his trade. Samples of the various designs, which are very numerous, are often framed and propped up against the tree under which he squats, so that his clients can choose whatever pattern or patterns they prefer. Some are very elaborate, and must involve considerable suffering on the part of the person who is tattooed with them. Many of the patterns are conventional designs, and I am assured that they have no special meaning, but are chosen according to individual taste and fancy. One pattern is called *esh-shagareh* (the tree), and is the one usually chosen by both men and women to decorate the back of the right hand. So far as I have observed, this pattern when used by women differs slightly from that used by men. The drawing given here (Fig. 21) I made from the hand of a woman; the marks were tattooed on her hand when she was a young girl.

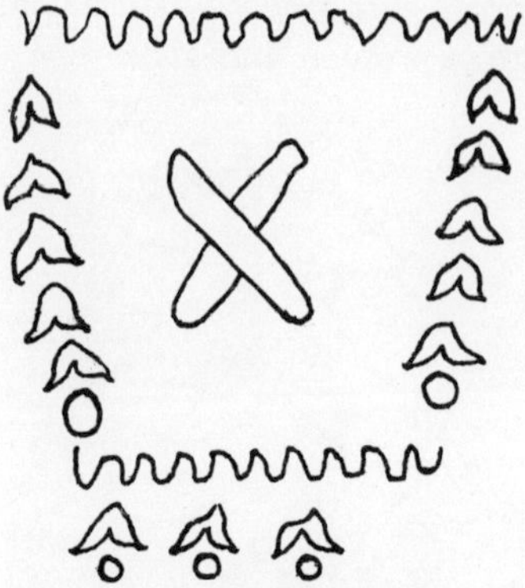

FIG. 21. TATTOO MARKS ON THE BACK OF A WOMAN'S RIGHT HAND AND ACROSS THE BACK OF THE WRIST

FIG. 22. TATTOO MARK FROM EDGE OF LOWER LIP TO BASE OF CHIN

The women are usually tattooed from the edge of the lower lip down to the base of the chin. The pattern shown in Fig. 22, copied by me from the same woman, is also called *esh-shagareh*. The tattoo on the back of the hand and wrist, as well as on the fingers and thumb, is said to make them strong.

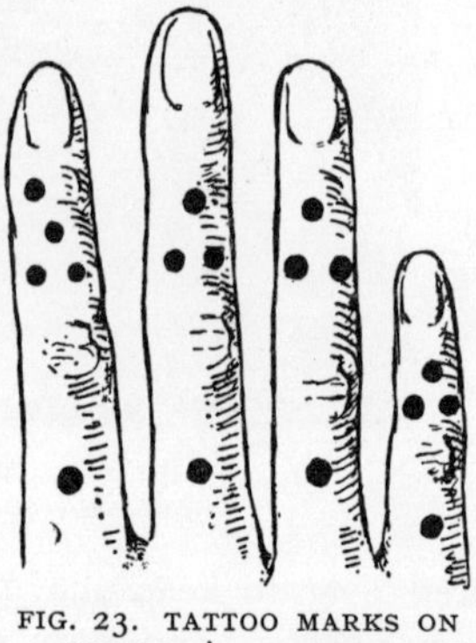

FIG. 23. TATTOO MARKS ON WOMAN'S FINGERS TO MAKE THEM STRONG

FIG. 24. TATTOO MARKS ON THUMB BELOW THE SECOND JOINT TO MAKE THE THUMB STRONG

A boy is often tattooed with a single dot on his chin and another near his right nostril; also most boys have three dots, thus ∴, tattooed on one arm, just above the wrist. Boys are tattooed in this manner when they are still very young (Fig. 25), for tattooing is considered to be of benefit to them. According to one of my informants, the dot tattooed at the side of the nostril is sometimes done as a cure for toothache. It is a very common mark among a large number of the Arabs; one of them told me that it was done as a sign of their race.

Many of the men among the *fellāḥīn* have a tattoo mark on either temple, the mark being often in the shape of a bird. This is sometimes purely a form of decoration, but it is also done as a cure for headache. One man I know has three short, straight lines tattooed near one side of his forehead. He told me that this was done when he was a boy, as the eye on the same side as the tattoo marks was very weak. He declared that it effected an almost immediate and quite permanent cure.

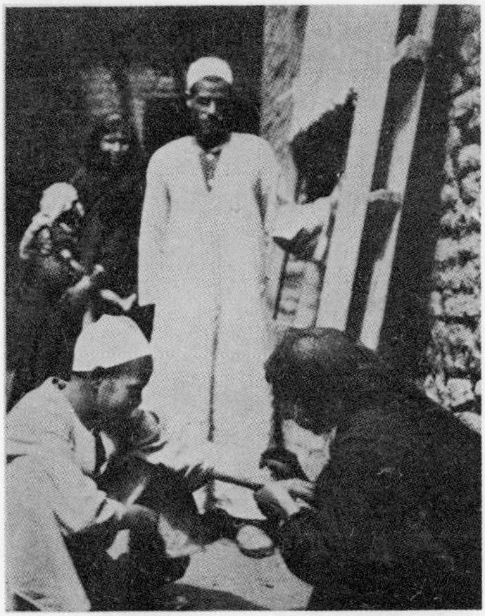

FIG. 25. WOMAN TATTOOING A YOUNG BOY

Another man I know had three dots tattooed about an inch and a half above each nipple, and three more in the centre of his chest. He also had three more dots tattooed on each shoulder-blade and one behind one ear. He gave me the following account of the history of these marks. One cold day he was warming himself over a fire on which was being cooked some fish which smelled unpleasantly. A woman glanced at his chest, which was bare, but he drew his clothes over it so that she should not see it. From that moment he began to itch, and the people said that he was affected by the fumes (*buhāḳ*)—those, I presume, from the fish. As a remedy for this he was tattooed with the dots as described above, which immediately cured him.

If a woman has lost several children in succession, when another one arrives she has it tattooed with a small dot in the centre of its forehead and another on the outer side of the left ankle. She believes that after this the child will live, because her *ḳarīneh*, seeing these marks, will not attempt to take her child.[1] The belief is that when King David had the interview with the queen of the *aḳrān* described in the following chapter she promised that any child that had these tattoo marks on the forehead and ankle should not be injured by its mother's *ḳarīneh*.

One man, who was a village guard far south in Upper Egypt, had a fish tattooed on the inner side of one arm, near the wrist. He told me that it was done some years before, when he was possessed by an *ʿafrīt*, that it quite cured him, and that he had never been troubled in that way since. This fish mark does not always serve a curative purpose, for in a village much farther north I saw a boy with a similar design tattooed on the back of one of his hands, and he assured me that it was done only as an ornament.

Most of the Copts have a cross tattooed on the inner sides of the wrists. There is a belief among some, if not all, of those Copts belonging to the *fellāḥīn* class that the Abyssinians will one day conquer Egypt, and will kill all the Copts as well as the Muslims if they (the Copts) cannot show this sign on their wrists. The Copts will, it is said, hold up their hands, thus exposing to view the sign of their religion.

One Coptic friend of mine, a man of good position, showed me some tattoo marks on his arm. There was an elaborate pattern on the inner side of his arm, below which were tattooed the dates of the two occasions on which he had gone on pilgrimages to Jerusalem—1911 and 1914. Another Copt told me that his little sister also had the year of her visit to Jerusalem tattooed on one arm, and that in future the year of each succeeding pilgrimage that she made to the sacred city would be similarly recorded. His mother, who had performed the pilgrimage on several occasions, had had each year of this event tattooed on one of her arms. Tattooing can thus be a means of record-keeping.

The operation of tattooing is an exceedingly painful one, and has very often unpleasant results, though the discomfort may be only temporary. One of my servants, a young man of about twenty-two years of age, was very anxious to have the back of his right hand tattooed this year. A specialist in the art was usually

[1] See pp. 69 ff. for explanation of *ḳarīneh*.

present at the weekly market, seating himself, with all his paraphernalia, on the outskirts of the market-place and under the shadow of a tree. A number of patterns were placed before the young man; he at once selected that called *esh-shagareh*, and the tattooer set to work. While working he had no occasion to refer to his pattern; long and constant practice had made him an adept. He would lightly prick out a small portion of the design, then work over it two or three times more, and so proceed until the task was completed. The first finger was not touched, and, when I remarked on this, my servant told me that that finger was never tattooed on a man's hand, but that it was done on a woman's. It took some time before the work was finished, the pain, which was great, being heroically borne by the unfortunate young man. However, I suppose that the thought of how beautiful he would look afterward helped him to endure! I rather fancy that the tattooing of the hand is a sign of manhood; it is certainly a painful initiatory rite. Soon after I returned to my house I found that the young man's hand, and indeed the whole of the right arm, had begun to swell, and that he was decidedly feverish. I made him lie down, and as the morning went on the fever and inflammation increased, and he was unfit to move. I wanted to send for a doctor, but he assured me he would soon be all right, and that most people got like this after having their hand tattooed. Toward the late afternoon he was much better, and by the next morning he had practically recovered.

Among the negroid peoples in Egypt, especially among the Berberines, cicatrization lines are often seen along the cheeks. These are probably tribal marks. Occasionally similar marks are to be seen near the ear or on the side of the forehead, and these have usually been made as a cure for bad eyes, headache, or other ills. Some Egyptians have the marks of two or three short cuts on the side of the face close to the ear. When I inquired as to the meaning of these cuts I was told that they were made because it was the custom. This practice is, I think, tending to die out.

It is quite a common sight to see notches cut along the outer edge of the ear—sometimes in one ear only, sometimes in both. The number of notches also varies, and in some cases only one has been cut. I have never noticed these notches in women's ears. I have observed that this kind of intentional deformation of the ear is common among many of the Arab tribes settled in Egypt, and with them it is possibly a racial mark, but the following information was given to me by an Egyptian woman whom I questioned on the subject. Among the *fellāḥīn* the notches are cut when there is supposed to be something wrong with the inside of a child's mouth, and the operation is performed in babyhood. A midwife acts as the surgeon in such cases. She cuts the notch, or notches, with a pair of scissors, and the blood from the wound is rubbed on the roof of the child's mouth. If the mouth is very bad more than one notch is cut.

Long hair is certainly considered a woman's glory in Egypt, though I have rarely, if ever, seen really thick, long hair among the *fellāḥīn* women and girls. However, this defect is easily remedied, and every woman buys long plaits of false hair, which hang down far below her waist. She cuts her hair short on either side of her face, and forms this short hair into flat curls against her cheeks. Over her head she ties a silk or cotton kerchief, a brightly coloured one if she is young, a more sombre one if she has passed her youth, and this keeps the side curls in position. The hair is not dressed every day, but when it is done a double wooden comb is used (Fig. 26), with fine and coarse teeth. The centre of the comb is usually decorated with coloured designs.

IIG. 26. DOUBLE WOODEN COMB

The long plaits worn by the peasant women are utilitarian as well as decorative. The house-door key is often attached to one of the plaits when the housewife goes off either to shop or to the fields, while from the others hang various charms, some of which are enclosed in small leather cases. One woman I know wore a charm against headache enclosed in a leather case, and also a large opaque bead to keep her husband's love and to make his mother pleased with her. Both these charms were attached to one of her plaits, and she gave me the bead after her husband died.

When a woman becomes a widow she immediately conceals the side curls ; in fact, no hair must be seen round her face—it is tucked away under a dark blue or a black kerchief. She wears it like this all her life, unless she remarries, in which case the curls again appear, and the mourning kerchief is replaced by one of brighter hue. Should a woman do this before her second husband is secured the whole village knows that she is anxious to marry again.

Women, especially when the hair begins to turn grey, often dye it with *ḥenna*, which stains it a bright red. This may be done by a woman who, wishing to obtain another husband, endeavours to obliterate the signs of advancing years. One day when visiting a village where I have often stayed for many weeks at a time I saw an old crone performing her toilet on the roof of her house. She was combing out her very scanty locks, which were dyed a bright red. Unfortunately, she had not been altogether successful with her hair-tinting, for considerable patches of white hair were still plainly visible. I asked a woman friend of mine, in whose house I was sitting, if the old woman wanted to marry again. She laughed, and said that she believed that this was so! I never heard that she met with any sort of success in that direction!

The men either have their hair cut quite short, or else they have the head shaved altogether. Some of them, however, leave one lock of hair at the back of the head, allowing it to grow quite long, even though the rest of the head may be closely shaved. One man told me that he wore this lock of hair so that when he died the men who washed him might not have to touch his head, but could hold it by this lock. I gathered that he thought that it would defile him if they caught hold of his head, but I am not sure about this point. My brother, Dr A. M. Blackman, tells me that a man told him that the object of the lock was to prevent those who washed a corpse from raising the head by putting a hand into the mouth and so possibly defiling the dead.

The men usually shave all the hair off the face, except the moustache. Old men, however, frequently allow the beard to grow, as it is looked upon as a mark of honour at that time of life. Most of the body hair of both sexes is shaved off, to ensure ceremonial purity.

A child often has the hair shaved off just above the forehead. In some parts of Egypt this is considered to be a good thing for the eyes, as it is believed that the hair growing on that part of the head is injurious to the eyesight when the child is very young. The shaven portion is often covered with *ḥenna*. Another special form of hair-cutting for very young boys is dealt with in the following chapter.

After a death the male relatives of the deceased will often allow the hair on the face and head to grow for some time as a sign of mourning.

An Egyptian woman who fears that her facial beauty is beginning to fade, and who wishes to obliterate lines on her face and to obtain a nice pink complexion, will proceed in the following way. She takes a quantity of sugar and a little alum, and boils them together in a small quantity of water till the concoction becomes thick and brown like toffee; the pan is then removed from the fire. When the toffee-like substance is cool enough she takes some of it and pinches it up between her fingers and thumb and applies it to her face, where it sticks; she then pulls it off. She massages the whole of her face in this way, or she may get a friend to do it for her (see Fig. 27), till the skin becomes very pink and also the soft, downy hairs are pulled out. Her husband, on coming home, will admire her complexion and be 'pleased' (*mabsūṭ*) with her, and the woman herself will thus be gratified. I know a woman who, in order to excite her husband's admiration, treats her face in this way every day! After being thus massaged the face is washed with pink soap, and then a pink powder may also be applied. Many of the vainer of the peasant women regularly make use of this treatment in order to beautify themselves. I have myself seen the face

FIG. 27. WOMAN HAVING HER FACE MASSAGED

being treated in this manner, and it seemed to be a somewhat painful process. However, "*Il faut souffrir pour être belle*," and these women do endure considerable discomfort in the course of their toilet.

The toffee-like substance described above is also used by women in a similar way in order to pull out any hairs that may be growing on their legs.

Most women and girls paint round the eyes with antimony (Arabic, *koḥl*). It is kept in a small bottle, generally of glass, called *mikḥaleh*, and is applied with a short stick with a blunt point. It is regarded not only as a beautifier, but also as a cure for sore eyes.

Scent is used by both sexes, some of it being of a very pungent nature. In some parts of Egypt it is taboo for a man to use scent while his wife is suckling her child. If he disobeys this rule the child, it is said, will come out all over in spots. A man whom I knew well used some scent on one occasion while his wife was still suckling their youngest-born. The child got nasty spots all over its body, and the mother told me that it was her husband's fault, because he had been putting some scent on his moustache!

I have sometimes heard English people remark on the dirty habit that the Egyptian peasant women have of wearing long dresses which trail over the ground, brushing up the dust in clouds as they go along. It is, of course, a very insanitary practice, but the wearing of short skirts would be looked upon as most immodest. A woman's legs should never be exposed, except from dire necessity. There is also another reason for the trailing skirts. Most peasant women walk barefooted, and so leave clearly defined footprints in the dry, dusty soil. A woman can be injured magically through her footprints, and so the long skirt acts as a safeguard, brushing over and thus obliterating them.

Little girls wear very bright-coloured cotton frocks, which reach almost to the ground (see Fig. 17). The women and older girls may wear such frocks indoors, but when they walk abroad, either to shop, to fill their water-jars, or to visit their friends, they wear a long black dress over the coloured one, and a thick veil, shawl-shaped, over their heads.

I was told by a friend some few years ago that in Sharḳīyeh Province the women wear long white veils, on which are several gold or silver ornaments. These ornaments are in the form of money, usually the Egyptian pound, and, according to my informant, they represent the money given to the bride before her marriage; thus the wealth of a woman may be estimated by looking at her veil. I have not yet visited Sharḳīyeh Province, and have therefore not had the opportunity of verifying this statement myself.

To draw the veil over the lower part of the face is a sign of respect for superiors, as well as a means of concealing the face from the gaze of men. For the former reason the women when passing me in the roads usually draw the veil over the face, however old they may be. Black and dark blue are mourning colours, and a dress of the latter colour is always worn in the house by a widow in place of the brighter coloured one which she wore before her husband died. She also wears a dark blue kerchief on her head, with a black veil over it when out of doors.

Men do not make any change in their attire after losing a relative, but some, as I have already stated, refrain from shaving, and let the head and facial hair grow long for some time after the death of a near, and especially a male, relative.

The loose, flowing robes of both men and women are admirably adapted to the climate, and it is much to be hoped that the custom of wearing the native dress will not die out. Much of the picturesqueness of the country would go if European dress became the fashion in Egyptian villages, and, moreover, the native costume is infinitely healthier and more comfortable in the hot, dry climate of the Nile Valley.

CHAPTER IV

BIRTH AND CHILDHOOD

CHILDREN occupy a very important place in Egyptian society, as will be seen in Chapter VI, which is concerned with the numerous methods employed by women to ensure their producing offspring.

When a woman becomes pregnant she often hangs up in various rooms in her house pictures of legendary persons who are renowned not only for physical beauty, but also for their loving and gentle disposition. The expectant mother believes that if she constantly looks at such pictures the child to be born will resemble them in face and character. Anything and everything that she gazes at for any length of time is believed by her to affect her unborn child.[1] The first year that I visited Egypt I was on more than one occasion somewhat embarrassed by the numbers of women who would sit or stand around me when I happened to be visiting a village, staring at me without moving their eyes from my face. I was afterward told by my servant, who always accompanied me and assisted me greatly in my work, that these women were all expectant mothers and desired to have babies resembling me in face—hence the rigid stares! Since then I have frequently been gazed at in this manner, but have now quite lost my first feelings of embarrassment.

"Ah," said one woman when thus engaged in studying my features, "if I had a girl like her I could marry her for a thousand pounds!"

"Look well, O girl," replied my servant, "and if you are in a state of yearning you may have one like her!"

For a similar reason most women in this condition will endeavour to avoid ugly or unpleasant sights or people, fearing that their unborn infants may be thereby adversely affected. If a pregnant woman should see a dead person, man, woman, or child of either sex, and not take the necessary precautions, it is the generally

[1] This is also a common belief in England.

accepted belief that the child will die directly it is born. Accordingly, a pregnant woman on seeing a dead person immediately breaks her necklace, so that the beads fall into her lap, and then dashes water on her face. This is believed to ensure the child living after it is born.

I have been told in many parts of Egypt that whatever an expectant mother 'yearns for' will appear on some part of the child's body at birth if the mother cannot obtain what she desires at the time of her craving. For example, I heard of a pregnant woman who had a great longing for grapes to eat, but could not obtain any, as the fruit was not at that time in season. Consequently the mark of a cluster of grapes appeared on the child's neck when it was born. My informant told me that he had seen this child himself, and that the bunch of grapes could be easily recognized. He also informed me that the mark of a single grape was commoner than that of a bunch, but that in either case the mark would swell out during the grape season and shrivel up again when the grapes were over! I have since ascertained that this periodical swelling and shrinking does not always occur, though my first informant, a very reliable man, assured me that he himself had observed this strange phenomenon. Again, if a woman craves for a special piece of meat and cannot obtain it the form of it will appear somewhere on the child's body. I myself have seen a child, whose mother craved for a pomegranate, marked with a shape of the fruit on one of its legs. I took a photograph of the child, but the mark, which was red in colour, unfortunately does not show up.

The women often have a craving to eat mud during their pregnancy. They go to the bed of a canal and break up into small pieces some of the clods of mud which have partially dried up since the inundation. They keep a store of these in their pockets or tied up in their veils, so that they may have them handy when the craving comes upon them. These pieces of mud are called *ṭīn iblīz* (alluvial mud). This curious craving by an expectant mother is common in some other parts of the world, as well as in Egypt.

A woman at her confinement may be attended only by her mother or some other female relative, or she may call in the help of a midwife. There are special training-centres for midwives at the present time in Egypt, all regularly inspected by a most competent Englishwoman.

If a midwife is called in to assist at a birth she brings with her the customary confinement chair (Fig. 28); for women in Egypt give birth in a squatting attitude. If this professional assistance is not required the woman squats without the chair, resting her arms on, and pressing upon, a sieve which stands on its side (Fig. 29). She leans forward on the sieve even if she squats on the chair. The sieve, which is a large one such as is employed in winnowing, plays quite an important part in all the birth ceremonies, as will be seen later.

FIG. 28. CONFINEMENT CHAIR

It is the business of the female attendant or midwife, as the case may be, to cut the umbilical cord. The afterbirth is dealt with in a variety of ways. In many parts, if not all over Egypt, it is often called *el-walad et-tāni* (the other, or second, child), and some people regard it as an unfinished infant. If a woman is anxious to make sure of having another child she buries the placenta of the latest-born under the threshold of her house. She does this in order that when she desires to have another child she may be able to step over the buried placenta three, five, or seven times; for the belief is that its spirit will then re-enter her body, to be born again as a complete child in due course.

FIG. 29. WOMAN LEANING ON SIEVE

If a woman has lost several children in succession at birth she thinks that somehow or other she has incurred the anger of her *ukht* or *ḳarīneh*, or both, and that they have taken the children away from her. She therefore consults a female magician, who gets into communication with these subterranean beings, and the mother inquires what she has done to make either or both of them angry. If the reply is that she has angered one or both of them she must then bring bread made of wheat flour, of which both she and the magician must partake. When the latter eats the bread it is as though the *ukht* and *ḳarīneh* ate it, for they eat it through her. After this ceremonial eating of the bread these beings make peace with the mother and tell her that the next time she gives birth to a child, and on all subsequent occasions, she is to act in the following way. She must bury the placenta, together with a round, bun-shaped loaf of bread, made of wheat flour, called *khubz*, and a *raṭl* (rather more than 1 lb.) of salt, in a bowl (Fig. 30), covered by another bowl of the same shape, under the floor of her house. By this means the *ukht* and *ḳarīneh* are appeased and will not take the woman's children from her.

FIG. 30. JAR IN WHICH THE PLACENTA, TOGETHER WITH BREAD AND SALT, IS BURIED UNDER THE FLOOR

If a woman's new-born children have survived birth the midwife, or a female relative or friend, throws the afterbirth into the Nile or into a canal. As she does this, however, she must laugh or smile, for then the child will always be happy and cheerful. If, on the other hand, she neglects her duty in this respect the child will always have an unhappy disposition.

Some mothers, in order to ensure long life to their children, will take a small piece of the umbilical cord and wrap it in a cotton wick. This they put in a pottery saucer-lamp filled with oil, light it, place it in a little boat, and leave it to float down the stream. Others again—and this is a very common practice—will take a short length of the cord and sew it up in a strip of cotton material, which is then hung by a string from the child's neck. After a short time this, together with certain other charms to be mentioned presently, is sewn up in one of the small leather charm-cases, and must be worn throughout life. It is usual to hang such a charm from the neck, the charm-case hanging under the right arm. I am told that a small piece of the placenta is sometimes used in this way instead of the cord, but so far I have not come across this usage myself.

Another method employed to prolong a child's life is the following. If a Muslim woman has had several children who have all died in early infancy, when another is born she asks a Coptic woman to give her *barakeh* (blessing, good luck), in order that the newly born child may live. The *barakeh* she asks for is either a part of a dress which has been worn by the Coptic woman or her husband, or else a dress which has belonged to one of their children. The dress *must* be that of a Christian, not of a Muslim. Among the Copts this custom does not exist. I asked why a Muslim should ask for the dress of a Christian, and I was told it was because they are good people.

A woman who has lost several children and wishes to ensure that the newly born infant will live acts as follows. She carries her baby in her arms, and, with a basket made of palm-leaves on her head,[1] goes from house to house begging for *ḥaseneh* (charity) for her child. She will do this however rich she may be, behaving as if she were a very poor woman. Some people may give her money, others *battaw* or *khubz* (two kinds of bread) and other articles of food. She will then distribute these gifts among the poor people of the village, even if she be as poor as they. She believes that, as the result of this action, God, or her *ḳarīneh*, will allow her to keep her child.

On many different occasions women have brought their babies to me with the request that I would spit into their mouths, in order to give them *barakeh* and make them live long! Also I found that many of my old clothes that I had thrown away were torn up, and small pieces of them given to various mothers in the village, who hung them on their babies as charms to prolong life. One expectant mother came and begged me to let her have one of my old frocks, in order that her child might be born on to it! She, poor thing, did not get her request granted, and I regret to say that her baby died very soon after birth!

Some women kill a puppy at the seventh month of their pregnancy. The puppy is killed over a cloth, on to which the blood flows. As soon as the child is born it is wrapped in this blood-

[1] The ordinary basket, called *maḳṭaf*.

stained cloth. When the puppy is killed its head is cut off and is pickled in salt, and it is worn by the expectant mother till after the birth of the child, when it is transferred from her to the infant. My informant, a clever, well-educated Egyptian lady, told me that this is done because dogs are regarded as very unclean animals in Egypt, and that therefore the mother's *ḳarīneh* would not come near her unborn child so long as she was wearing the puppy's head ; and for the same reason the child will not be attacked or injured by its mother's *ḳarīneh* while it wears this charm.

Another protective charm, worn by an expectant mother if all her children have died before they have attained the age of seven years, consists of the head of a hoopoo, a *ḍufr* [1] of a snake, a small piece of the under lip and of the ear of a dead donkey, a *'nāb* (double tooth) of a camel, a *ḥirbāyeh* (chameleon), and a written charm. All these are hung under her right arm while she is pregnant. After her confinement the child wears these charms.

I saw a set of these charms which had been worn by a woman during the last two months of her pregnancy, only in addition to the above-mentioned articles there were seven threads of silk, which may be of any colour. While the expectant mother was wearing these charms they were divided into two packets, each done up in cotton material. When I saw them they had been transferred to her child, and had all been put together into a raw hide case. The child must wear this until death, and it is supposed to ensure it a long life.

It is the custom in many parts of Egypt for a mother to wear an iron anklet if she has lost all, or most of, her children ; or one of her surviving children may wear the iron anklet, which, it is believed, will protect the next child that is born. The photograph (Fig. 31) shows two such anklets which I obtained from villages in Middle and Upper Egypt.

If a woman has arrived at the time for her delivery, and she suffers much, but cannot give birth, she may sometimes crawl under the body of a camel seven times backward and forward, after which performance the child is born. The woman crawls from side to side of the camel, so I was told, not between its hind-legs.

If a birth is delayed for three days, and the woman is in constant pain, her husband must wash his right heel and she must drink

[1] The word means 'nail' or 'claw,' but here, perhaps, a 'horn' of a cerastes.

the water in which he washed it. Then he must walk round the village seven times, and while he thus perambulates he must not speak to anyone. If a passer-by salutes him in the usual way he must reply by touching his forehead with his hand, but he must not speak.

Immediately this walk is accomplished the child will be born.

It is said that a protracted birth never occurs if the husband and wife are both good people, but even if only one of them is bad it may still occur.

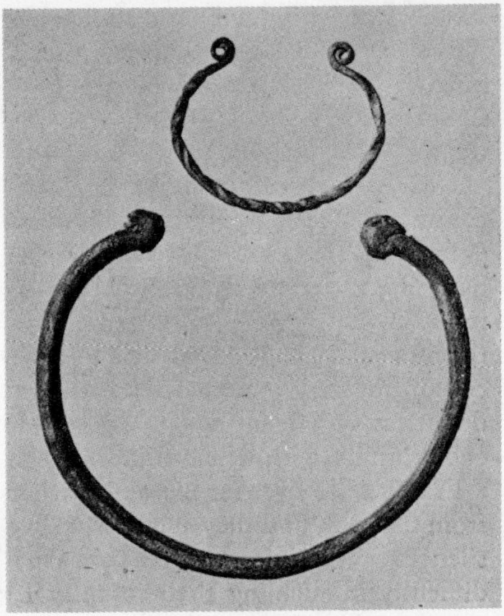

FIG. 31. IRON ANKLETS

If a woman has one miscarriage after another she places the last-born embryo in a niche in the wall inside the house. She takes a red brick—*i.e.*, a brick that has been baked in a kiln, not sun-baked only — and pounds it into powder. She then mixes honey with this powder and eats some of the mixture every day for seven days. At the end of this period she takes the embryo and puts it in a bath, into which she steps, and, squatting over the embryo, she washes herself all over her body. The belief is that the spirit of the embryonic child will enter her body again, and that she will immediately conceive. It is necessary, however, that she and her husband should have marital relations directly after she has had the bath. The body of the embryo is put back into the niche in the wall after she has had the bath and before marital relations take place. It remains there always, but soon falls into dust.

When a child is born it is said that a new star appears in the sky. When the child dies, whether in infancy or at any later period, its star falls. Hence the falling stars.[1] The star falls two or three

[1] The same belief is current in some parts of England.

minutes after the death of the person to whom it belongs. Another explanation of falling stars is that they are darts aimed by God at unbelievers. Lane says [1] that they are believed to be darts thrown by God at evil *ginn*, usually called *ʿafārīt*.

Certain precautions must be taken by a woman after she has given birth to a child. A woman who has lately lost her baby must not enter the room where a woman is being confined, nor for seven days after this event. If this taboo is broken the woman who was last confined will have no milk for her baby.

If a cat gives birth to kittens which all die, and a woman gives birth to a child in the same house in which the cat had its kittens, the cat must be taken away from the house or the baby may die. Or, if it lives, the mother will have no milk.

Near a small village in Asyūṭ Province there is a stone, roughly conical in shape, standing in the fields, and surrounded by whatever crops are being cultivated on that spot. It is said that men have often tried to dig it up, excavating to a considerable depth all round it, but no one has ever been able to come to the bottom of the stone. It is believed by the peasants to be very ancient. A certain mystery is attached to it because of these beliefs, thereby doubtless enhancing its magical value. Women who have not enough milk with which to nurse their children visit this stone on a Friday. They must not speak when coming to and going away from the spot, and they should step over it, still preserving absolute silence, seven times. After this, it is believed, they will have no difficulty in suckling their infant. I was told that the stone has been visited for this purpose, among others, for a hundred years or more.

If a woman or child brings meat to a house where there is a woman who has a child under seven days old that person must not go into the mother's room, but the latter must come out of her room and step over the meat three times. If she does not do this she will have no milk.

When a woman who is a Christian, whether Copt, Protestant, or of any other denomination, has given birth to a child her relatives take some wheat flour and mix it with water. Out of this dough they make several crosses, sticking them on the walls of the room occupied by the mother and child. The greatest

[1] *The Manners and Customs of the Modern Egyptians* (London, 1871), vol. i, p. 283.

number of crosses is placed in that part of the room where the child lies. It is believed that by this means no *ʿafārīt* can come near the child and that the mother's *ḳarīneh* cannot injure it.

Every human being is said to be born with a double, which is quite distinct from the *ʿafrīt*,[1] and it is called, in the case of a man, the *ḳarīn* (colleague, companion), in the case of a woman *ḳarīneh*. The man is always born with his male, as is the woman with her female, counterpart, according to the prevailing belief among most of the *fellāḥīn*. The *ginn*, or *ʿafārīt*, are often called "our brothers and sisters beneath the earth," but they are separate beings from the *aḳrān* (plural of *ḳarīn*), though the two communities are in touch with each other.

The *aḳrān* are believed to be of different colours, some being white, some black; their looks also vary, as some are beautiful and some are ugly. This belief is easily accounted for, as each person's *ḳarīn* is a facsimile of himself or herself, and doubtless the colours are racial distinctions. The *aḳrān* are not, I believe, always malevolent, though stories of their mischief-making propensities are commoner than accounts of their good deeds.

Not only do the *aḳrān* resemble their prototypes on earth in person, but also in character—in fact, they faithfully reflect in themselves all the actions, both good and bad, of their earthly duplicates. Thus, if a man or woman gets into a temper his or her double does the same; if he or she suffers pain and sickness, so does his *ḳarīn* or her *ḳarīneh*. This point was brought out clearly one day three years ago when a large number of women had come to see me and to have their eyes doctored. One of them was speaking about her *ḳarīneh*, so I said, "But your eyes are very bad now, what about those of your *ḳarīneh*?"

"Oh," she replied, "her eyes also are bad."

"Poor thing," I said. "But who is looking after her eyes?"

"Why, your *ḳarīneh*, *ginīb es-sitt* [honoured lady]," the woman immediately answered.

The following is another example of the intimate connexion between a human being and his or her double. When an argument begins between two or more men or women and a mischievous bystander wants to lead them into a real quarrel he will take two bricks and place them on their ends, each tilted against the other, or he will take off one of his shoes and place it on the

[1] See p. 237.

ground upside down—*i.e.*, with the sole uppermost. This will make the disputants quarrel violently, and finally they will resort to blows. As soon as the bricks are taken apart or the shoe replaced on the foot of its owner the quarrelling will stop. My informant himself had witnessed an experiment of this kind. A friend of his, seeing two men arguing in the cultivation, placed one of his shoes, sole upward, on the ground. The disputants immediately started a violent quarrel, hitting out and striking each other. Then the friend replaced the shoe on his foot, and at once the quarrel ceased.

The belief is that when people start quarrelling their *aḳrān* come up above the ground and quarrel also. They are, of course, invisible, but they see the bricks or the shoe, as the case may be, and as long as the bricks remain together, or the shoe remains on the ground, they will continue to fight. As long as the *aḳrān* quarrel the people to whom they belong must quarrel too.

Again, a man's *ḳarīn* marries the *ḳarīneh* of his wife, and when a man or woman dies his *ḳarīn* or her *ḳarīneh* dies also. I had been informed of these facts several times, and the reality of the belief was brought home to me in the following way. An Egyptian friend of mine died some three and a half years ago, and I was sitting with his wife one day after his death when a woman magician came to pay us a visit. I suggested a *séance*, whereupon the magician seated herself in a corner of the room and asked for a blanket, with which she completely covered herself. Presently she clapped her hands two or three times, thus summoning her familiar and some of the *ʿafārīt*. They spoke to her, and after various messages from them had been conveyed to us through the magician my friend's wife asked her to inquire what had become of her husband's *ḳarīn*.

"Oh," was the reply, "he is dead also, and your *ḳarīneh* is a widow."

The magician was something of a ventriloquist, and her voice changed completely when the subterranean beings spoke through her.

As I have stated above, the *aḳrān*, besides being like their human prototypes in colouring and physical features, also resemble them in character. Most of the Egyptian peasants are of a very jealous disposition, and this quality is strongly marked among the women with regard to the possession of children. Childlessness is a real terror to them, and the more children they have the happier they are. They are often very jealous of the offspring of another, and therefore precautions are taken to protect the children from the ill effects of the evil eye, or eye of envy.[1]

A woman's *ḳarīneh* may also be jealous of the human children, in spite of the fact that if a child is born to a woman the *ḳarīn* or *ḳarīneh* of that child represents the offspring of the mother's *ḳarīneh*. Various measures are taken to safeguard the human child from the possible machinations of its mother's double. Indeed, the mother herself during her pregnancy must also be protected, for her *ḳarīneh*, in a fit of jealousy, may come at night while she sleeps and strike her "on the belly," thus causing premature birth. This is curious, as, presumably, the mother's *ḳarīneh* would also lose her child. But, at any rate in some parts of Egypt, the belief is that when a child dies it goes to the mother's *ḳarīneh*, who would in this way possess at least one child, even if her own child (*i.e.*, the human child's double) died at the same time as its human prototype.

Sometimes the *ḳarīneh* speaks roughly to the expectant mother, but refrains from striking her. In such a case the woman will go at daybreak to see a magician or a sheikh, and will ask him to write a protection for her. The protection (or written charm) is the agreement of the queen of the *aḳrān* with King David. For it happened one day that David saw one of them unfasten her hair, and fire was issuing from her mouth.

So he asked her, "What is your work?"

She answered, "If a woman is pregnant I come by night and strike her on her belly, so that she will give birth to a dead child. And if I do not do this, but allow her to bear the child safely, I may perchance come and strike the baby, or cause a snake to bite or a scorpion to sting it, so that it will die."

Then David said to her, "If this is your work I will kill you," and he spoke threateningly to her.

So she made an agreement with him and said, "If a mother carries your words on her person I will never do her harm."

So David consented to this suggestion and let her go on his way. Therefore if a pregnant woman thinks that she has cause to fear that her *ḳarīneh* will do her an injury she will apply for a charm (*ḥigāb*) and wear it till her child is born, when she will give it to

[1] See Chapter XIII.

the infant, hanging it round its neck till it is seven years old, after which period it will be immune.

The *ḳarīneh* seen by King David was the queen of them all, and the promise she gave is binding on all her subjects. She herself is not, according to my informant, the double of any human being ; she is by herself, and, like the king of the *aḳrān*, lives for ever.

A woman's *ḳarīneh* may do good or evil to her children till they have passed the age of seven years She does harm, so I was told, only if the mother has been doing something wrong, or has been jealous of another. For instance, if the *ḳarīneh* clutches a child by the throat it means that the child's mother has been ill-tempered, and so on.

A man's *ḳarīn* does not affect his children ; it only affects him. If he should lose his temper with his wife or family, or with his friends, or does wrong in any way, and goes to bed unrepentant, he may wake up in the morning and find that some illness has attacked him. This has been caused by his *ḳarīn*. When he is sorry and has expressed his repentance, or has called in a magician, who will give him a charm to wear under his left arm, he will be cured.

If a child seems sickly and gets thinner and weaker every day the mother knows that her *ḳarīneh* is trying to draw her child away from her. Various methods are employed to mitigate this evil. Near a small village in Asyūṭ Province there is a large stone which is called the stone of the Sheikheh Fāṭimeh, who is believed to be buried here. If a child is being drawn away by its mother's *ḳarīneh* the mother will take it on a Friday to this stone, near which she will place the child, she herself staying to watch over it. If the child goes to sleep quietly the mother knows that it will recover, but if it cries and refuses to sleep she takes it home again, knowing full well that it will shortly die. I have myself seen a child lying near the stone fast asleep, with its mother sitting by.

In a village in Middle Egypt there is an old, disused graveyard, crowned by the domed tomb of a celebrated local sheikh. The other graves are now fallen into ruin, and many of them show large, gaping hollows (Fig. 32). A woman whose child is affected by her *ḳarīneh* will take it and place it in one of these cavities, the results being the same as in the case of the stone of the Sheikheh Fāṭimeh. This is a common custom in many parts of Egypt.

A child under eight years of age may suddenly begin to shake all over, gasping, and catching at its throat, as if it could not breathe. When this happens the grandmother, or, if there is no grandmother, a neighbour, is called in, and she takes the child, or, if there is more than one child under eight years of age, each one in turn, on to her lap and folds her *gallabīyeh* (native dress) over it. Then she takes a spindle and the implement (*maḥalleh*) on to which the wool is wound after it is spun, and winds the wool on to it; if there is no wool she will simulate the action of winding.

FIG. 32. RUINED GRAVES, IN THE APERTURES OF WHICH CHILDREN ARE PLACED WHEN AFFECTED BY THE MOTHER'S ḲARĪNEH

Then she will break both the spindle and the *maḥalleh*, and the child will recover.

A woman's *ḳarīneh* may sometimes perform a kindly action, for a certain woman who is related to a man whom I know always declares that her *ḳarīneh* is very good to her. This woman has ten boys and two girls, and she is a widow and very poor. Her *ḳarīneh*, so she says, often comes to her when she is short of money and cannot do anything to help herself or her children. On one occasion when she was in this plight she heard her *ḳarīneh* call her by name three times while she was sleeping at night. Her *ḳarīneh* then took her by the hand and led her down the street in which she lived. When she got to the end of it the *ḳarīneh* put some money in her hand and left her. The woman then returned to her house.

Another example of kindness shown by a *ḳarīneh* to her human prototype is described on p. 102 (see also p. 235).

The following is a translation of the written charm (Fig. 33) worn by an expectant mother who has reason to fear harm being done to her offspring by her *ḳarīneh*. The charm is obviously Coptic, but it is used by Muslim mothers as well as by those professing Christianity. " In the Name of God of Triune nature, He is the Mighty Benefactor, Creator of all the powerful witches [evil women], Whom eye does not see and thought cannot conceive [mix with], Who knows what is before it is, before Whom the angels tremble with awe, and Whom the devils fear for His Power. All things in Heaven and on earth worship Him, and He is Ruler over all things. O God, by Thy Mighty Name and Powerful Arm and the Beneficent Light of Thy Face protect the bearer of this my charm—what is in her womb and who drinks [will drink] of her milk—from the devilish, cursed *ḳarīneh* by the power of this magic square and what of Thy Mighty Name it contains."

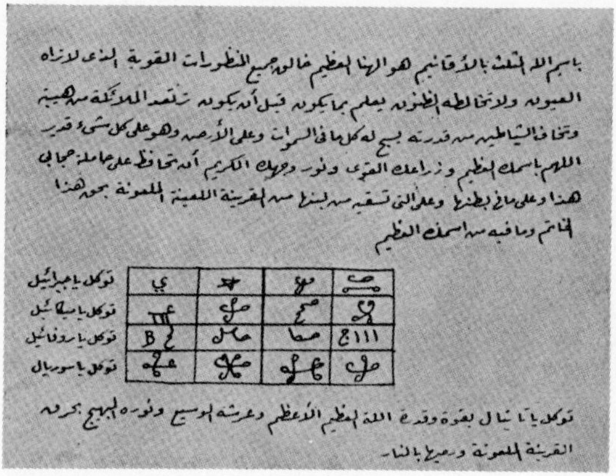

The probable meaning of the square in the illustration is, so I was told : " Make it your charge, O Gabrāīl, make it your charge, O Mikhāīl, make it your charge, O Rūfāīl, make it your charge, O Sūriyāl, make it your charge, O Māniyāl, by the power and might of the Mighty God, the Almighty, and His broad Throne, and His dazzling Light, to burn the cursed *ḳarīneh* and cast her into the fire."

There is another personality besides the *ḳarīn* or *ḳarīneh*, called the *ukht* (sister), which is believed to be born simultaneously with each human being. There is, however, no *akhkh* (brother), but the *ukht* only is attached to each individual, whether male or female. According to my informants among the *fellāḥīn*, the *ukht* of each person lives underground,[1] though it comes up on occasions. It resembles in character the human being to whom it is attached. Thus, if a man or woman is good his or her *ukht* is good, if bad the *ukht* is bad also. It is quite distinct an entity from the *ḳarīn* and *ḳarīneh*.[2]

The following incidents happened last year in connexion with a woman and her husband, both of whom are well known to me. The woman in question was expecting to become a mother, and she and her husband were having a meal together one day when a cat came into the house and tried to eat some of their food. The woman hit the cat, which disappeared immediately. Being surprised at this sudden and miraculous disappearance of the animal, the woman consulted a well-known female magician who lives in her village. This magician got into touch with the "people beneath the earth," who informed her that the *ukht* of the woman mentioned above was angry with her, and wanted to know why she had hit her when she had come to her house in the form of a cat. The woman then said that she was very sorry, but she had not known that it was her *ukht* who had come in that form. The *ukht* said, "Why did you hit me? Did you not want me to eat?" She also complained that the woman to whom she was *ukht* had no *kūz* for her *zīr*, so that she (the *ukht*) could not drink when she came to the house. (A *kūz* is a large tin mug, and anyone who wants a drink dips it into the *zīr*—a large pottery jar, often kept in a special kind of cupboard, and containing the household water—and drinks from it.) The magician told the woman that she must buy a *kūz* and put it with the *zīr* in the cupboard, which was to be locked so that no one could get at it, and the *ukht* could drink without being disturbed.

It also transpired that the woman's *ukht* and also the *ukht* of her husband were both very jealous, because the man and his wife were always laughing together. The two *ikhwāt* (plural of *ukht*) said they did not like it, and that if this merriment between the pair continued all their children should die. The woman was to laugh only occasionally, and then all would be well. To my own know-

[1] See also pp. 69, 184, 186, 227.

[2] See my article on the subject, "The Ḳarīn and Ḳarīneh," in the *Journal of the Royal Anthropological Institute*, vol. lvi, January–June, 1926, pp. 163–169.

ledge this woman is of an exceedingly jealous disposition, which no doubt accounts for that particular trait being exhibited in her *ukht*! Her husband is a decent man, but I have had no opportunity of judging as to whether he is jealous or not. However, one must presume that he is so, in view of the fact that his *ukht* appears to possess this quality in so marked a degree!

As will be seen below on p. 186, some of the subterranean beings also have each an *ukht*.

FIG. 34. CHILD WEARING FROCK AND HOOD OF SACKING

A woman remains unclean for forty days after giving birth to a boy and for thirty days if the child is a girl. I have also been informed that the husband must not enter the room occupied by his wife for seven days after the birth, and that if he wishes to speak to her he must do so from a distance. I am not sure if this is always the rule, but it is so among some of the *fellāḥīn*.

A child is not washed at all until the seventh day after birth, and then the face, hands, and feet only are washed. When I endeavoured to make the women understand how unhealthy this was they declared that they were afraid to wash a child until it was seven days old, and then only to the limited extent just mentioned, for fear of its catching cold. On one occasion a child was brought to me in a most filthy state, and covered from head to foot with suppurating sores. I told the mother that I would not give her any medicine until she had washed the child. On hearing this she became terribly distressed, and declared that she could not wash it. I remained firm, however, in my refusal to give her anything until she had made the child cleaner. It transpired that the child's father had had spots on his body when he was younger, and from what the woman said I fear that it was syphilis from which he was suffering. Anyhow, she told me that if the father or mother suffered in this way their children were never washed at all until they were old enough to wash themselves. Two doctor friends of mine confirmed this, stating that they knew the practice to be a common one among the peasants. As for the child which was brought to me, I am glad to say that I at last persuaded the mother to wash it to a certain extent, and I gave her some medicine. This happened a few years ago, and on my visiting the same village again some time later I was glad to hear that the child was well and flourishing.

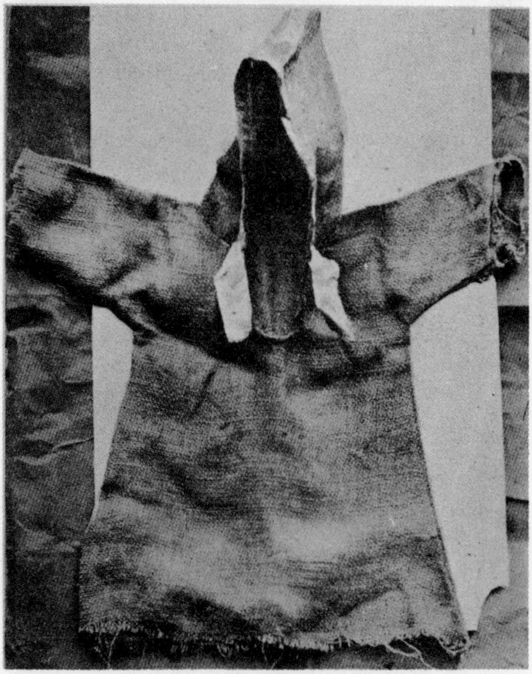

FIG. 35. FROCK AND HOOD MADE OF SACKING

The same woman had lost several children in early infancy before this particular infant was born. The child was wearing a peculiar dress, made of sacking, and with a hood in one piece with the frock (Fig. 34). The woman informed me, and I have been told the same thing by others, that this dress was put on the child to make it live. The dress must always be made out of a sack which has contained raw cotton; no other kind will do. Two such dresses were made and given to me (see Fig. 35).

On the seventh day after the birth a midwife comes and washes the child, as stated above, and also the mother. The water used for washing the child is obtained the night before and put into a metal jug with a long spout called an *ibrīḳ*. This is stood in a metal basin, and both are placed near the mother and child. The water is called *moiyet el-malāyikeh* (water of the angels), angels meaning in this connexion the *ḳarīn* of the father, the *ḳarīneh* of the mother, and the *ḳarīn* (or *ḳarīneh*) of the child. The *ibrīḳ* is decorated in different ways according to the sex of the child. On the occasion of the birth of a boy I observed that a rosary (*sibḥeh*) belonging to the father was twisted round the *ibrīḳ*, while a handkerchief belonging to the boy's sister was tied round the top of the vessel. On another occasion, when a girl was born, the mother's gold necklace and some brightly coloured silk handkerchiefs were fastened round the *ibrīḳ* (see Fig. 36). This decoration is done, so I was told, to appease the *malāyikeh*, who would then do no harm to the child or its mother. After the child has been washed a man of the same age as the father of the infant must drink the water that remains over in the *ibrīḳ* It is believed that this will ensure the child's growing up into manhood.

FIG. 36. YOUNG MOTHER AND CHILD WITH DECORATED IBRĪḲ

On the seventh night (*i.e.*, the evening preceding the seventh day) two or three large baskets, each containing salt, beans, seed of *ḥelbeh* (fenugreek), lentils, wheat, clover, and maize, are placed in the room occupied by the mother and child. Sometimes one of the baskets may be filled with bread, this being often in the form of rings. On one of the baskets is placed a large winnowing sieve, in which the child sleeps all night. When the midwife comes on the following morning, and both mother and child have been washed, some of the grains from one of the baskets are put in the sieve, the baby also being placed in it. The midwife then tosses and shakes the baby in the sieve, its mother meanwhile banging the edge of the metal basin with a tin mug. The striking of the basin by the mother is not, I believe, always done, but on one occasion when I was present at this ceremony the mother acted in this way. The tossing and shaking of the child in the sieve is repeated several times, after which the grains are returned to the basket. The midwife now takes the child in her arms, and covers it with a cloth of white cotton on which are placed some of the grains from one of the baskets. Having first carried the child into all the rooms on the ground floor, she then goes outside the house, sprinkling some of the grains wherever she walks, and repeating "*Ṣalla ʿa 'n-Nebi*" ("Bless the Prophet") over and over again during the whole of her perambulation.

FIG. 37. UMBILICAL CORD IN COTTON WRAPPING, AND OTHER CHARMS SUSPENDED FROM IT

Left to right: twisted iron wire, string of seven grains of beans, and bag containing samples of the seven ingredients of one of the baskets.

The child is now taken back into the mother's room, and the midwife blackens its eyes with *koḥl*, a bottle of which she has brought with her. She dips a feather into the *koḥl*, and, having opened the child's eyes, passes the feather across each of them in turn. After thus painting the eyes she fastens round the child's neck the cotton case containing a piece of the umbilical cord, to which are attached a string of seven grains of beans and a little cotton bag containing a small quantity of the seven ingredients of one of the baskets (Fig. 37).

The midwife's fee consists of a large basket (Fig. 38) of maize, bread, dates, various nuts, and occasionally a little money.[1]

Some of the six various grains, together with the salt, are often given to the father to scatter over his fields. This is a fertility charm, and is believed to ensure his having good crops.

FIG. 38. MIDWIFE CARRYING HER WAGES ON HER HEAD

In addition to the charms mentioned above, the child sometimes has another one made of thick iron wire twisted into a particular shape (Fig. 37). This is also hung round the child's neck, but only so if, when it cries, it clenches its hands and shakes itself.

In some parts of Upper Egypt the following mixture is put into a child's eyes by the midwife on the seventh day. The woman brings an onion with her and squeezes the juice from it into a small coffee-cup, mixing with it salt, oil, and, usually, *koḥl* also. Then, taking a feather, she dips it into the mixture and, opening the child's eyes, brushes the feather right across them. It is believed that this will give the child wide open and beautiful eyes.

The naming of the child is part of the seventh-day ceremony. If the parents are anxious to discover the best and luckiest name for their offspring they proceed as follows. Candles, usually four

[1] Sometimes she is, I believe, paid only in grain.

in number, sometimes of different colours, are procured, and a different name is inscribed on each. All these candles are lighted at once, and the name on the candle which burns the longest is the one eventually bestowed on the child. After it has received a name the birth is entered in the Government archives, the name of the child's mother only being given ; the father's name is not entered at all.

Boys are more highly valued than girls, and special precautions have to be taken when a male child is born to protect him from the evil eye. Sometimes the midwife is bribed to keep the sex of the child a secret, and if she is paid a sufficiently large sum of money she will consent to give out to the villagers that the child is a girl. I was told of a case of a woman who had given birth to a boy not knowing the sex of the child until it was thirty days old or more, and her husband was equally ignorant.

As a further protection from the evil eye a boy is often dressed as a girl for two years or so, all the villagers, presumably, being led to think that the child is a girl.

Women are supposed to suckle their children for two years, but if a woman again conceives before the end of this period she must, of course, wean her last-born child. When this happens she hangs a ' date of jealousy ' round the child's neck to prevent its being jealous of the baby when it is born. I once witnessed a most frantic display of jealousy on the part of a very young child when he saw his mother with the newly arrived infant in her arms. He flung himself upon her in a fury of envious rage. The ' dates of jealousy ' in some parts of Egypt are acorns ; in other parts they are made of a kind of earth moulded into the form of a date stone.

If a child cries very much the mother will sometimes purchase a very small copy of the Ḳorān and hang it round the child's neck. It is believed that if the child begins to cry and then looks at the Ḳorān which it is wearing it will immediately stop weeping. Such small editions of this sacred book are also worn by a child to keep it well and to ensure its living. When used for this purpose the book is sewn up in a cotton case.

If, after long waiting, a woman at last bears a son a festival, or *mūlid*, is held. There are various kinds of *mawālid* (plural of *mūlid*) held for different reasons and on various occasions, and among them is that held in celebration of the birth of a son. It is a kind of thanksgiving on the part of the parents, and is also believed to be beneficial to the child. I have been present at one or two such ceremonies, and the following description is typical of all.

A ram had been purchased for sacrifice, and the services of a butcher engaged for the slaughter of the animal. When I arrived at the house I was conducted on to the roof, where various members of the family were awaiting me. The ram was also there, in happy ignorance of its fate. Presently the butcher arrived, and when he had ascertained that his knife was sufficiently sharp the poor animal was made to lie on the ground on its back. Then with a "*Bismillāh er-Raḥmān er-Raḥīm*" ("In the Name of God the Compassionate, the Merciful") the butcher cut the ram's throat. I must confess that I did not see this part of the performance, for I closed my eyes and blocked up my ears, telling the people to let me know when it was all over. The carcass of the animal was then hung up and skinned. The skin was, I believe, given to the butcher, in recognition of his services. A good deal of the blood was preserved in a large bowl, and the house-door was sprinkled with it, a large dab of it being smeared on the centre.

The reason for the slaughtering of the ram at a *mūlid* for a child may be that a life is thus given for a life, and so this sacrifice of the animal will ensure the life of the child.

The child's mother and some of her female relatives now set to work to prepare the meat and cook it for the large number of guests who would assemble at the house in the evening, while I retired for a short rest. At about seven o'clock I returned to the house, where great preparations had been made, and where a considerable number of visitors had already assembled. The seat of honour had been reserved for me, and soon after I arrived a sheikh celebrated for his excellent chanting of the Ḳorān entered with his assistants. I had brought a number of boxes of cigarettes with me, and some of these were now handed round by my servant, while coffee was brought for me. Newcomers constantly arrived, till every available seat had been taken, both on benches and on the floor, and then the sheikh began to recite. Such recitations are always intoned, and are repeated entirely from memory. The performer nearly always places a hand against one side of his face while he recites, and sways in rhythmic accompaniment to his chanting. This particular sheikh is renowned for his voice, and warm exclamations of approval were heard on all sides as he proceeded. Finally he stood up on a high bench, and, one hand against his face and the other holding a rosary, worked himself up to an even greater pitch of fervour, gesticulating with the hand which held the beads. The audience too became more and more enthusiastic, and there were constant cries of "*Yā sheikh!*" ("O sheikh!"), "*Aiwa, keda!*" ("Yes, thus!"), as we might say, "Yes, go on!" One man at last got so beside himself with emotional fervour that he rose abruptly from his seat, tore off his turban, which he hurled at the sheikh, and then clasped him by the knees. Others too followed his example, flinging themselves in admiration on the sheikh.

When the recitations had gone on for some time there was a pause, and more coffee was handed round, and also more of my cigarettes. During this interval one of the sheikh's assistants went the round of the guests, to inquire of each whether he desired a *Fātiḥeh* to be repeated for himself, or for friends, the latter being mentioned by name. Each person presented the assistant with a small sum of money. Very many *Fātiḥehs* were said for me and for my family, while I made similar requests for several of my village friends. Then the recitations began again, and shortly after there was another pause as before. I am afraid to say how many boxes of cigarettes I distributed, but I do know that they were thoroughly appreciated.

This performance was continued till nearly midnight, when at last I rose to take leave of my friends. My departure broke up the assembly, and the rest of the guests quickly dispersed to their several homes. I was told afterward that it was one of the most successful *mawālid* that had ever been held; never had they had so many cigarettes to smoke, and never had the sheikh and his assistants received so much money! I regret to say that the child for whose benefit this *mūlid* was held died rather suddenly before I left Egypt.

Among the Copts the child receives its name at baptism, when the parents take it to the church. Total immersion is the recognized form of baptism among the Copts, and, according to Dr A. J. Butler,[1] the rite is permissible only in certain seasons of the year, and no child should be baptized during Lent, Holy Week, or at Eastertide. The same authority also states that a boy must be

[1] *The Ancient Coptic Churches of Egypt* (Oxford, 1884), vol. ii, p. 264.

forty days old and a girl eighty before they can receive this sacrament.[1]

Exception to this rule is made in cases of grave illness. According to my informant, the water for baptism is contained in a tank in the ground. After asking the mother what name is to be given to the child the priest dips the infant into the water three times, each time repeating the name chosen for it. The child is then returned to its mother, who dresses it, and then the priest takes a silken thread, which the mother has brought with her, and places it round the child, passing it under its left arm. He then ties this thread into a knot with a loop. A certain number of prayers are repeated, after which a few drops of the Eucharistic wine are given to the child to drink. Most of the people who have been present at this ceremony now take their departure, but the parents, with the child, remain in the church while the choir sing certain chants. The priest then questions the parents as to their willingness to bring up the child with a knowledge of the Christian religion, impressing on them how great their responsibility is with regard to the proper religious instruction of their child.

When the ceremony is over the parents give the priest some money, the amount varying according to their means, and then the priest unties the knot he made in the silken thread.

In all Egyptian villages a number of little boys may be seen with their heads shaved save for a few tufts of hair, which are left untouched. Each of such tufts is dedicated, in the case of Muslims, to a sheikh, or to a saint if the child's parents are Copts, or sometimes all the tufts are dedicated to one sheikh or saint. I am told that there is no *special* age for the hair to be cut in this way, but I believe it is always done in very early childhood, probably as soon as the hair has grown, for I have never seen any but young children with these tufts of hair left on their heads. The ceremonial cutting off of the tufts is not, so far as I have discovered, performed at any particular age of boyhood, but the date of the performance seems to depend on whether the father can afford the expense that the ceremony entails, such expense in some parts of Upper Egypt being considerable. It has never been suggested to me that the ceremony takes place when the boy has reached the age of puberty. Indeed, as far as my own experience goes, the tufts were removed long before that period was reached.

[1] *The Ancient Coptic Churches of Egypt* (Oxford, 1884), vol. ii, p. 263.

When it is desired that the tufts shall be shaved off quite an important ceremony takes place—at least, according to my informant, in Asyūṭ Province. When possible the child is taken to the tomb or tombs of the sheikh or sheikhs to whom the tufts of hair are dedicated, and the tufts are removed just within, or just outside, the sacred building (Fig. 39), or the child may be taken to a mosque, where the ceremony can also be performed. If the child is a Copt it is taken to the church or churches named after the saint or saints to whom these tufts of hair have been dedicated. In the case of the Muslims the village barber is called in to remove the hair, but with the Copts a priest performs the rite. The removal of these tufts takes place if possible when the hair is four to five centimetres long, but in parts of Upper Egypt the ceremony is so expensive for a poor *fellāh* that the child may have to wait some time longer before the tufts can be removed. Bread and meat are taken to the tombs or mosques where the ceremony is to be performed, and then a feast is held to the accompaniment of dancing, beating of the drum (*darābukkeh*), hand-clapping, and *zaghārīṭ*.[1] The barber on these occasions may demand quite a large sum of money, and altogether the ceremony rarely costs less than six pounds, often more.

FIG. 39. CHILD ABOUT TO HAVE ITS TUFTS OF HAIR CUT OFF AT THE TOMB OF THE SHEIKH UMBĀRAK

The man on the right is the barber.

[1] The shrill cries of joy uttered by women on all festive occasions.

I myself witnessed the performance of the rite in Fayūm Province, where the proceedings were simpler. The child whose tufts were to be removed was taken to the tomb of the sheikh Umbārak, to whom they had all been dedicated. The barber arrived and shaved off the hair just within the entrance to the tomb. On this occasion the child was held by the sister-in-law of the child's mother, but I do not think there is any fixed rule as to who should act in this capacity. There was no feast or dancing, but such festivities may take place also in this province, though they are not necessary, as I was told was the case in Asyūṭ Province. The child's mother is a friend of mine, and as I paid the barber's fee myself I managed, with the assistance of the woman who held the child, to secure half the hair that had been cut off. The cut-off hair is always buried outside the tomb or mosque where it has been cut off, and is put in the ground either loose [1] or else is first enclosed in a clay ball. On the occasion when I was present at this ceremony the hair was enclosed in a clay ball and buried outside the sheikh Umbārak's tomb, and half was kept back and put in another clay ball and presented to me. The ball in my possession is somewhat flattened at the base, owing to the fact that the clay of which it is made was rather moist, and the placing of the ball outside the house to sun-bake naturally flattened that portion which rested on the ground.

As stated above, Coptic parents take their children to have the tufts removed at the church or churches, or sometimes it may be to the tomb or tombs, of the saint or saints to whom the tufts of hair are dedicated. The priest, as has also been stated, officiates as barber, the father presenting a gift of money to the church or churches where the tufts are removed. On such an occasion a special service is held at the church, and oxen and fowls are killed outside the building, the meat, together with bread, being distributed among the assembled crowd of friends and the poor. If the parents are not rich enough to supply such a munificent feast they will bring a smaller quantity of meat with them, and will distribute it and the bread to the crowds which always collect outside the building on these occasions ; in such cases no sacrifices are made. Among the Copts no dancing takes place at this ceremony as among the Muslims, but the women utter the cries of joy (*zaghārīṭ*), and there is a good deal of singing.

I have been told that if a woman remains for a long time after

[1] See my article in *Man*, vol. xxv, Pl. E, Fig. 4.

marriage without the prospect of a child she will pray for a son, promising that, in the event of her prayer being answered, she will have the boy's hair shaved, leaving only the tufts, which she will dedicate to the sheikh or sheikhs, or to the saint or saints, with whom she has interceded. When offering such prayers she will probably repair to the tomb of the sheikh, or to the church of the Coptic saint, to whom she wishes to appeal. I was told in Fayūm Province that if a boy is seen with his hair cut into tufts it means that he is an only son, and that this style of headdress will ensure him a long life. The initial cutting of the hair, it should be pointed out, is performed at home.

Among the Copts the rite of circumcision should be observed before baptism, according to Dr Butler.[1] The actual ceremony closely resembles the Muslim rite, so that the following description applies to the followers of both religions, the only difference being that whereas the Coptic child should have this operation before baptism, for the Muslim there is no limitation as to age, though it is always carried out during the early years of a child's life. The ceremony entails a certain expense, and is therefore sometimes carried out conjointly with a marriage ceremony, so that the cost may be shared.

The boy who is to undergo this operation has his hands and feet dyed with *ḥenna* at sunset two days before it takes place. On the following day the barber comes and cuts the boy's hair in a particular way, called *muḳarraṣ*, which means 'made into little loaves or cakes.' I do not think that this form of hairdressing is in any way connected with the tufts of hair described above. After the haircutting the boy is washed, and, so I was told, coins are put on his face. This is probably the same custom as is observed at weddings, when the female visitors who wish to present the bride with small sums of money go up to her and place the coin they wish to give to her on her upturned face. In the case of the boy the money presented in this way is taken by the barber. The boy then has a particular kind of felt cap placed on his head. This cap, which is white in colour, decorated with yellow designs and tassels (Fig. 40), is purchased by the parents especially for the occasion, and worn only for this rite. The cap is further decorated by the attachment of scraps of coloured paper or bits of cloth or muslin. The boy, thus attired, is then placed on a horse, usually, I believe, with his face toward the animal's tail; he is covered up with a shawl, and, with one man holding him securely and another leading

[1] See my article in *Man*, vol. xxv, p. 263.

the horse, he is paraded through the village, accompanied by musicians. If two brothers are to have this operation at the same time they ride together on one horse. When the perambulation of the village is over the boy is taken home, and all the friends who have placed money on his face, and also the barber, are provided with supper. Music plays an important part at this ceremony, and the musicians keep up a constant beating of drums, clashing of cymbals, and blowing of bagpipes. When the guests have finished supper they all, including the musicians, take their departure. On the following morning the barber only comes to the house and is first paid by the parents, who give him anything from one or two pounds upward. The child is then taken hold of and told not to be afraid. Some one tries to attract his attention, while the barber seizes this opportunity to cut off the foreskin. The boy wears a white *gallabīyeh* for this occasion, with long sleeves, in one of which the foreskin is tied up. The barber then ties the boy's mother and maternal aunt together by binding a turban round their throats, and drags them outside the door of the house. Friends, who by this time have collected outside, come into the house and present the barber with more money, and he then takes his departure. The wound is washed every day, and is anointed with some healing powder, which is, I fancy, *ḥenna*. The foreskin remains in the sleeve of the boy's *gallabīyeh* until the wound is healed, during which period the white gown must also be worn.

FIG. 40. CAP WORN BY A BOY AT HIS CIRCUMCISION CEREMONY

A charm consisting of short lengths of the mid-rib of a palm-branch, deeply notched along one side, is worn by boys after they have been circumcised to keep the wound from going septic, and to ward off the evil eye. Such a charm is worn for seven days after the operation, being suspended from the neck by a string.

No reason could be given as to why the mother and maternal aunt were tied together by the throat and thrust out of the house.

I suggest that it may possibly be a way of emphasizing the fact that the boy has now definitely joined the male community by undergoing this operation, and that therefore he is no longer under the control of his mother and her female relatives. This is a pure guess, and is brought forward only as a possible explanation of this somewhat curious custom.

It is a common belief all over Egypt that the souls of twins when they have passed babyhood often leave their bodies at night and enter the bodies of cats. These animals, therefore, are usually very kindly treated. The following stories were told me in connexion with this belief, and my informant declared that they were true and that he knew the people concerned.

In a small village in Asyūṭ Province there was a boy who was one of twins, his twin, however, being dead. One night a cat came to a house and clambered on to the flat roof, upon which were some of the usual mud granaries. Some *kishk*, which is made of wheat mixed with milk, dried in the sun, and then cut up, was stored in one of these receptacles. It is often offered to visitors as a great delicacy. The cat knocked the lid off the granary which contained the *kishk*, jumped into it, and began to eat some of the contents. A member of the household happened to go on to the roof, and, seeing the granary uncovered, immediately put the lid on it without noticing that the cat was inside. It remained covered for three days, keeping the cat a prisoner. During this period the boy mentioned above remained motionless and unconscious on his bed, his soul being in the body of the imprisoned cat.

After the third day some visitors arrived at the house where was the granary in question, and one of the family went to get some of the *kishk* out of it to offer the guests. When the lid was removed the cat jumped out and ran away. Immediately after this the soul of the twin returned to his body, and he rose from his bed quite well.

One evening a cat in whose body the soul of a twin happened to be temporarily incarnate was struck on the head by a woman. On the following day the twin in question came to this woman and accused her of striking him the previous night, pointing out to her exactly where she had hit him, and complaining that the blow had caused him considerable pain.

If a cat is killed while the soul of a twin is in its body the twin dies also. For this reason cats are rarely killed.

CHAPTER V

MARRIAGE AND DIVORCE

I HAVE already stated that girls at a very early age dress themselves up in order to attract attention to themselves and so secure a husband. These children are often married to quite elderly men, old enough to be their fathers or even their grandfathers. Such disparity in age is most unsuitable, and frequently leads to great unhappiness. In their attempts to obtain husbands the girls are aided and abetted by their mothers, who resort to magic and trickery of all sorts to secure a desirable man. The two following incidents, which occurred while I was in Egypt in 1926, illustrate a device often employed by women who want to catch a man, either for themselves or for one of their daughters.

A certain woman living in a village in Middle Egypt was walking out one day when her glance fell on a young man (Fig. 41) to whom she took a great fancy, and who, she thought, would make an excellent husband for her daughter. She therefore went to a magician and begged him to write a charm, which she buried under the threshold of her house. She then persuaded one of her male relatives to bring the young man to her house on the pretext that he desired his company when he went thither on some business matter. The young man acceded to this request, and the elder man, who knew the exact spot where the charm was buried, stood at the door of the woman's house in such a position that his companion, when he entered, must step over the buried charm. The girl made some coffee for the two visitors, and either brought it in herself or allowed the young man to get a glimpse of her in some other way. The youth then went home, and on the way there began to think of the girl whom he had seen, and to desire her as his wife. By the time he reached home he wanted her still more, and by the evening was quite mad about her, refusing to eat or sleep, and saying that he must have the girl as his wife. I saw him several times after this, and he was in a most forlorn and love-sick condition, imploring me to intercede with his father, who was not inclined to pay the bride-price, partly because the girl had been married before, but chiefly, I think, because he did not want to part with the money. The love-stricken young man, who had already got his portion of his father's house allotted to him in view of his marriage later on, would often enter these apartments to clean and tidy them, meditating the while on the girl whom he so desired.

The effect of this device on a man is, I am told, always the same; and even if he is already betrothed to another girl he will break off his engagement.

FIG. 41. THE YOUNG MAN WHO WAS THE VICTIM OF A LOVE-CHARM

In Egypt betrothal is almost, if not quite, as binding as marriage, and the people speak of the dissolving of such a tie as a divorce. A man who has been affected in the way described above will, if he is betrothed, pay a large sum of money to get rid of the girl whom he was originally to have married. I was told that the man is quite unaware that a charm has been used to catch him. He just gets mad about the girl without any knowledge that such a trap has been set for him.

On the other occasion the mother and brothers of a young unmarried girl were very anxious that she should secure a husband, but hitherto none had been forthcoming. One of my servants, a young man of twenty-two, had been seen several times by the various members of this family and by the girl herself. He is rather a nice-looking young man, and, moreover, has a certain amount of land and a good house. The eldest brother of the girl had been to my servant's village and visited his home, and had seen that his family was very superior to most of the other villagers. One day when my servant was walking through the garden of the house which had been lent to me by the Government he noticed a piece of paper lying on the ground under one of the palm-trees. He picked it up and saw that it was a charm of some kind. He cannot read or write, but he can sign his name, and he noticed that his name was written on this charm. One of the Government *employés* who lives near by has a considerable knowledge of such matters, so my servant took the paper to him. The man read it and said that it was a charm written to make my servant love the girl mentioned above. It had been placed high up in the palm-tree, but had not been securely tied to the branch, and so had fallen on to the ground. However, it would not have been effective in any case, as the name of my servant's father was written in it, and not the name of his mother, which must always be inserted in such charms. The man said that it was a charm of terrible potency, and that, but for this slip, due probably to their not knowing the mother's name, it would have been disastrous in its effect! Unfortunately, my servant tore it up before he told me about it. I reproached him for not giving it to me, as he knew I was anxious to collect such things, but he was obviously frightened, and felt that he must destroy it. I may mention that this young man is now safely married to one of his cousins.

As I have stated before, the girls when they have reached marriageable age are more restricted in their freedom. If there is an unmarried cousin, especially one in the paternal line, a girl is usually married to him. When a marriage is contemplated the relatives of the two parties discuss how much money either is prepared to provide. When this has been settled the prospective bridegroom, or rather his father, pays the bride-price agreed upon to the bride's parents. They then repair to the *ḳāḍi*, as the village judge is called, and he writes out the agreement between the two parties. The couple are now betrothed, a betrothal, as I have already stated, being almost as binding as a marriage.

Among the Muslims there is no religious ceremony at a wedding, for with them marriage is not regarded as a sacrament; the actual marriage takes place when the bride goes to her husband's house. The bride is usually, so I am told, taken to her husband's house at sunset, but I have often seen her being conveyed thither in the daytime. She is usually taken there on a camel, being seated in a sort of tent-like erection fixed on to the animal's back, and she is accompanied by some of her girl friends. This erection sways from side to side as the camel walks along. Other camels, with similar erections on their backs, follow, bearing other female relatives and friends, many of the women uttering their *zaghārīṭ* as they proceed. I am told that a bride is thus conveyed on a camel if her husband lives in another village, but that she rides a horse if he lives in the same village as her parents. I have myself, however, never seen a bride on horseback.

Now that Ford cars are so common in Egypt even the *fellāḥīn* sometimes use them for conveying the bride and her friends to the bridegroom's house, the wedding procession thereby losing a great deal of its old picturesqueness. Cartloads of furniture are carried from the bride's house to that of the bridegroom, usually on the day before she goes there herself. Everything is left uncovered while it is being conveyed to the house, so that people may see what good furniture the bride is taking with her !

Music plays an important part in all the marriage festivities, and the bridal procession often includes a band. The groom gives a feast in his house to all his male friends, the bride remaining in a room at the top of the house with her female relatives and companions. The women dance a peculiar dance on these occasions, usually known to Europeans as the *danse à ventre*. It is exceedingly ugly, and must require a special development of abdominal muscles. A woman or girl who performs in this way first ties a sash tightly round her waist, then, holding out a stick in front of her in both hands, she jerks her stomach up and down, turning round and round as she does so. As I have said before,[1] the bride's friends present her with small sums of money, placing these gifts on her upturned face. As evening advances guns are fired, the women utter their *zaghārīṭ*, and the musicians likewise contribute to the general din. An awning is usually erected outside the house, and here the men congregate, congratulating the bridegroom and drinking coffee and smoking. The festivities are usually kept up for two or three days unless the people are very poor.

Among the Copts the preliminary arrangements are much the same as among the Muslims, but with them there is, of course, a marriage service in the church. Among the *fellāḥīn* the bride is brought to church on a camel if she and her bridegroom live in different villages, but on a horse if their homes are in the same village. The bride is followed by her female friends similarly mounted. I am told that the service takes place in the evening,

[1] See p. 87.

and that the procession is accompanied by men carrying lanterns and candles. As they proceed the women utter their *zaghārīṭ*. The priest addresses the pair, but before he does so he takes a silken thread and passes it over the right shoulder of the bridegroom and under his left arm, where he ties the thread into a knot with a loop. After the address from the priest is over the bridegroom pays him a sum of money, and then the priest undoes the knotted thread. He then takes the two engagement rings which the bride and bridegroom gave each other at their betrothal and ties them together with a silken thread. After putting certain questions to the pair he returns them their rings, and each puts his or her ring on; the bridegroom does not place the ring on the bride's finger.

After the service is over the priest invites anyone present who may wish to do so to speak. Perhaps one man may get up and deliver an oration, in which, in addition to various other complimentary remarks, he will probably compare the bride to the moon, and the bridegroom to the sun. Others will follow his example, and even women are permitted to speak on such occasions. The bridegroom then either himself thanks his friends for their kindly speeches or asks his father or his brother to do this for him.

Both bride and bridegroom wear new clothes on the occasion of their marriage, and they wear these garments for seven days after the wedding. When this period has elapsed these clothes are put away for several days, and then they can be worn at any time.

When the bride is on her way to the bridegroom's house her unmarried female friends who accompany her thither pinch her on one of her thighs. By doing this they believe that they also will soon get a husband. The bridegroom is pinched in the same way by his unmarried male friends, who hope that this will ensure each of them a bride. I am told that this is a common custom among the *fellāḥīn*.

On the morning after the marriage night the bridegroom when he goes out pulls a branch off a palm-tree, tears off all the leaves, and then cuts off a long length of the thicker end of the mid-rib as a stick. He then splits up one end of it several times, so that these split ends stand out slightly. With this split stick he strikes any of his unmarried male friends whom he happens to meet. Those whom he thus strikes will, it is believed, shortly marry too. This, according to my informant, is a very old custom which was formerly common to all classes in Egypt, but now survives only among the *fellāḥīn*.

Among the Copts divorce is never permitted, but among the Muslims it is not a difficult matter to arrange, though it is necessary for a man or woman to produce some valid reason for taking this course of action. The parties, or perhaps the husband or the wife only, go before the *ḳāḍi* and say that they wish to be divorced. A sum of money is sometimes paid to the other party by the one who applies for the divorce. A man is permitted to divorce his wife if she is childless; that is to say, if he wishes to get rid of her. If after such a separation the parties wish to marry again they can do so. The 'triple divorce' is a much more serious affair, as will be seen in the following story.

FIG. 42. THE OLD MAN WHO DIVORCED HIS WIFE

An old man whom I have known for several years (Fig. 42) came to me in great distress when I arrived in his village. He is eighty years of age or more, and owns most, if not all, the looms in the place. I thought he seemed very bent, and he hobbled along with the aid of a stick, followed by a grinning crowd of villagers. He fell down at my feet and began to kiss my boots, and appeared to be beside himself with grief. It appeared that shortly before my arrival he had got into a temper with his wife (Fig. 43), who is considerably younger than he is, and in a fit of rage had divorced her by the triple divorce. This divorce is obtained by a man saying to his wife " I divorce you " three times over, in the presence of witnesses. Once this is done he cannot remarry his wife, however much he may wish to do so, unless she first marries another man, who must consummate the marriage. After this, if the parties agree, they can be divorced, and the original husband can marry the woman again.

The old man begged me to see if I could do anything to help him, but I told him that there was nothing I could do, and that, in any case, at his age he ought no longer to be contemplating marriage, but had better direct his thoughts to preparing himself for death. I was told by some of the villagers that the divorced wife had been to a magician, who had written a charm to make the old man mad with love for her. Nearly every time I went to this village I found the old man mooning about the street near the house where his divorced wife was staying, and the villagers told me that he was always sitting there, in the hope of getting a glimpse of the woman, and that on market days he would buy her presents of meat and material for dresses, which he left at her house. I made the acquaintance of the wife, a tall, rather fine-looking woman. She appeared to be very happy and cheerful, and quite amused at the display of love on the part of her late husband. Just before I left Egypt there were rumours that her son by a former marriage, a grown-up man with a wife and family of his own, was negotiating for the marriage of his mother with another man! If this takes place I fear the worst for my poor old friend!

FIG. 43. DIVORCED WIFE OF THE OLD MAN

CHAPTER VI

FERTILITY RITES

RITES to ensure the birth of children are practically world-wide, and are of great variety. The failure to produce offspring involved the weakening of the tribe, which in early times depended upon its numerical strength for its defence against hostile neighbours. Hence the importance of the possession of children, especially of the male sex.

Love for their children is a marked trait in the character of the modern Egyptians. I have often seen the roughest *fellāḥ* handle his sick child with remarkable tenderness when he has brought it to me in the hope that I might be able to cure it of some complaint.

Muslim law permits a man to put away his wife if she has no children, and a woman divorced for this cause has small chance of obtaining another husband when once the reason for her divorce has become known. Hence the prospect of childlessness is a very real terror to a wife, and the methods to which women resort in order to prevent such a catastrophe are numerous.

Some years ago, when I was working at a large collection of charms and various magical appliances at the Pitt-Rivers Museum in Oxford, it occurred to me that certain so-called pendants which my brother had brought me from Egypt might have some magical powers attached to them. These pendants are modern copies of ancient Egyptian blue glazed amulets, representing gods, goddesses, sacred animals, or scarabs. I showed these objects to an Egyptian sheikh then resident in Oxford, and asked him what they were used for. After some hesitation he told me that they were women's charms, and were used in Upper Egypt as a means of ensuring the birth of children. I have found that such charms are in great request in all the provinces south of Cairo that I have visited. The sheikh also told me that a man travelling about Upper Egypt with such charms in his possession would be besieged, as he approached a village, by crowds of women begging to be allowed to step over these amulets.

On my first visit to Egypt in 1920, soon after my arrival at my brother's camp on the high-desert slope in Asyūṭ Province, a certain number of childless women sent appealing messages to me, asking if I would let them have one of the bones which were scattered in great numbers about the ancient burial site on which the camp was situated. Their object was to step or jump over the bone in order to ensure, as they believed, the production of offspring. I acceded to their request, and then suddenly thought of my pendants, which I had unfortunately forgotten to bring out to Egypt with me. However, I sent a message to the women to say that I had written to England requesting that certain very potent charms that I possessed should be sent to me as soon as possible.

FIG. 44. THE FOUR CHARMS OVER WHICH THE WOMEN STEP

When the parcel arrived I caused the fact to be known in the various villages of the district, at the same time intimating that I should be glad to see any of the women who wished to make use of them. From then onward women, sometimes as many as ten at a time, would come from various villages in the district, crossing the lower desert, and climbing up to our camp on the hills which rose into the upper desert. They were usually accompanied by a middle-aged man or woman, sometimes by both. The man was not present at the ceremony, but the woman chaperon stayed with them all the time.

The ritual was as follows. The women first repaired to one of the ancient decorated tomb-chapels, conducted thither by one of our servants, who had the key. On entering they each stepped seven times backward and forward over what they supposed to be the mouth of the shaft admitting to the subterranean burial chamber. When this performance was over they returned to the undecorated tomb-chapel in which I lived. Here I produced the charms, two of which were placed on the ground at a time. Then each woman solemnly stepped over them backward and forward seven times. Four charms in all were used, representing the head of Isis, a mummified divinity, a scarab, and a cat (Fig. 44). When this was accomplished the lower jaw-bone of an ancient Egyptian skull was placed on the ground. The same ceremony was yet again performed, being repeated with two complete ancient Egyptian heads, one a well-preserved mummified head, the other a skull. A glass of water was then brought, into which the blue glazed charms were dropped. Each woman drank some of the water, and then picked out the charms and sucked them, and some rubbed their bodies with these magical objects, and also applied the water to their persons.

It may interest my readers to know that on my return to Egypt the following year one of the first items of news communicated to me by my servant was that at least two of the women who had had resort to my charms would shortly bear children.

Great efficacy is attached to the Pyramids, and childless women will repair to one of them and walk round it seven times, believing that this perambulation will assist them to become mothers. Women sometimes beg to be allowed to remove small portions of the decorated walls in ancient tomb-chapels to assure their bearing children. It appears that ancient things in Egypt are credited with great potency in this respect, but it is difficult, if not impossible, to obtain any reliable information from the people themselves as to why they attach such magical power to antiquities. The stepping over the tomb-shaft suggests a belief in reincarnation, and this belief does exist among the peasants, as will be seen later on ; but there is also the idea that *barakeh* is attached to anything that is old, or sacred, or even peculiar. The word *barakeh* means blessing, and *barūkeh* is a lucky coin, a thing to bring good luck.

Women who have no children will sometimes visit a sheikh's tomb, entreating him to intervene on their behalf, and vowing to make some gift in return if their wish is granted. A cord or cords are often to be seen hanging across the inside of such a building, and from it are suspended a variety of objects, including coloured handkerchiefs. These are, in many cases, the votive offerings of women, which they have hung up in the tomb when their prayers for offspring have been answered.

Lane [1] records the practice of visiting tombs or mosques to obtain

[1] *The Manners and Customs of the Modern Egyptians* (London, 1871), vol. i, pp. 300 f.

a blessing, or to urge some special petition, such as the gift of children. He states that the suppliants believe that a more favourable reception to their prayers will be granted if offered up in such sacred places.

Barakeh is also occasionally believed to be possessed by, or attached to, living people. Over and over again women have come up to touch me because they believed I had this virtue. Among the numbers of women who in 1926 came to me to step over the blue glazed charms which I always take about with me was a young married woman who was in a state almost verging on madness because she had no children. Five years ago she had given birth to a child which survived only a few hours. Since then she had had no hope of becoming a mother. She was in a desperate plight, and her fears were increased because she suspected that her husband would shortly divorce her as there seemed to be no prospect of a family. She begged and entreated me to help her, so I suggested the charms, over which she stepped seven times. She came a second and a third time, becoming more and more frantic as time went on.

The last time she visited me she said, "O gracious lady, I know you *can* help me if you will; we all know you have so much *barakeh*!" She then seized my hand, pressing it against her, and saying, "You *can* give me *barakeh* if you will!"

I expressed my sorrow for and sympathy with her, and she took her departure. Not long after I heard from one of her fellow-villagers that her wish was at last realized, and that she had hopes of becoming a mother. It was all put down to me, and she called it *my* child! Many people after this came to me from her village for the same purpose, and all, so I heard, met with the same success. The population of that village should be appreciably increased through my supposed *barakeh*!

It is a popular belief in Egypt that if a dead child is tightly bound in its shroud the mother cannot conceive again. Therefore the shroud and the cords binding it are always loosened just before burial, dust also being put in the child's lap. The dust is put there, so I was told, in order to keep the body lying on its back. The woman who gave me this information said that sometimes a body twists round when decomposition sets in, and if this happens the mother cannot have another child. If, in spite of precautions, the woman as time goes on seems to have no prospect of again becoming a mother she will go to the tomb of her dead child, taking a friend with her, and request the man whose business it is to do so to open the tomb. The disconsolate mother then goes down inside the tomb where the body lies, and steps over it backward and forward seven times, in the belief that the dead child's spirit will re-enter her body and be born. Here we see a definite belief in reincarnation.

A very similar practice has been noticed among the Bangalas, a tribe to the north of the Congo. On one occasion a woman of this tribe was seen to be digging a hole in a public road. Her husband explained to a Belgian officer who was present that his wife wished to become a mother, and begged that she might be left unmolested, promising, on his part, to mend the road afterward. The woman continued to dig till she had unearthed the skeleton of her dead child, which she affectionately embraced, begging it at the same time to enter her body to be reborn.[1] In this case we see a very similar rite, accompanied by the same belief, as in modern Egypt.

Among the Copts, if a child dies while it is a baby and after it has been baptized the body is enclosed in a coffin. However, the mother of the child instructs the men who take it to be buried in the graveyard (generally near a monastery) that they are to remove the body from the coffin and inter the latter only in the vault. The body of the child is then buried in the sand near the vault, and sand is placed under its armpits and its chin and on its thighs. This, the mother believes, will ensure her having another child. It seems as if the Copts have a belief similar to that of the Muslims mentioned above, and that the sand is used to keep the body from twisting and thereby preventing the mother from bearing another child.

Again, among the Copts, if a child dies before it is baptized it is placed naked in a *ḳādūs* (an earthenware jar, several of which are attached to water-wheels). This jar is buried under the floor of one of the rooms in the house, it does not matter which, and is covered again with the mud of which the floors are usually made in the houses of the *fellāḥīn*. This is believed to ensure the mother having another child.

Sometimes if a woman has no children her friends will take her

[1] Quoted by Sir J. G. Frazer in *The Golden Bough*, "Adonis, Attis, and Osiris," 3rd edition, vol. i, p. 92.

to the railway and make her lie down between the lines in order that the train may pass over her. One reason given me for this somewhat dangerous procedure is that the fear which the woman experiences assists conception, for it is said to cause the blood to circulate quickly through the body, making the womb expand, with the result that she will more easily conceive. Another ex-

FIG. 45. FERTILITY RITE: LIGHTING THE 'CANDLE'

planation given me for this rite was that when the mother is thus frightened her *ḳarīneh* comes to her with the soul of one of her dead children and causes it to re-enter its mother's body. The soul of a dead child, so I have been told, goes to its mother's *ḳarīneh*. Probably these explanations are accepted by some of the people, but in many cases, I fancy, such rites are merely carried out because they are customary and recognized cures for childlessness.

The water with which a corpse is washed before burial is, if possible, obtained from a mosque or from a sheikh's sacred well. After the washing is completed a barren woman will seize the opportunity to step over this water seven times. I was told of one who resorted to this device and who became pregnant a month afterward.

Not long ago I was fortunate enough to witness the following curious performance to which a Coptic woman had recourse; she had been married for some time, but had had no children.

A secluded spot behind the house was selected, and a blanket spread on the ground for the woman to lie upon. Such a performance would usually take place inside the house, but, as the light indoors was not strong enough for photography, the woman consented to it taking place outside. She lay down upon the blanket on her back. Her clothes were then drawn up to above her waist, and the lower part of her body was covered by a rug, her abdomen being thus left exposed. Some flour was put into a small bowl and mixed with water into a firm paste. One of the two women who officiated took the paste and formed it into a flat, round cake, which she then placed on the recumbent woman's stomach, just over the navel. Meanwhile, the second woman selected a head of maize (*dura*) from which the grain had been removed and placed it upright in the centre of the cake, where it was held in position by the first woman. Her companion now struck a match and lighted the head of maize, which they called a 'candle' (Fig. 45). They held this lighted 'candle' in position while they placed over it a pottery jar, pressing this well into the cake. In this way the jar remained upright without further support, and it was left in this position for about one minute (Fig. 46). The Coptic woman called out more than once for the jar to be removed, but her two friends urged her to be patient and to keep the jar on her stomach a little longer.

FIG. 46. FERTILITY RITE WITH JAR

One of the women then got up from the ground where she had

been sitting and proceeded to lift the jar from off the woman's stomach. It took a very strong and somewhat lengthy pull to do this, and as it was finally removed there was a resounding pop, like an explosion. It was explained to me that one possible reason for the woman not having conceived was that she had "wind in her stomach." The noise caused by the removal of the jar was this wind coming away, as they supposed, from the stomach through the navel. The performance was repeated two or three times, and on each occasion when the jar was pulled away the noise was very loud, and the two attendant women remarked on how much wind the patient had in her stomach. As I have said, the woman who removed the jar had to exercise her full strength to get it away, and this part of the performance must have caused the patient a good deal of discomfort, if not actual pain, for her stomach was dragged up with the jar in the effort to remove it, the suction, of course, being caused by the vacuum created by placing the jar over the lighted 'candle.' I was sorry to hear, when making inquiries later on, that the operation had failed to produce the desired effect!

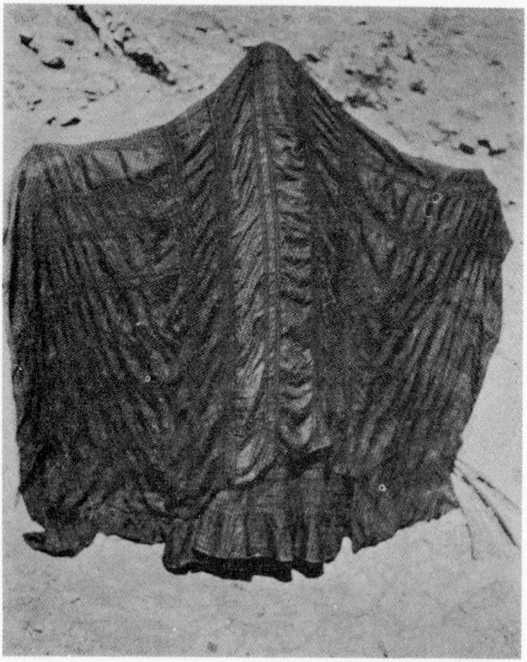

FIG. 47. WOMAN WITH OUTSTRETCHED ARMS COMPLETELY ENVELOPED IN A TŌB

Childless women frequently have recourse to this fertility rite, at any rate in some parts of Egypt. I do not yet know if it is a widely spread custom, for, being a somewhat private operation, it would not be talked about freely, and one must have been on very familiar terms with the people for a long time before being invited to be present on such an occasion.

Quite recently I was present at another rite performed by two childless women. A third woman held a long, wide piece of black material over her head and outstretched arms, so that she was completely covered (Fig. 47). This garment is called a *tōb*, and is the one worn by women out of doors. The woman who thus officiates must be one who has had children that have died. One of the childless women then crept underneath the *tōb* and walked round the officiant seven times, always keeping well under the garment (Fig. 48). The second woman then followed suit. No woman who has walked round another woman in this way must in her turn thus hold the *tōb* for another, for if she did the benefit she had hoped to secure by walking under this garment would be taken from her.

FIG. 48. WOMEN CREEPING UNDER THE TŌB

These two women, hearing that I was coming to the village in which the ceremony was to take place, delayed carrying it out until I could be present, in the hope of getting the additional benefit of my *barakeh*. I am happy to say that in both cases the performance was crowned with success!

I have already mentioned that the peasants appear to believe that ancient things are specially endowed with *barakeh*, and that on that account they may be efficacious in curing childless women of their barrenness. On the site of an ancient temple in Middle Egypt is a pool of water in which large inscribed stones are partly submerged, while others lie on the ground close by. The site is

FIG. 49. WOMEN PERAMBULATING THE POOL ON THE SITE OF AN ANCIENT TEMPLE

called *el-Kenīseh* (the Church) by the peasants, probably because it became known that it is the site of an ancient temple. This pool is believed to possess miraculous powers, and every Friday childless women flock thither from all the surrounding villages. They clamber over the stones on the edge of the pool and also over those which are partly submerged, performing this somewhat arduous feat three times, and going more or less in a circular direction (Fig. 49). After this they hope to conceive.

Curiously enough, women come to this spot and act in the same manner to prevent conception. On the occasion of my visit to the pool one of the women who was there told me that she had come for this latter purpose. She did not want to have another child for some time, as she had one or two very young children living

Women also come here if they are experiencing difficulty in suckling their children, and donkeys which are not producing sufficient milk for their young are likewise driven here. The ceremony is the same as that for childlessness, and after its performance the milk is supposed to be much increased in quantity.

Many years ago my brother, Dr A. M. Blackman, recorded a custom of hanging skins of foxes over the doors of houses in Lower Nubia.[1] On inquiry he found that they were believed to be charms "to protect the women of the household, preventing miscarriages, and helping them in labour." In some parts of Egypt if a mother wants another child she will attach a small piece of fox's skin to the head of her last-born living child. After doing this she hopes that her wish will be granted.

The pollen of a male palm is used as a charm to produce fertility; some of it is mixed in water, which is drunk by the woman who wishes to have a child. The fertilization of the female palm with such pollen might naturally account for the belief in its efficacy as a charm to cure a woman of barrenness.

It is believed that if a woman who has lately had a child goes to see another woman who has recently given birth to a child which did not survive, the latter will not conceive again. The happy mother whose child lives must wait until her friend's child has been dead for fifteen days, when all danger of seeing her will be over. However, should such an unfortunate visit be paid before the fifteen days have expired, the bereaved mother must counteract the danger of future childlessness by visiting the tomb of her dead child and going through the ceremony of stepping over its body already described. She may as an alternative choose one of the other rites for the same purpose.

I will now describe some of the methods employed to prevent conception. One I have mentioned already in connexion with the stones in and beside the pool. If an expectant mother wishes to have no more children for a certain period she will take the seeds of a castor-oil plant and, on the day after her child is born, she will eat one of the seeds if she wishes to be without another child for one year, two if for two years, and so on. This is believed to be invariably effective. If a woman has a spite against another who wishes to have a child she may secretly insert some castor-oil seeds into her food, and so render her unable to conceive.

[1] *Man*, vol. ix (1909), pp. 9 f.

If a woman when she gives birth to a child does not want to conceive again for some time she takes some date stones and covers them with some of the blood of her confinement, and then, tying them up in a rag, conceals them in a wall of her house between the bricks. The chink is then stopped up with clay. Each date stone she thus conceals represents a year, and the number, of course, varies according to the number of years she wishes to remain without offspring. When she wishes to have a child again she removes the date stones from their hiding-place, steps over them seven times, and then, placing them in water, bathes in it. I had the opportunity of witnessing such a performance once. The woman, to enable me to take a photograph in a better light, placed the date stones on the threshold of her house, and then stepped over them. Some of these date stones, with the rag in which they had been tied up, were afterward given to me.

A man who is well known to me divorced one of his two wives a year or so ago, and this woman resolved to have her revenge on the other wife. She accomplished her purpose in the following manner. She consulted a female magician, who wrote a spell on an egg and another on a palm-leaf. A male member of the divorced woman's family (probably her brother) took the egg and the leaf and hid them in a tomb. The hiding-place is kept secret, so that no one can remove them, for if they were discovered and taken away they would no longer remain effective. It has come to the knowledge of the man's wife that the divorced woman has acted in this way, and the spells, so she says, have made it impossible for her to bear a child. Possibly the firm belief she has in the potency of such spells has brought her into a neuropathic condition.

The fact that so many methods of curing barrenness are employed by the peasants is an indication that, despite the high birth-rate, infertility in women is not uncommon in Egypt. As has been pointed out to me by a doctor who is in daily touch with the poor, venereal disease, which is, unfortunately, very prevalent in some villages, is largely responsible for this state of affairs. A proper organization, involving treatment and instruction in simple hygiene—at present, so far as I know, entirely lacking in the country places—is badly needed to prevent the further spread of this terrible scourge.

CHAPTER VII

DEATH AND FUNERARY CEREMONIES

WHEN a male or female Muslim is dying it is the custom to give him or her some water to drink. So far, despite careful inquiries, I have discovered no definite belief associated with the practice ; all that I have been told is that it is a custom that must always be observed. It may originally, perhaps, have been a purificatory or vivificatory rite. In certain parts of Egypt it is the custom for some of the people sitting or standing near a person who is *in extremis* to squeeze his or her body with their hands, in order to force the soul out of it. Men do this for a man and women for a woman. When death has actually taken place the eyes and mouth of the deceased are closed, and the legs drawn down straight and laid close together. The body is then washed, the water for this purpose being obtained, if possible, from a mosque or from some sacred well or pool connected with a sheikh. In Upper Egypt the corpse may be washed by a *fiḳīh*, who takes as payment all the clothes of the deceased, and also the remains of the soap used in the washing.

As Egypt is a very hot country burial takes place very shortly after death. For instance, if a death has occurred in the morning or early afternoon the funeral takes place the same day. On the other hand, if death resulted from some injury due to accident or an act of violence burial is not permitted till the Government doctor and police officials have made full investigations.

If some one is dying in the village the news soon spreads, and friends and relations flock in crowds to the house. The moment the breath is out of the body female relatives and a number of professional mourners begin to shriek and scream (Fig. 50). Many of them leave the house of death and perambulate the village seven times, uttering the while piercing cries, and waving handkerchiefs, usually black, blue, or green in colour, as they go along. This perambulation of wailing women is not, anyhow at the present day, consciously associated with any idea of driving the spirit or ghost of the deceased away from the village. I am told that it is merely the way of making it known that a death has taken place.

When the corpse has been washed it is wrapped in cotton or silk cloths, the first wrapping being usually white, the outer green. Green is the sacred colour among Muslims, being associated with the Prophet Muḥammed. His descendants, or perhaps I should say those who lay claim to be such, very often wear a green turban.

FIG. 50. WOMEN WAILING OUTSIDE AN ENGINE-HOUSE, WHERE A BOY HAD JUST BEEN KILLED

Note the uplifted arms of the dead boy's mother, in the centre, a characteristic attitude of grief. See below, p. 236, and Fig. 137.

The Muslims do not bury in coffins. The corpse, when wrapped, is laid on a bier with low sides, and this is covered with a shawl by way of a pall. The sex of the deceased is indicated by slight differences in the draping of the shawl.

When a man or a woman dies a ram must be killed and some of its blood sprinkled on the place where the death occurred. If this is not done the *rōḥ* (soul) will remain in the house and cannot go to heaven. If the people are too poor to afford a ram a kid is killed instead. When the father of a rich man whom I know died a ram and some other animals were killed at the house, and, in addition, a camel was slaughtered near his grave and the meat distributed among the poor

The clothes which the man or woman wore when he or she died must be washed, and then a *fiḳīh* comes and recites passages from the Ḳorān, having the clothes close to him and one of his hands resting on them. He also recites over the place where the person died. If these precautions are not taken the *rōḥ* of the dead person cannot leave the house. When a child dies a hen is killed instead of an animal, the rest of the procedure being the same as on the occasion of the death of an older person.

I have given this information as it was repeated to me, but I

FIG. 51. STRING OF WAILING WOMEN IN A FUNERAL PROCESSION

fancy that it is really the *ʿafrīt* of the dead person that is meant in this statement, not the *rōḥ*, which is the soul, the *ʿafrīt* being the ghost, and quite separate from the *rōḥ*, according to the popular belief.[1]

The corpse is borne to the grave by four male bearers, who are constantly changed during the procession to the cemetery, for to assist in thus carrying the dead is considered a pious act, and he who performs it thereby acquires considerable merit. The funeral procession is headed by men, those who are relations walking as near as possible to the bier. Immediately behind the bier walk the female mourners (Fig. 51), their faces, hands, and arms dyed blue, and their heads, breasts, and arms plastered with mud ; they hold handkerchiefs, usually blue or black, and sometimes green, which they wave in the air as they give vent to their piercing

[1] See below, pp. 237 ff.

ululations of grief. Among them are professional wailers, whose lamentations are the loudest of all.

It should be noted here that the wailing and general uproar made by women at a death is quite contrary to the teaching of the founder of Islām, and many men among the peasants in Egypt have often expressed to me their disapproval of the practice. As will be seen later, this custom is one of the many survivals from ancient times

FIG. 52. THE HALT FOR PRAYER ON THE WAY TO THE CEMETERY

It is surprising for how long a time the women can keep up their wailing, which is pitched in a very high key. As a matter of fact, their throats are often so affected by the continuous uttering of these piercing cries that at the end of one day of mourning they can speak only in a whisper.

On its way to the grave the funeral procession halts at a specially chosen spot, and the bier is placed on the ground (Fig. 52). The men stand in rows, one behind the other, and assume a deeply reverential attitude, while a *fiḳīh* (plur. *fuḳahā*; see p. 172) recites passages from the Ḳorān, the assembled men often joining in. When these recitations are finished the bearers come forward and raise the bier from the ground, and the procession is continued to the grave. As they proceed the men chant the profession of faith: " There is no God but God, and Muḥammed is the Apostle of God. The blessing of God upon him and peace, a thousand blessings upon Muḥammed." These words are repeated over and over again till the graveside is reached.

It is believed that the dead, while being carried to the grave, can make their bearers walk fast or slowly. If the bearers are made to go quickly it is said to mean that the deceased is a good man or woman, who wishes to go as fast as possible to the tomb, and does not fear the visit of the two angels Nākir and Nekīr, who are believed to come to the tomb on the first night after burial to examine the deceased as to the life he spent on earth and to question him as to his religion.

When the bearers suddenly feel themselves being dragged back, or even unable to move at all, it is believed to be that the deceased does not like the spot chosen for the grave.

During a funeral procession in a village well known to me the bearers were not able to advance a step, owing to the dead man objecting to the locality of his grave; however, as it had already been dug, and the bearers were not willing to pander to any such whim, they carried the bier round and round in a circle, thus making the dead man so giddy that he lost his power over his bearers and did not realize where they were conveying him! They were thus able to rush him into his grave without more ado!

On another occasion, in the road running past my house, I saw the bearers being dragged back by constant jerks. The reason given was that the dead woman who was being carried to her grave was upset that her son, a very young boy, was not in the procession. Some one, therefore, had to fetch him, and then the *cortège* proceeded on its way without further interruption.

There appears to be a belief, at any rate among some of the peasants, that a man's shadow is a separate entity. It walks with him through life, dies with him at his death, and then enters with him into his tomb. When discussing this point with some of the people I gathered that no one knew what became of it afterward. I was told that there is no belief, such as is found in some parts of the world, that a man may be injured by some one stepping on his shadow.

On returning to the house of the deceased the men seat themselves outside the doorway, where they are joined by friends, all observing almost complete silence, except on arrival, when they may say, "*El-baḳīyeh fi ḥayātak*"—literally, "May what remains over be in your life!"—*i.e.*, "May the rest of the days of the dead be added to your life!"

The female mourners, including the professional wailers, congregate together, either inside the house or in some secluded spot outside. Here they continue to utter their piercing cries, and usually also engage in a dance. The dancers, each one swaying slightly backward and forward, move in a circle, smiting their cheeks the while with both hands in rhythmic accompaniment to their chanting and cries. I have seen women thus beating their cheeks till blood flowed. One of the dancers often beats a *nadam*, a single-membrane drum, resembling a tambourine, but without jingles.

The mourning ceremonies are continued for seven days, though very occasionally they may last for three days only. The first evening after the burial *fuḳahā* come to the house, one of them bringing a large rosary, called a *sibḥeh*, consisting of five hundred to a thousand large beads. They repeat passages from the Ḳorān a thousand times, keeping count of the recitations by means of the beads. The merit of this religious exercise is conveyed to the deceased. During the period of mourning *fuḳahā* come daily to the house to recite the Ḳorān, but the ceremony with the rosary is performed on the first night only.

The *fuḳahā* are usually given a small sum of money for their services, and also at intervals in their recitations they are refreshed with coffee and cigarettes, but no one, either performer or listener, would ever think of smoking while they are in progress. I have been present several times on such occasions, and have been much impressed by the excellence of many of the voices, as well as by the reverent attitude of all the people present. The *fuḳahā* sit cross-legged on a bench inside the house, and, as they recite, sway from side to side, holding one hand against one side of the face. One of them usually acts as leader, and the others join in as a chorus; or sometimes the chief *fiḳīh* will tell one of his subordinates to take his place and recite. The recitations last for an hour or more.

On the seventh day after a death the mourning at the house ceases, and the women, accompanied by their male relatives, visit the grave. They bring loaves of bread, called *kaḥk*, which are either round and somewhat flat or ring-shaped. A number of very poor people and *fuḳahā* follow the mourners to the cemetery. The bread is given away to the poor in the name of the dead, and the *fuḳahā* also receive their share in return for recitations from the Ḳorān at the graveside. These men may receive small sums of money for their services in addition to the gifts of bread. The visit is repeated on the fifteenth and fortieth days after the death (see also pp. 117 ff.)

It is customary to engage two or three *fuḳahā* to give recitations regularly two or three times a year in a house where a death has taken place, to ensure the welfare of the deceased. Some people arrange for even more frequent recitations.

I will now briefly describe the various kinds of graves I have seen. The structure varies according to the nature of the ground in which the cemetery is situated. In some parts of Egypt the dead are buried along the lower desert. In this case the grave is not usually prepared beforehand, but a number of men, carrying the necessary implements for digging, accompany the funeral procession. When they arrive at the selected spot the bier on which the body lies is placed on the ground, and a shawl is fixed on sticks stuck into the ground to act as a temporary wind-screen. The diggers then set to work, and, after removing the covering of sand, dig a rectangular pit in the underlying limestone rock, oriented east and west. On the south side of the pit[1] a recess is cut, large enough to admit the corpse, which is lifted into its last resting-place by some of the men present, and with its head toward the west—*i.e.*, looking east toward Mecca. The recess is then bricked over in such a way that a chamber is formed of sufficient size to admit of the deceased sitting up in it. This is necessary on account of the belief that when the two examining angels visit the grave on the first night after burial the dead must be able to sit up while they question him. For this reason also the cords or tapes which are bound round the wrappings of the dead must be unfastened as soon as the body is laid in the grave. When the recess has been bricked over the pit is filled up and the sand piled in a mound over it, palm-branches being stuck into the sand to surmount the whole.

Sometimes instead of the mound of sand a brick superstructure such as is described below is erected above the grave. The above-

[1] So in the case of two interments that I have witnessed.

mentioned palm-branches, which are often carried in the funeral processions, are placed over the graves (see Fig. 53) because they are believed to bring a blessing to the dead. For the same reason plants of *ṣabr* (aloes) are often planted, either in earthenware pots or in the ground itself, close to the mound.

Sometimes these rock-hewn burial-places are of a more elaborate design. Instead of the pit giving direct access to the burial-chamber there may be an intervening passage, the outer end of which, not the immediate entrance to the chamber, is bricked up before the pit is filled with sand and the excavated *débris*.

If the cemetery does not lie in the lower desert, but in, or on the edge of, the cultivation, the graves are somewhat differently constructed. A large chamber is excavated underground and surmounted by a flat-topped or vaulted superstructure, which varies considerably according to the taste or wealth of the owner of the tomb. The chamber constitutes a family vault, and most of the members of one family are buried in it, the sexes being usually divided, the men lying together apart from the women. This is the general rule, but I have been told that it is not always strictly adhered to by the *fellāḥīn*. Above the ground, at one end of the superstructure, is a recess, which indicates where the opening to the grave is situated underground. Palm-branches are placed in front of this recess, and plants of *ṣabr* are often planted on either side of it. At this spot, too, the relatives and friends assemble and sit down during the periodical visits to the graves discussed on pp. 117 ff. and 263 ff.

That the dead should appear to their relations and fellow-villagers soon after death is looked upon as a matter of course and an event of common occurrence. I have heard of many such appearances, which are much welcomed by, and are a great comfort to, the mourners. The following account of an after-death appearance which led to the detection of crime was given me by an old friend, who swore that it was quite true.

Two years before the story was told to me a man in one of the provinces in Middle Egypt married a woman of questionable character. After the marriage he found out that she was unfaithful to him, so one day, accompanied by a friend, he took her out for a walk. She wanted to go one way, but they insisted on her going the way they chose. They went on till they arrived at a newly dug well, into which they threw her and then filled up the pit. Shortly after this she appeared first to her brother, then to her mother, and then again to her brother, to whom she related the circumstances of her death and the exact spot where they would find the filled-in well at the bottom of which her body lay. The brother reported this to the proper officials, who went to the spot, had the well excavated, and found the woman's body at the bottom, just as she had told her mother and brother. The husband and the friend who had assisted him in the murder were convicted on this evidence, and sentenced to fifteen years' imprisonment.

One day a week—in some parts of Egypt on Thursday, in others on Friday—the villagers pay a visit to the graves of their relations and friends. The ceremony is called *eṭ-Ṭalaʿ*, meaning the coming forth or the going up. Many of the cemeteries are situated in the lower desert, and this name may have been given because the people always speak of ' going up ' to and ' descending ' from the desert. On the day of *eṭ-Ṭalaʿ* the souls of the dead are believed to return to their graves, and they expect their relatives to meet them there. I have often taken part in these ceremonies, and the following description of one of my visits shows what the proceedings are on such occasions.

The cemetery where the events described took place is situated in the lower desert, and it runs parallel to an ancient burial site lying rather nearer the upper-desert slope. It is a sand- and wind-swept place, and the palm-branches stuck into the mounds above the graves quickly wither and assume the pale tawny colour of the surrounding desert. But from the high-desert slope above, where I was camping with my brother, the shadows cast by these branches are so dark that they give the impression of black-clad figures kneeling in perpetual grief, keeping silent watch by each grave. From the camp I could see the people on their way to visit the graves, and also much that was going on in the cemetery itself. Early in the morning processions of women, often accompanied by their male relatives, were to be seen wending their way from the neighbouring villages toward this desert graveyard. Some were walking, some, mostly men, were riding on donkeys. As soon as the sound of the still distant wailing reached our camp I would mount my donkey and start off to meet the mourners in the cemetery. A number of *fuḳahā* were always present on these occasions, as it was their business to recite various passages from the Ḳorān by the gravesides, for which purpose they are hired by the visitors.

Some of the women brought with them large baskets full of bread-rings, and with these they rewarded the *fuḳahā* for their recitations, which are believed to be of great benefit to the dead. The bread used on these occasions is in this part of Egypt nearly always made in the ring shape, and sweets of all kinds, cakes, etc., are also brought for distribution, especially by the richer people. There was usually a certain number of the very poorest people present, as well as children, who had come in the hope of receiving a share in the gifts. One of these suppliants might say, "*Iddīnī*

FIG. 53. WOMEN CROUCHING OVER A GRAVE

ḥaseneh, yā sitt" (" Give me *ḥaseneh*, O lady "). The word *ḥaseneh* means charity, and is a general term for the bread, etc., given away on these occasions ; the bread, as I have mentioned above, being called *kaḥk*.

On presenting bread to the *fuḳahā* or to the poor the giver will say, "*Khud kaḥk ʿala rōḥ el-fulān*" (" Take a cake on behalf of the soul of so and so "), mentioning the name of the dead relation. It is quite a moving sight to see the faces of the women contorted with grief, the tears streaming down their cheeks, as they crouch over the graves, swaying backward and forward (Fig. 53). They hold in their hands coloured handkerchiefs, generally of silk, used only on these occasions or at a funeral. Sometimes a large one, often black with a coloured border, is doubled cornerwise and placed round the neck of the mourner. With this she can vary her movements, taking hold of the handkerchief at either end and drawing it backward and forward, like a saw, while she sways rhythmically from side to side. It should be mentioned here that all these movements, including those of the *fuḳahā* when reciting, are strictly rhythmical.

With the smaller handkerchiefs with which the women wipe the tears from their cheeks they also pat and stroke the grave. On one occasion I saw a young woman acting in this manner just as if she were affectionately stroking a living person. She then knocked on

FIG. 54. DISTRIBUTION OF BREAD-RINGS AT THE GRAVESIDE

the grave as if to attract the attention of the dead man who lay below, crying, as she did so, "*Yā abūi, yā abūi!*" ("O my father, my father!"). Some of the apparently grief-stricken mourners were professional wailing women, and often as I passed them, in the midst of what sounded like heartbroken sobs, they would look up at me, smiling in a friendly way, only to resume their sorrowful attitude the moment I left them.

Those who can afford it often bring several large baskets of bread for distribution. I have seen six or seven such baskets piled up on a single grave, where a large party was assembled, a number of wailing women being seated at one end, while at the other was a group of men and boys. The men were *fuḳahā* who, swaying from side to side, were reciting passages from the Ḳorān, accompanied, as is very often the case, by the boys. When one set of recitations came to an end each performer had two or three bread-rings doled out to him by a man and one or two women, who appeared to be the chief mourners.[1] Then the recitations began again, ending with a similar reward. All this time the women at the other end of the grave kept up their piteous cries, receiving in return exactly the same compensation as did the *fuḳahā* (Fig. 54).

Presently one of the women who had been assisting in the distribution of the bread-rings took up a basketful and, placing it on her head, started off, accompanied by another woman, to present the contents to the mourners at other graves. They perambulated most of the cemetery, giving bread-rings to women who had none. The acceptance of such a gift implies that the receiver is willing to be on friendly terms with the giver. Sometimes the donor meets with an angry refusal from the woman to whom she presents the bread. This implies that there have been quarrels between them. In such cases bystanders will intervene, urging the acceptance of the gift and the duty of living at peace with each other and making up the quarrel. These peacemakers are usually successful, and the gifts are finally accepted, though sometimes it requires considerable persuasion before a reconciliation is effected.

This weekly ceremony usually lasts from two to three hours, after which time the women take up their now empty baskets, the men who have donkeys mount them, and the whole procession returns to the villages, the women sometimes wailing as they go.

In another part of Egypt where I have attended this ceremony the cemetery does not lie in the desert, and the graves have large superstructures, with the recesses, or false doors, as described above.[2] On more than one occasion when I have visited a particular grave I have observed the widow of the man who is buried there squatting down close to the false door and addressing her dead husband thus : "*Nahārak saʿīd, yā Hideyb ! Ēy-zēyak ?*" and so on, these being the usual salutations on greeting a living person. They may be rendered, " Good day, O Hideyb ! How are you ? " This woman told me that she is happy to be able to go to her husband's grave on this day and meet him there, which shows how definite a belief it is that the dead return to their graves on the day of *eṭ-Ṭalaʿ*. The care of the dead is a strongly marked feature of Egyptian life generally, for these ceremonies are performed largely for the benefit of the departed, to ensure them happiness in the life beyond.

[1] See *Discovery*, vol. ii, p. 211, Fig. 3.

[2] See p. 116.

That the souls of the dead come to the cemeteries is again shown in the following belief. I have been told by two or three of my village friends that when the people go to visit the cemetery, and they see a number of small green birds near the graves, they believe that these birds are the souls of the dead who lie buried there. Lane [1] says that "Souls of martyrs (*shuhadā*) reside in the crops of green birds, which eat of the fruits of Paradise and drink of its rivers." This is the belief as he heard it. It was definitely stated to me that the green birds *are* the souls of the dead.

There are certain taboos on mourners, two of which are the following. If a person, male or female, has attended a funeral and walked in the procession, or even only gone part of the way, he or she must not enter the house where a woman has a baby under seven days old, for this will cause the mother to have no milk. Such a person must inform the mother of the child that he desires to enter her house, and she must then go outside to meet the visitor, who can then come into it without any evil consequences.

Again, no such mourner must enter a house in which there is some one suffering from sore eyes, for in that case the sufferer will lose his or her sight. Such intending visitors must wait outside the house, and the man or woman who has sore eyes must come out and meet them there first, and then they can enter without danger.

The death and funeral rites of the Copts are in many respects very similar to those of the Muslims.

The following incidents were witnessed by me several years ago when I was staying in a small village in Fayûm Province, and this account of what I actually saw will best describe the ceremonies incident to the death and burial of a Copt. It must always be remembered that these are accounts of death and funeral rites as practised by the peasants only, and that they are not meant to be a description of the ceremonies which take place among educated people on similar occasions.

Early one morning a visitor brought to the house where I was staying the news of the death of a poor but much respected Copt who lived in an adjacent village. It was suggested that his relations and friends would much appreciate a visit from me, so I started off on my donkey as soon as possible after the sad tidings had reached me. It was not long before I arrived at the house of

[1] *The Manners and Customs of the Modern Egyptians* (London, 1871), vol. i, p. 83.

mourning, which could easily be distinguished by the number of men seated outside it; these observed almost complete silence, instead of carrying on an animated conversation as they would have done in happier circumstances.

I was courteously received by the men and conducted to the apartment in which the women were assembled. The house was one of the type always to be found in Egyptian villages, built of crude bricks, and with steep, rough steps inside the building leading up to the roof. In the first room which we entered lay the coffin—a long, narrow box, made of planks of wood hastily nailed together, over which was stretched a covering of black cloth decorated with white crosses and other designs in *appliqué*. We passed through this room into an inner apartment, in which a large number of women were sitting on the ground, uttering from time to time piercing cries of grief. The sister of the dead man came toward me, her hair and dress dishevelled. As she advanced she swayed from side to side in a kind of dance, keeping both arms extended. She at once conducted me into a small room which led out of that occupied by the women. It was dark except for a glimmer of light which penetrated through the half-open door. A mattress was on the floor—indeed, it occupied most of the available space—and on it was stretched the body of the dead man, covered with a coloured sheet. From the end of the room, which was in pitch darkness, came the piercing cries of wailing women. Presently the sister drew aside the coverlet and invited me to take a seat on the mattress beside the dead man. This was no doubt very polite of her, but it was rather more than I could stand—not that I feared the dead, but because the mattress was almost certain to be covered with vermin. I managed to evade the offer without hurting anyone's feelings, and returned to the larger concourse of women in the adjoining room. Each of these women had a coloured handkerchief—green, blue, or purple, or some of these colours combined—such as are carried by women at all funerary ceremonies. Some of them possessed two such handkerchiefs knotted together. They held them in front of them, stretched out at full length, and as they swayed from side to side, wailing and bemoaning the dead, they would wave the handkerchiefs up and down. The faces of the women, as well as their hands and arms, were smeared with blue dye.

Presently I went out to speak to the men, who evidently disapproved of the way the women were conducting themselves. They asked me if such things were done in Oxford when there was a death. I said " No," and explained that at such times there was always perfect quiet in a well-conducted household.

" *Aḥsan, aḥsan khāliṣ* " (" Better, much better "), they replied.

Just then a number of women came running out of the house, followed by the dead man's sister. They rushed into a small palm-grove which faced the house and began a weird dance, the sister standing in their midst. The last-mentioned had, on leaving the house, made for a muck-heap which lay near the entrance, and, thrusting her hands into it, covered her face, arms, and clothes with mud, and finally clapped a large lump of it on to the top of her head. As the women went round and round in a circle they chanted a mournful song, violently smiting their cheeks with both hands, in rhythmic accompaniment to the singing.

They soon worked themselves up into a perfect frenzy ; the sister fell back two or three times, almost fainting, whereupon the men entreated me to induce her to return to the house. This I at last succeeded in doing, with the assistance of one of the male relations, who were apparently thoroughly ashamed of this wild exhibition of grief. When we had got her safely into the house she sat down on the ground with some of the other women, including the dead man's wife. The latter, by the way, took quite a secondary place in these ceremonies. The blood-tie is the strongest in Egypt, and the wife has to take second place to the sister on such occasions.

The sister now began a long oration in praise of her dead brother, in which the other women joined at intervals, in a kind of chorus. She kept on pointing wildly toward the door of the room in which the dead man lay, while she and her companions uttered cries of "*Yā akhūi, yā akhūi !* " (" O my brother, my brother ! ").

By this time two or three men were busy washing the corpse and preparing it for burial. Presently one of them came out to fetch the wrappings, which had been placed on the floor of an outer room. These wrappings consisted of white and green cotton cloths, as the relations of the dead man were too poor to afford silk, the white being wound round the body first, the green cloth providing the outer covering, as is also the case with Muslims. After a few minutes the door again opened and the men came out to get the coffin. As they were carrying it into the death-chamber the women became frantic (they had by this time been joined by the dancing women from outside), and the men had some difficulty in getting past them into the room again and closing the door. The sister got up and rushed toward the door leading into the room where her dead brother lay, crying out to him, "*Taʿāla, taʿāla!*" ("Come, come!"), the mourning women at the same time uttering their piercing cries of grief, so that the din was deafening. As the men came out with the coffin, which now contained the body, the pandemonium became greater than ever

FIG. 55. COPTIC FUNERAL: COFFIN ON CAMEL'S BACK

The women shrieked, and the sister tore off her veil (at other times considered a most immodest thing to do), wrenched her dress open at the throat, and rent her garments to such a degree that her female companions, for decency's sake, were obliged to restrain her. The coffin was then placed on the ground, and the women seated themselves round it. They hammered with their fists on the lid, shrieking to the dead man, and flinging their arms wildly about in the air. The sister so completely lost her self-control that I urged the men to advance and take up the coffin. After some difficulty they managed to hoist it up on to their shoulders, and, followed by a crowd of screaming women, at last got out of the house. The coffin was placed on the back of a donkey, though a camel is more often used (see Fig. 55), and the procession set off for the Coptic monastery situated in the desert a few miles away.

I mounted my donkey and accompanied them. The women went only a short way with us, and we left them, the hysterical sister in their midst, huddled together on the high road which led through the cultivation, still shrieking, smiting their faces, and waving their arms aloft. As we passed on toward the peaceful desert their cries grew fainter and fainter in the distance, till at last no sound broke the stillness save the occasional singing of a hymn by the men who formed the funeral *cortège*.

When we arrived at the gate of the monastery every one passed within the precincts, and the bearers carried the coffin into the church, setting it down in front of the curtain behind which was the altar. We all entered the sacred building, and a seat was offered to me close to the corpse. There was a large assembly of both Copts and Muslims, for the dead man was much respected by the followers of both religions among whom he had lived. We waited and waited, but still there was no sign of a priest. The men beguiled the time by talking and smoking, and, though I am sure it was not at all intentional, there was an extraordinary lack of reverent demeanour in those present. At last the priest arrived. The whole congregation immediately rose to their feet, and after the priest had shaken hands with me the others came forward in turns and kissed his hand. The lid of the coffin was now removed, and the body disclosed, wrapped in its white and green coverings. A very dirty cloth, on which was sewn a cross in green, was placed over the body, and candles were lighted and stuck to the sides of the coffin—six on each side and one each at the head and feet. This was accomplished by dropping some of the melting wax from the lighted candles on to the coffin and sticking the candles on to it. Two larger candles were fitted into large candlesticks placed on either side of the head of the coffin. These candlesticks were possibly of silver, but were in such a dirty state that it was impossible to guess with any certainty of what they were made.

The service then began. It was very long, lasting for three hours or more! The priest was accompanied by the *ʿarīf*, as the man who leads the singing in a Coptic church is called. The latter was quite blind, and had a very resonant voice. When he sang he accompanied himself on a pair of cymbals. There was a great deal of this 'music,' and also recitations by the priest of portions of the Gospels. Furthermore, another man, whom he singled out from among those present, likewise read passages from the

Scriptures. After interminable readings and chantings there was a pause, and one of the mourners present clapped his hands, thus commanding the attention of every one in the church. He then began the funeral oration, extolling the dead man and mentioning many of his good deeds. He spoke with great fervour and sincerity, though he was himself a Muslim, and I much admired his restrained gestures, his fluency, and his clear enunciation. He was really a good speaker and entirely devoid of self-consciousness. After the speech was ended the candles were put out and removed from the sides of the coffin, the lid was replaced, the bearers hoisted the coffin on to their shoulders, and, preceded by the priest and the *ʿarīf*, walked three times round the church, followed by all the mourners. After the third perambulation they came down the centre of the building, and so out of the church to the place of burial.

There is no service at the grave among the Copts, and after loud-voiced and conflicting advice from every man in the crowd assembled round the grave the coffin was at last successfully lowered to its final resting-place, a vault in which a number of interments had already been made. Finally the opening to the vault was bricked up and the earth flung back into its place again, and we all set off for our several abodes.

The mourning at the house usually lasts for seven days, as with the Muslims, though the period is sometimes reduced to three days only. During those seven or three days, according to one of my Coptic informants, no food is cooked in the house of mourning, but supplies are brought in by village friends. According to the same informant, prayers are offered up in the church by the priest on the third, seventh, fifteenth, and fortieth days after a death; these prayers are believed to be the means of saving a lost soul. During the fifteen days the house of mourning is not swept, but no reason was given for this custom.

On the third day after a death has taken place a priest, attended by the *ʿarīf*, goes to the house of the dead man or woman. Some of the uneducated Copts believe that the priest on this occasion dismisses the soul of the dead person from the house, where it is believed to remain until that day. I was present for this ceremony after the death of the Copt whose funeral I described above. As his relations were very poor people the ceremony was doubtless far less elaborate than it would be in the case of people in a better position.

The priest, I was told, was to arrive at 3.30 P.M., so I started off for the house early in the afternoon. I found a number of women seated in an inner room, wailing and waving their coloured handkerchiefs with the usual rhythmic movements. The sister of the dead man began a long dissertation in his praise, speaking of all his good qualities and good deeds. She would speak for a short time, then pause, whereupon the wailing women would join in a rhythmic chorus of cries, occasionally uttering the customary piercing cries of grief. The sister would again take up her theme, followed shortly by the wailing women as before.

FIG. 56. COPTIC PRIEST HOLDING CROSS

Meanwhile, one of the men seated outside the house came in and handed round cigarettes. Several of the women smoked, but this form of enjoyment did not in the least interfere with, or interrupt, the wailing and screaming. Still the priest did not come, though all the arrangements for his visit had been made—a large metal basin of water being placed on a chair, with a glass decanter of water standing in it. At last, after four o'clock, he arrived with his *ʿarīf*, both of them having come from the monastery in the desert a few miles off. The priest read some prayers, after which the *ʿarīf* chanted certain passages, and then portions from the Bible were read aloud by one of the men present. Immediately upon his arrival the priest had placed a small silver cross (see Fig. 56) in the basin of water, and it remained there all the time the reading and chanting were in progress. When these were ended he removed the cross, which was, of course, dripping with water, turned to me, and pressed it on my forehead, making the sign of the cross on me at the same time. He repeated this ceremony with each of the men in turn, and then, turning toward the crowd of women, sprinkled them with some of the water from the basin. Incense had been kept burning from the moment of the priest's arrival, and he now took up the censer and advanced with it toward the room in which the man had died. Every one was censed as he passed toward the room, and one of the men, who accompanied him, carried the basin of water. The priest censed this room and sprinkled the whole of it, together with the mattress on which the dead had lain, with the water. This terminated the ceremony, and the priest and his *ʿarīf* departed for the desert monastery.

There is a common belief among the Copts of the peasant class that this sprinkling of the water in the house drives away the soul of the person who has died. This use of the water together with the incense is probably in origin a purificatory rite, cleansing the house and the inhabitants from the contamination of death, though such a belief, at any rate among the peasants, does not appear to exist at the present day.

CHAPTER VIII

INTER-VILLAGE FIGHTS. THE LAW OF REVENGE

THE Egyptian *fellāḥīn* are by no means a military people, but in their inter-village fights, which are not of infrequent occurrence, they sometimes display a quite surprising ferocity. It must be remembered that to the Egyptian peasant his own village is the centre of the universe, and people of other villages, though treated with hospitality and courtesy as visitors, are, in some cases, looked upon with as much suspicion as if they were positive aliens. As will be seen later on, hostilities between adjacent villages were no less a marked feature of Egyptian life in antiquity than at the present day.

The inhabitants of some mutually hostile villages hardly ever meet without at least attempting to pick a quarrel, and I have been myself a spectator of such conflicts on more than one occasion. In most parts of the world it is usually found that the market-place is neutral ground, and that there even the most antagonistic peoples will meet unarmed. In some parts of Egypt, however, not only is the market-place the site regularly chosen for village conflicts, but fights which take place there are by no means confined to non-market-days! Various weapons (Figs. 57 and 58) are used at these inter-village encounters. The commonest are the *nabbūt* (a very stout single-stick), a primitive type of spear, and a battleaxe. The spear consists of a long wooden shaft terminating in a slender iron point or in a plain or barbed leaf-shaped blade. The axe is a long pole surmounted by a winged iron head. Stones too are used, and are thrown with deadly effect.

The first battle of this kind that I witnessed took place in connexion with the sinking of a large boat in a canal, the muddy bottom of which held it fast. An attempt had to be made to raise the vessel, to which two strong ropes were attached by divers. Large crowds had collected on either side of the canal, and the services of some of these people were enlisted in the efforts to raise the boat, but most of them, like myself, were mere spectators.

The two ropes attached to the boat by the divers were very long, as well as strong, and one was held by either group of helpers (Fig. 59). First one rope was pulled by the men on one bank, then, after a few turns, the other was tugged from the other side of the canal. This went on regularly for some time, the whole proceeding being well organized by the officer in charge of the district. However, as it turned out, the two groups of people facing one another across the canal belonged to two antagonistic villages, and, before long, stones of considerable size began to fly from one bank to another. The officer, an old friend of mine, rushed up and begged me to take shelter while he settled the matter, but I was far too interested to beat a retreat, as I wanted to see what would happen. He, armed with a stout *kurbāg* (a very powerful leather whip), rushed in among the crowd that had actually started the fray, slashing right and left. By this display of promptitude and courage he put an end to what might have been a serious and bloody fight. Meanwhile, I dodged about trying to get a snapshot of the combat, but the excited crowds, rushing hither and thither, frustrated all my endeavours. Eventually the villagers who started the fight were no longer allowed to assist, and were made to squat in rows at a distance, in dire disgrace They appeared utterly unmoved, and when I spoke to them and

FIG. 57. WEAPONS USED IN BLOOD-FEUDS AND INTER-VILLAGE FIGHTS

asked them why they had behaved so badly I was met by the friendliest grins.

On another occasion I happened to be present at a fight which took place at the annual festival held in honour of a local sheikh. One of the villages mentioned above again engaged in battle with the people in whose village the festival was taking place. The chief guard of that village, a hospitable man as well as an excellent disciplinarian, invited me to visit his house after I had seen the various shows which are an important feature of such festivities.

FIG. 58. ATTITUDE OF COMBATANTS IN INTER-VILLAGE FIGHTS

His house had a good balcony overlooking the whole fair, and, as the weather was very hot, I was only too glad to be able to watch what was going on from so sheltered and comfortable a position. Suddenly, without apparent warning, out came the *nabābīt* (plural of *nabbūt*), and the fun began. The head guard, however, is skilful in using the *kurbāg*, and he was soon in the thick of it, slashing right and left, accompanied by a soldier, similarly armed, who had been sent as my bodyguard. Presently the combatants fled helter-skelter down side-passages—anywhere, in fact, to get out of reach of the well-directed lashes of the whips! Peace again reigned, but not for long. A crowd composed of members of the two antagonistic villages again collected, and sticks once more had free play. This fight was stopped in the same manner as the previous one, but there were two or three repetitions before a final armistice was enforced.

One of the customs that one would be glad to see die out in Egypt is the blood-feud. As far as I can gather from scholars acquainted with the ancient history of the country, this custom does not seem to be a native one. I fancy it must have been introduced into Egypt at the time of the Arab conquest. It is a very terrible custom, and one that will be very difficult to abolish, for many of these family feuds have persisted for several generations, and still continue with no sign of abatement. The weapons used in con-

FIG. 59. CROWD PULLING THE ROPES TO RAISE THE SUNKEN VESSEL

nexion with blood-feuds are often the same as those used in inter-village fights, though firearms are sometimes employed. The rule is, so I was told, that the murderer, or a member of his family, must be killed by the avenger with exactly the same form of weapon as he (the murderer) used, and, if possible, on the very spot where the murder to be avenged was committed.

One day, as I was riding through the cultivation, an Egyptian friend of mine who was with me pointed to a certain place in the fields where a man had lately been strangled by a large handkerchief being tightly knotted round his throat. Shortly afterward, my friend told me, vengeance was taken by a member of the victim's family, who killed one of the murderer's relatives in the same way and on the exact site of the crime. Moreover, the same number of knots was tied in the handkerchief used by the avenger as had been tied in the handkerchief used by the original murderer.

On another occasion the train in which I was travelling stopped close to a certain village in Middle Egypt. I noticed that the place was in great commotion; crowds of people had collected in the streets, and there were two or three motors drawn up, evidently belonging to Government officials. In a palm-grove opposite the village were groups of people, mostly women, seated round objects covered up with black cloaks such as are often worn by the men. Presently my servant came to the door of my carriage to tell me what was the matter. His information, collected from various persons on the spot, was practically the same as what I was told later by the officials themselves. It seems that in the village in question there is a long-standing feud between two families, one of which is weak, the other strong. About eight months previously the strong family had fought with the weaker one, and had either killed or severely wounded—I forget which—some of its members. The weak family was not in a position to take immediate revenge, but bided its time, determining to retaliate sooner or later. During the night before my visit fifteen members of the more powerful family had been out in their fields, as water had been turned on for irrigation purposes. It is always necessary on these occasions to see that the water is conducted into the proper channels, and also that no one steals it by altering its course. The men thus employed were widely separated from each other, and during their watch they all fell asleep. The weaker family knew that this might well happen and so give them the long-desired opportunity of taking their revenge. A number of them, therefore, set off from the village at night, and, creeping up to their sleeping enemies, beat them so severely with *nabābīt* that those they did not kill outright they injured so terribly that they were not expected to live—I never heard definitely how many actually were killed, though one rumour, happily an exaggeration, I believe, put the number as high as twelve.

The law of blood-revenge is one of the greatest obstacles to justice with which the police officials have to contend. It is most difficult to obtain evidence, because the witnesses know that, should what they say result in a criminal's conviction, his relatives will certainly take revenge. It is not to be wondered at, therefore, that criminals sometimes escape punishment, in spite of the skill and patience displayed by many of the officials in unravelling the mass of conflicting evidence. To this skill and patience I can myself testify, and also to the obstinate refusal of witnesses to give any incriminating evidence, for I have been present over and over again at criminal investigations.

However, we must not pass too harsh a judgment on the attempts of the villagers to frustrate the aims of justice. Even in England people would hesitate to assist the law if it were known that to give evidence against even the most depraved criminal meant almost certain death at the hands of the avengers. Foreigners who have little or no knowledge of the customs prevailing among the peasants are inclined to be too severe in their criticism of the Egyptian officials when they fail to obtain sufficient evidence to convict almost undoubted criminals. But English officials who have lived in the provinces of Egypt and in close contact with the people realize how difficult a matter this is. To my mind the wonder is not the number of crimes that go unpunished for lack of evidence, but the number of criminals whose crimes are detected and who are brought to justice.

CHAPTER IX

INDUSTRIES. THE VILLAGE MARKET

ONE of the commonest industries in Egypt is pottery-making, and the methods employed are usually very simple. There are, roughly speaking, two kinds of pottery—hand-made and wheel-turned. When no wheel is employed the potters may be men or women, but the wheel is used only by men. I shall deal with this industry at some length, for, despite their importance for archæology, the methods employed by potters in modern Egypt have hitherto received little attention from archæologists. Several of these, however, have recently told me that my researches in this subject will form a valuable addition to the study of ceramic art, and will throw light on the different methods of pottery-making employed in much earlier times, not only in Egypt itself, but in other parts of the Mediterranean area also.

The processes in the manufacture of pots vary in different parts of Egypt, and I will endeavour to give as detailed a description as possible of those which I have studied in Fayūm, Minia, Asyūṭ, and Ḳena Provinces.

In one village in Asyūṭ Province there is a large pottery-making establishment in which both men and women are employed, and where hand-made as well as wheel-turned pots are manufactured. The potters carry on their art in charming surroundings, the scene of their labours being a beautiful palm-grove, the trees of which afford them a welcome shade.

The clay used for the pots is obtained in the neighbourhood, and is prepared for use by a woman. It is put in a hollow in the ground, and a certain amount of finely chopped chaff is mixed with it, as well as sufficient water to make it of the proper consistency. One of the women then kneads this preparation with her feet until it is thoroughly mixed.

In this particular locality only women make the hand-made pots, and the process is as follows. When the clay is ready for use one of the potters forms portions of it into flat, round cakes, from two to three inches thick. Another woman takes one of these cakes and places it on an upturned pot with rounded base which stands in a shallow pan filled with chaff. The upturned pot can be turned round and round in the pan at the will of the potter. The cake of clay is moulded over the base of the upturned pot, and the potter pats and smooths it into shape with one hand and with a potsherd held in the other hand. When this part of the process is completed she removes the clay, now formed into a hemispherical shape, and places it on the ground beside her. She goes on dealing

FIG. 60. SMOOTHING OVER THE JOIN IN POT-MAKING

with the cakes of clay in this way until she has a number of such shapes prepared. She then takes two of these, and bends the edges of both inward, moistening them, as she does so, with water from a bowl placed near her. The two shapes are now put together, rim to rim, the woman again moistening her hand with water to effect the join, which she first smooths over with her hand and then with a potsherd or a curved piece of wood[1] (Fig. 60).

The vessel is now a perfect sphere. The opening is cut with the woman's thumbnail (Fig. 61). She keeps her hand steady with the thumb in position, and turns the pot round rapidly as it rests on the ground, or in the pan, thus making a perfectly circular

[1] See below, p. 141, footnote.

incision. The disk cut in this way is removed, whereupon the woman inserts her hand inside the pot to smooth away the interior ridges formed by the joining of the two hemispheres. A rim is then added round the opening, and small handles are fixed to the sides (Fig. 62). The pots are left to harden in the sun before being fired in the kiln. No slip or glaze is used for decoration.

FIG. 61. CUTTING THE OPENING WITH THE THUMBNAIL

I found the same technique employed in another village in the same province, the site chosen for the factory being also a palm-grove. Here men as well as women were making the hand-made pots. This is somewhat unusual, as in most parts of the world the men confine themselves to pottery-making with the wheel.

In both these villages men were making pots with wheels on the same site as that occupied by the women, but at a short distance from them.

The clay used for the wheel-turned pots is the same as that used for the hand-made. The circular table on which the clay is placed is rotated by means of a flywheel worked by the potter's foot (*cf.* Fig. 72). When large vessels, such as *ziyār* (singular *zīr*),[1] are to be made the man first moistens the circular table with water,

[1] Very large jars, in which the household water is stored.

sprinkles on it a certain quantity of chaff, and then puts a large lump of clay on it to form a strong base for the pot. When smaller vessels are to be made the process is different, as will be seen later. He then takes some more clay and forms it into a thick, flat sausage, which he coils round the lump of clay forming the base (Fig. 63). As he rotates the wheel the pot begins to take form, the potter drawing up the clay as he works to make the sides. Having completed the work so far, he takes another lump of clay and presses it on to the base to strengthen it still further in this part. To increase the size of the vessel more coils of clay are superimposed round the pot, one at a time, the man pouring a little water from his hand over each added roll to effect a join. This is repeated until half the intended height of the vessel is attained, when cords are coiled round it spirally with the aid of the wheel (*cf.* Fig. 77). This half-pot is now removed from the wheel and placed on the ground, where it is left to dry for several hours. When sufficiently hardened it is again placed on the wheel, and the upper part completed by superimposing thick sausages of clay as before, the shape of the vessel being obtained by decreasing the length of each additional roll of clay. The *zīr*, having been finished off with a

FIG. 62. PUTTING ON THE HANDLES OF A POT

thick rim, is now put to sun-bake again, the rope being still left coiled round the lower half. No rope is put round the upper part, but large nicks are impressed in the clay with the thumbnail just below the rim.

After the sun-baking is completed the vessels are placed in a kiln to be fired, the cords being previously removed (Fig. 64), though the impress made by the cord remains on the pot even after baking.

FIG. 63. COILING THE FLAT SAUSAGE OF CLAY ROUND THE LUMP OF CLAY ALREADY ON THE POTTER'S WHEEL

A pattern similar to that effected by the rope is employed for the decoration of pots in many countries; but this practice of strengthening and supporting the weakest part of the pot, or the part which receives the greatest pressure, by coiling rope round it probably suggested this decoration in the first instance. When such a practice has died out, possibly owing to greater skill achieved by the potters, the pattern originally made by the impress of the cord upon the pot is imitated for purely decorative purposes.[1] With the Egyptian potters the use of the cord is, as I have already stated, simply to support the thicker and heavier part of the *zīr* while sun-baking, and the impress left on the vessel does not seem to have any æsthetic value attached to it.

[1] I am indebted to Mr Henry Balfour, Curator of the Pitt-Rivers Museum, Oxford, for this suggestion.

Smaller vessels, such as the *ḳulleh* (see below, Fig. 79), are also made on the wheel, these being formed out of a single lump of clay. The potter, from long experience, knows exactly how large the lump must be for the formation of each vessel.

Near another village in Asyūṭ Province I saw the three following processes employed in the manufacture of a single pot. The vessels being made were large and globular in shape, and three people, a

FIG. 64. REMOVING THE CORDS FROM THE POTS BEFORE PLACING THEM IN THE OVEN

woman and two men, were each responsible for one process, besides a fourth person, a man, who prepared and kneaded the clay. The clay was obtained in the neighbourhood, and chaff only was mixed with it. There was a kiln near by for the firing of the vessels (Fig. 65).

The first part of the pot was made by the woman. She took a large lump of clay, placed it in a round, shallow hollow in the ground, previously prepared and made very smooth, and then pounded the clay into the shape of this mould by means of an object, rather like a cottage loaf in appearance (Fig. 66), made of hard baked clay. By this means the base of the pot was constructed. She then took a potsherd, and with it and the other hand drew up the clay all round, thus forming a shallow bowl with thick sides.

Her share of the work was now completed, and she handed the

FIG. 65. MAN PREPARING AND KNEADING THE CLAY: KILN IN THE BACKGROUND

pot on to a man, who thinned the sides by drawing the superfluous clay upward. This he did by holding the palm of one hand flat against the interior surface, while he beat the exterior side with a curved piece of wood[1] held in the other hand (Figs. 66 and 67). He continued this process until he had formed a large but rimless jar.

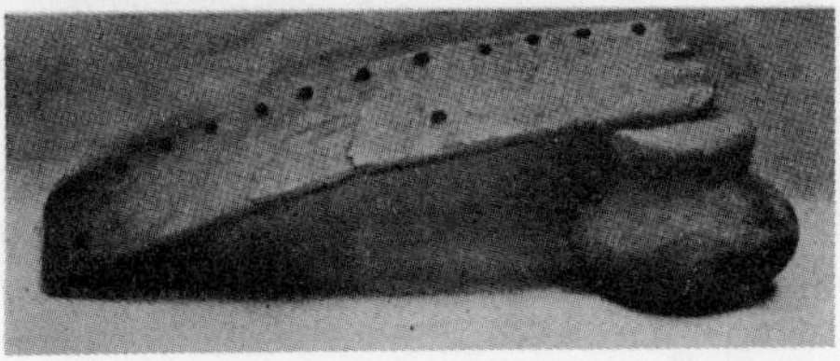

FIG. 66. TWO IMPLEMENTS USED BY POTTERS

The man now handed the jar on to another man, who placed a thick coil of clay round the opening, and, turning it on the wheel, formed it into a rim (Fig. 68). He finally added one or two small

[1] This piece of wood is a portion of the rim of an old sieve used for winnowing.

handles to the vessel. The pots were then sun-baked before being placed in the kiln.

It is interesting to observe that there are three distinct stages in the manufacture of the single vessel, and to note that a man again takes his share in the hand-making process. I should mention that, owing to the skill of the potter, these jars, though almost entirely hand-made, are quite symmetrical.

The method of shaping the first part of a vessel in a carefully

FIG. 67. DRAWING UP THE SIDES OF A POT

prepared hollow in the ground, as described above, is common in many parts of Egypt.

As a rule the Arabs do not make pottery, but rely on the Egyptian *fellāḥīn* for the pots they may require. So far there is only one place where I have found this industry among the Arabs, and I came across it quite accidentally. I was staying in a locality in Middle Egypt where Arabs have been settled for several generations, and in one of their villages, situated close to the desert, I found an old man engaged in the manufacture of the large jars (*balālīṣ*, singular *ballāṣ*) in which women carry water to their houses. In that part of Egypt the *ballāṣ* is globular in shape. I visited the old man's 'factory' and found him hard at work. He had his supply of clay, mixed with chaff, ready prepared inside a hovel, and carefully covered with sacking to prevent evaporation. A potter's wheel also stood inside. The prepared hollow was just outside the hut, and it was made there to enable me to take photographs of him at his work; he usually had one inside, where there was not sufficient light for photography. The hollow was circular and shallow, and was lined with chopped straw well beaten into

FIG. 68. FORMING THE RIM WITH THE AID OF THE WHEEL

the ground, until the surface was smooth and firm. The potter took a large piece of clay, which he formed into a cone shape by rolling it in the hollow (Fig. 69). He then took the implement made of hard baked clay and began to hollow out the cone of clay from the thick end into a thick, shallow bowl. Laying aside the clay implement, the potter now began to draw up the sides of the vessel with his left hand and the wooden implement, in the manner described above (Fig. 70). This process was continued until a large globular water-jar was formed. The somewhat small circular opening was carefully nipped into shape with the fingers and thumb, and then the jar was put in the sun to dry and harden for some hours before the rim was added on the wheel (Fig. 71). It

FIG. 69. THE ARAB POTTER WITH CONE-SHAPED LUMP OF CLAY

FIG. 70. THE WATER-JAR NEARING COMPLETION

should be noted that in this case the pot was not taken out of the hollow in the ground until it was ready for sun-baking.

Similar jars are made by another family of potters in this Arab village, where the women assist their menfolk by preparing the clay for use. The method employed in the manufacture of these jars is the same as that just described.

Much farther south I saw a somewhat different method. The pots, which are of various shapes and sizes, are not only all entirely

FIG. 71. WATER-JARS SUN-BAKING

wheel-turned, but the material of which they are made differs from that used farther north ; also, the vessels are covered with a slip and painted with simple designs.

The pots are made of *ḥamr* (a reddish clay), which is brought in large lumps from the adjacent desert. These are broken up, soaked in water, and then kneaded into a clay of the right consistency. No chopped straw is mixed with it. After the pots have been turned on the wheel (Fig. 72) they are placed on hard clay disks to sun-bake for half a day, and during this period they are tilted slightly from time to time, so that the air may circulate underneath. This is done so as to ensure an even evaporation of the superfluous moisture from all parts of the vessels; otherwise the pots would crack while being baked in the kiln.

When the pots have thus been dried in the sun they are handed over to a woman, who takes each one in turn and smooths the base of the vessel with a knife, cutting off the superfluous clay. The pots are then returned to the disks and left to sun-bake again for two or three days. They are then passed on to another woman, who paints them all over with a slip (Fig. 73). This is made of powdered *ṭafl* (a yellow clay) mixed with water. The pots are

FIG. 72. THE POTTER MAKING HIS WHEEL REVOLVE

now left to dry for ten minutes or so, when they are passed on to another set of women and girls, who polish them both inside and out with a smooth pebble of basalt (Fig. 74 and p. 152, Fig. 80). When this process is completed they are handed on to a woman artist, who paints them all over with simple designs (Fig. 75). The paint, which is made of a material called *mughreh* (red ochre), pounded up and mixed with water, is applied with a feather. 'The designs are freehand, and are put on very rapidly, without any pattern to work from.

The pots are now ready for the kiln, where they are fired as soon as the oven is ready for them, but they can be put on one side for a short time without any detriment if the preparation of the kiln is not complete.

FIG. 73. WOMAN PUTTING THE SLIP ON A POT

FIG. 74. POLISHING THE POTS

Dried maize-stalks (*būṣ*) are used as fuel for the furnace, which is lighted under a large circular oven, in which the vessels are placed in rows, one above the other. Cakes of buffalo- or cow-dung are placed on the top of the last layer of pots. The oven, be it noted, is roofless. The furnace below is kept open and constantly supplied with fuel for some hours. Then the furnace is closed, and the fire left to burn out. Meanwhile, the cakes of dung get gradually hot from the heat of the furnace below, and this ensures a good heat at the top as well as at the bottom of the oven.

FIG. 75. WOMAN ARTIST PAINTING THE POTS

On the site of this pottery factory a large number of tiles are also made (Fig. 76), the material being ordinary clay mixed with finely chopped straw. Men only are employed in this industry.

Each tile is shaped in a shallow wooden mould with a handle very similar to that used in brick-making (see p. 154, Fig. 81). The tiles are turned out of the mould on to the ground, and there left to sun-bake for two weeks during the winter and for one week in the summer. They are then placed in piles in the oven, the baking being carried out in exactly the same way as described above. The furnace is kept open and constantly supplied with fuel for five to six hours in the case of smaller ovens, and for seven to eight hours when the ovens are larger. The whole process of baking occupies about forty-eight hours from start to finish; by that time the tiles have cooled down and can be removed from the oven.

On another pottery-making site in Fayūm Province which I visited large *ziyār* and pans, as well as *ḳulal* (see p. 151) and other small vessels, are made. Both hand- and wheel-made methods are employed here. The clay used in the manufacture of the larger vessels is obtained from Kīmān Fāris. This clay is soaked in water till it is of the right consistency, then *mūṣ* is mixed with it and well kneaded. The words *mūṣ* and *tibn* both mean finely chopped straw, but the former is so finely chopped that it is more like a powder. This mixture is left to soak for one day in a large hollow in the ground. It is then removed and left piled up in a heap for four days before it is ready for use. Each potter takes a large quantity of this prepared clay and places it conveniently near the spot where he is working, keeping it covered with sacking to prevent further evaporation.

FIG. 76. MAN MAKING TILES

The *ziyār* and large pans are made on the wheel, the former in the manner described earlier in this chapter ; they are, however, decorated with simple designs on the upper half of the vessel. This decoration is done with the aid of an implement called a *garūt* (see p. 152, Fig. 80), which consists of a thin, flat piece of iron bent at a right angle at the top.

For maḳing the pans the process is as follows. The revolving table is covered with a thin layer of clay, and on this a thick pillar of clay is placed upright, and gradually hollowed out and moulded into shape. Long experience enables the potter to know the exact amount of clay required for making a pan, so that there is no necessity to add more. The pillar of clay is rapidly hollowed out and drawn outward and upward into the required shape, and it should be noted that the rim is not added, but is in one piece with the rest of the pan. The base, however, is strengthened by the

FIG. 77. BINDING CORD ROUND THE PAN

addition of another lump of clay smoothed over by the hand, and the outside and inside of the pan are finished off by smoothing with a potsherd. Cord is then bound round the pan spirally, as the vessel revolves on the wheel (Fig. 77). Care is taken that the cord should encircle the outer edge of the pan just below the rim. The vessel is now dried in a shady place for two days, and in the sun for one day, after which the cord is removed (Fig. 78). Before being placed in the oven, however, the superfluous clay is scraped off the base with the *garūt*. The fire is constantly kept going with the usual fuel of *būṣ* for two hours, after which time the furnace is closed and the fire left to burn itself out. When the vessels are cold they are removed from the oven.

The custom of binding the cord just below the rims of the larger pans may have been also practised in former times when making the upper part of a *zīr*. As I stated earlier in the chapter, the potter usually makes incised marks with his thumbnail just below the rim of a *zīr*, the marks roughly resembling those made by the impress of the cord. This impress may have suggested a pattern, which the conservative mind of the potter demanded should always appear on that portion of the pot, even when the cord was no longer wound round it. Thus the marks made round the base of the rim by the thumbnail may be an imitation of somewhat similar markings left by a cord bound round this part of the *zīr* in earlier times.

FIG. 78. PANS BOUND WITH CORDS DRYING IN THE SUN

Smaller vessels, such as *ḳulal* (singular *ḳulleh*) (Fig. 79), are also made at this factory, and the clay used is obtained from Begīg, or Abgīg, as this village is sometimes called. *Ṭafl* (yellow clay) brought from Kīmān Fāris is mixed with the ordinary clay, the proper proportions being two-thirds ordinary clay to one-third *ṭafl*. These two materials are laid in water to soak till they are quite soft. They are then removed to a deep cavity dug in the ground, where a man kneads them with his feet. The mixture is taken out and piled in a heap, so that the superfluous moisture may evaporate.

When it is ready for use each potter takes a quantity from this store, and places it in his hut, covering it, as usual, with sacking. A large lump of clay, worked up into a thick bolster shape, is taken and placed on the round table above the wheel. From this quantity of clay a number of *ḳulal* are made, each one, on completion, being cut off from the mass of clay by a string attached to a short stick (Fig. 80).

FIG. 79. TWO TYPES OF ḲULLEH OR WATER-BOTTLE

The potter begins by hollowing out the upper portion of the clay with his thumb, turning the wheel with his foot all the time, and slowly drawing up the sides of the vessel, which at the first stage resembles a bowl with thick sides. Then this is gradually shaped into a slender vessel by drawing up the sides, which, of course, become much thinner, until the *ḳulleh* is formed. The grooving

FIG. 80. POLISHING STONE, SĀDIF, GARŪT, AND STRING FOR CUTTING OFF FINISHED POTS

and final shaping is done with the aid of an implement called a *sādif*, a small, thin square of iron perforated in the centre (Fig. 80). The *sādif* is also used for incising the simple designs to be seen on the *ḳulal* made in this locality. The *ḳulleh* is then, as stated above, cut off by a string. The *ḳulal* are sun-baked for one day, then put into the oven, the fire being kept alight for four hours and then left to go out. The vessels are removed from the oven when they are cold.

The water-jars (*balālīṣ*) manufactured at this place are entirely hand-made, and for this process a circular hollow in the ground, such as has been described previously, is used. Large, shallow saucers and bowls are made in the same way.

A large lump of clay, sufficient to form the whole *ballāṣ*, is placed in the hollow, and beaten into a preliminary shape with the cottage-loaf-shaped clay implement. The curved piece of wood is also used here to beat up the sides of the vessel. When bowl and saucers are being made the rims are beaten into shape with it likewise. A *garūt* is used to cut off any superfluous clay that may appear during the formation of the *ballāṣ*. These jars are then left to sun-bake for a short time before the rim is added with the aid of the wheel. The *balālīṣ* are baked for the same length of time as the *ziyār*.

I asked a potter who worked with the wheel how long it took to become proficient in the art, and he told me that he had learned it from his father, and had taken five years to become really skilled in his work. He, however, said that if he had learned it from some one else it would have taken him ten years to become an expert. His father, he remarked, was a good teacher as well as a very skilful workman.

The granaries, which are usually erected on the roofs of the houses, are made by the women out of clay and chopped straw, well mixed together. Each granary takes some time to complete, as it can only be made piecemeal. The finished portion must remain exposed to the sun until it is fairly dry before another can be added. When the whole is constructed it is left in the sun to harden thoroughly.

The granary has a circular opening at the top, covered by a clay lid, while near the base there is a small opening which is closed with a mud stopper. This latter opening is used when the supply of grain in the granary is low, the grain being more easily extracted through it than through the opening at the top, for many such granaries are from four to five feet high.

These granaries are usually roughly circular, with straight sides, the top slightly domed ; but in some parts of Egypt many of them are globular, a shape possibly derived from certain basket granaries described below. Farther south, near el-Kāb, I saw some much larger granaries, which stood on the ground. They, again, were made of sun-baked clay. Many of these must have been from seven to eight or ten feet high.

Brick-making is also an important industry. The clay is mixed with chopped straw, and is prepared and kneaded as for pottery-making (see above, pp. 135, 151). So far as I know, men only are employed in this work. The bricks are shaped in a wooden mould with a handle, and are left on the ground to sun-bake (Fig. 81). Most of the houses of the *fellāḥīn*, and even some of the better-class residences, are built with these crude bricks, though the owners of the latter type of house more usually prefer to use fire-baked bricks.

FIG. 81. BRICKS LEFT TO SUN-BAKE: WOODEN MOULD WITH HANDLE IN FOREGROUND

When the walls are being built each bricklayer is assisted by a fellow-workman, who stands below and throws up to him one brick at a time (Fig. 82). I have often watched walls being built in this way, and I do not remember ever seeing a bricklayer miss a catch!

I have referred more than once in preceding chapters to fuel manufactured out of cow- or buffalo-dung. This dung is made into round, flat cakes by the women and young girls. Very young children are often to be seen in the villages, their hands and arms plastered with dung, busily engaged in making these cakes, which are left on the ground to dry and harden in the sun. Every housewife is careful to see that she has always a plentiful supply of this fuel, which is neatly stacked in large quantities on the roofs of the houses.

Basket-making is a very large and important industry. Certain kinds of baskets are made in almost every village throughout the country, but a few types are characteristic of certain localities only. Many of the commoner kinds of baskets are strong and well made, but the finest work is to be found in the more southern provinces; indeed, the farther south one goes the better the workmanship. Baskets are made by both men and women, though I have found that in some localities this work tends to be monopolized by one of the sexes only; and one type of basket at least, so I was told, is made only by men. Baskets are constructed mostly out of date-palm leaves and the mid-ribs of palm-branches, but one variety in the south is made from the leaves of *dōm*-palms. These particular baskets are easily to be recognized by the shiny surface of the material employed in their manufacture.

FIG. 82. BUILDING A WALL

The commonest and one of the most useful baskets in general use is called the *maḳṭaf* (Fig. 83). It is used in field-work, for the clearing away of rubbish, for removing *sibākh* (the earth obtained from ancient rubbish mounds, used as a fertilizer), and for the transport of grain ; in it, moreover, a woman generally places the dry roots which she collects in the fields to bear home for fuel, and also the goods which she conveys to and from the market. A woman always carries this basket on her head (see p. 80, Fig. 38),

FIG. 83. A MAKṬAF

the varied contents sometimes including even a small child (see p. 37, Fig. 14).

The habit of carrying their burdens on their heads gives the women their wonderful poise. The heaviest loads are thus carried with apparently the greatest ease. For example, the large water-jars, filled to the brim, are conveyed home in this way by the women without any support from their hands, and without a drop of the contents being spilled (see p. 41, Fig. 16).

Children begin to carry burdens in this way at a very early age, smaller jars, and perhaps somewhat smaller baskets, being used by them. If the heads of the female Egyptian peasants were systematically measured it might be shown that this method of carrying heavy weights from early childhood has made a definite impression on the shape of the skulls, those of the women being possibly much flatter on the top than those of the men. I do not know if any physical anthropologist has discovered this peculiarity in the head-form of Egyptian women or not.

The *maḳṭaf* is made, as I have said, of palm-leaves. These are torn off the main stem and split into the desired width, and are then woven into a very long plait. Extra leaves are constantly incorporated, till the necessary length is completed. Any very narrow

FIG. 84. SEWING THE PLAIT INTO A SPIRAL

strands left over as useless for this purpose are carefully put on one side, to be utilized in the following manner. When the plait is completed the basket-maker takes these strands and forms them into a cord by twisting them together between the palms of his hands. He then takes a large iron needle, which he threads with this cord, and proceeds to form the basket by sewing the plait into a spiral. The cord is inserted through the plait in such a way that it forms a thick spiral rib round the basket (Figs. 84 and 86). The work is often so cleverly done that, unless one has witnessed the whole process, it is exceedingly difficult to discover how the basket has been made. Two rope handles are attached to each basket (Fig. 83), the rim of which is often strengthened with the same material, any ends that remain over being laced into the sides of the basket below either handle. The base of the basket on the outside is also sometimes reinforced with cord coils.

I should mention that a basket in my possession, from the oasis of el-Farāfreh, displays the same technique as the *maktaf*. It is of very fine workmanship and the plaits are very small.

FIG. 85. BASKET-GRANARIES

A similar technique is employed in the making of basket-granaries. These are of great size, and are made, so I was told, exclusively by men and, so far as I know, in Fayūm Province only; I have never, as yet, come across them elsewhere. Numbers of them are sold at the weekly markets, and their size may be estimated by comparison with the height of the people standing near them in the photograph (Fig. 85). I have frequently seen these basket-granaries on the roofs of houses in Fayūm. Sometimes they are quite globular in shape and are entirely covered with clay, this being done, so one of my servants told me, to keep the wind and dust from penetrating through the interstices. Only when small pieces of clay have fallen off is the original structure of basket-work revealed. All the basket-granaries that I have seen are extremely well made, and are very strong.

Many baskets in use all over Egypt are made in the following way, the materials employed being taken from the palm-tree.

A number of the mid-ribs of palm-branches are split up lengthways, the leaves likewise. The basket-maker takes a certain number of the split mid-ribs, the number varying according to the required thickness of the coil, these forming a foundation. An iron needle, somewhat more slender than that used for the plaited baskets, is threaded with one of the split leaves, which is sewn over and over the foundation, almost, if not quite, concealing it. This type of basket is again built up spirally, each stitch being passed through the preceding coil (Figs. 86 and 87). Such baskets are made in a large variety of shapes, from flat, round trays to large receptacles with lids. They are often decorated with simple designs in colours, the leaves being, of course, dyed before they are sewn into the baskets.

FIG. 86. UNFINISHED BASKETS, SHOWING METHODS OF WORKING

FIG. 87. BASKET WITH OPEN WAVY-LINE PATTERN

Some baskets, which I was told are made only in two small villages in Fayūm Province, have the base made in the way described above, while the sides show an open wavy-line pattern (Fig. 87). These also are made in a large variety of sizes and shapes, and are very attractive and decorative. The wavy line consists of mid-rib foundations closely bound round with the leaves. It must be remembered that both the leaves and the mid-ribs are fresh when the baskets are made, and are therefore pliable enough to be bent into whatever shape the basket-maker desires.

In one very small village in Fayūm I found a large number of people engaged in this industry. There is also a basket-merchant in this village, and his trade extends all over the country. He informed me that he sent large consignments of baskets abroad, even, he declared, to England, but I am not in a position to be able to verify his statement. I bought a certain number of baskets

FIG. 88. BASKET-MAKERS IN A SMALL VILLAGE IN FAYŪM

from him, including one which, he said, had come from the oasis of Sīweh. This basket, the workmanship of which is very superior, is to be seen in the adjacent illustration on the right (Fig. 89).

Baskets of the variety called *ḳafaṣ* (plural *aḳfāṣ*) (Fig. 90) are used as temporary cages for fowls, pigeons, rabbits, and so on. Oranges and other fruits may also be packed in these baskets, as well as household utensils. In the manufacture of these baskets, which are made of the mid-ribs of palm-branches only, men are more usually employed than women. The baskets can be made very strong, and therefore may be used for carrying heavy weights. Vertical lengths of mid-rib are inserted into holes pierced through horizontal bars of the same material forming the four sides; no nails or fastenings of any kind are used. The lid is made in a similar way. I always have my kitchen utensils and stores packed in such baskets when travelling from village to village, as they have the advantage of being light in weight as well as durable.

FIG. 89. VARIOUS BASKETS: TRAY (AT BACK), FRUIT-BASKET (IN CENTRE), BASKET FROM SĪWEH (ON RIGHT)

Beds, chairs, and small tables are made of the same material and in a similar way to the *ḳafaṣ*.

Native rope is usually made out of the fibre of the palm-trunk (*līf*). The *līf* is picked over and torn into strips, which are twisted into a cord between the palms of the hands (Fig. 91 and Frontispiece). There is a large rope-making industry in Fayūm Province, and the ropes made in this village are traded over a large area.

Strong woollen cloth is woven in a great many villages, but the weaving of finer materials, such as silk, is mostly

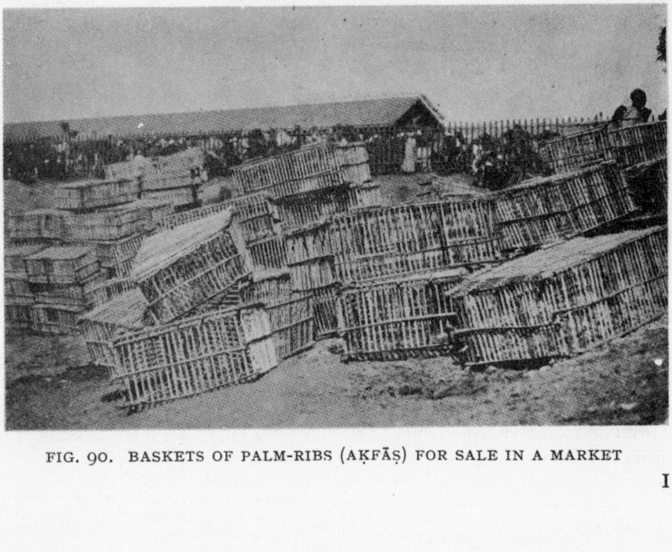

FIG. 90. BASKETS OF PALM-RIBS (AḲFĀṢ) FOR SALE IN A MARKET

confined to a few localities, where such work is done by specialists.

The looms are usually set up indoors, but, though hand-worked, they cannot be said to be very simple or primitive, and I feel that I must devote a great deal more study to the methods of working them before describing them in detail.[1]

FIG. 91. YOUTH MAKING ROPE

Very small looms are used for weaving narrow bands or for adding borders to silk handkerchiefs (Fig. 92).

Looms such as are used by the Arab women for the weaving of carpets are of a more primitive type. They consist of four pegs driven into the ground, on which the warp is extended, and two stones on which the heddle is balanced (Fig. 93). An excellent description of such a loom has been given by Mrs Crowfoot in *Sudan Notes and Records*.[2] The carpets and rugs woven on these simple looms are very strong and durable, and the colouring is quite attractive.

Spinning is, so far as I have yet observed, more often done

[1] For an excellent photograph and description of a modern upright loom see A. C. Mace, *Ancient Egypt* (1922), pp. 75 f. and Pl. 2.

[2] April, 1921, vol. iv, No. 1, pp. 25 ff.; see also H. E. Winlock, *Ancient Egypt* (1922), pp. 71 ff.

by men than by women in Egyptian villages, though I have seen one or two women engaged in this occupation. One year, when visiting a tribe of Arabs, I saw more than one woman spinning yarn.

I have referred in previous chapters to two kinds of bread made by the peasant women. Wheat- and *dura*-flour blended, or the latter ingredient only, are used, mixed of course with yeast, and

FIG. 92. SMALL LOOM FOR ADDING BORDERS TO SILK OR COTTON HANDKERCHIEFS AND THE LIKE

water is added till the dough is of the right consistency. The dough is then put to rise in the sun.

When the round, bun-shaped loaves of bread, called *khubz*, are made the dough is formed into cakes of the required size, which are then put to rise in the sun before being baked in the oven (Fig. 94). Wheat-flour is the main ingredient of *khubz*, which is the bread usually eaten by the wealthier peasants.

The making of *battaw* is a more laborious task. When ready for the oven a small dab of fairly moist dough is placed on a large, fan-shaped object made of palm-ribs. The woman then tosses the dough on the fan until it has spread in a thin layer all over it. The ' fan ' is then handed to another woman, seated before the mud oven, who slides the flat, round sheet of dough on to the open oven shelf.[1] A large fire, made of dry *dura*-stalks, is kept burning in the furnace below the shelf. When one side of the bread is done the bakeress turns it over with an iron rod (called *bashkūr*), made for this purpose, till the other side is cooked. When quite finished she removes it with the aid of the *bashkūr* and places it on the ground beside her.

FIG. 93. ARAB WOMAN WEAVING A CARPET

The dough for the *battaw* is usually kneaded in a very large basket, and a great quantity is always made and baked at a time. Thus the task entails many hours of hard labour, and the women often begin the work in the afternoon and continue through the night until daybreak or even later. The baking takes place once or twice a month, and female relatives and friends usually come in to assist. Such bread, if made in a cleanly way, is excellent when fresh. It is crisp and thin, somewhat like the oatcake made in the North of England and in Scotland. No one who has not made the attempt can realize how difficult it is to toss the dough on the 'fan.' I have myself made one or two efforts to assist in this breadmaking, but I made a hopeless failure of it, much to the amusement of my village friends.

Most villages, and all towns, have a weekly market, where a great variety of goods are for sale. The market-place is usually situated just outside the village, and is either Government property or belongs to some private individual. Every one who brings

[1] The oven is open in front, but is covered at the top. The smoke goes up through a hole in the ceiling, which opens on to the flat roof.

goods for sale pays a small sum to the owner of the property on which the market is held.

There is no more animated scene than a village market (Fig. 95). Some of the traders bring their goods the evening before, packed in *akfāṣ* (plural of *kafaṣ*) and other receptacles, and these, together with bundles of sugar-cane and the like, are deposited overnight in the market-place, being left in the charge of village guards. Others who have goods for sale begin to assemble very early in the morning, bringing sacks of onions, bundles of cotton cloths, cheap jewellery, household and kitchen utensils, tomatoes and other vegetables, as well as cattle, sheep, goats, donkeys, and camels. The butchers are usually among the first to arrive, for they slaughter the animals on the spot, hanging up the carcasses on huge wooden tripods (Fig. 95, and p. 32, Fig. 11). While thus suspended the meat is cut up, and the purchaser is able to select any special portion that he or she requires.

FIG. 94. LOAVES OF UNBAKED BREAD PUT IN THE SUN TO RISE

Each trade has its own particular location in the market-place, which is thus divided up into sections, such as the market of camels, the market of meat, the market of sugar-cane, and so on. Women take their full share in the business of selling, and may be

FIG. 95. A VILLAGE MARKET: SUGAR-CANE IN THE FOREGROUND, THE BUTCHERS BEHIND

seen squatting on the ground, often accompanied by their male relatives, with their goods spread out before them. The market of cheese and *semn*—the latter clarified butter regularly used in cooking—is conducted solely by the women, so far as I have seen, and they bring these provisions in metal pans carried on their heads.

Large numbers of pottery water-bottles are nearly always to be

FIG. 96. A SHOEMAKER ON THE OUTSKIRTS OF THE MARKET

found for sale at the markets, the better ones being made at Ḳena, in Southern Egypt, and exported thence far down the Nile.

The tinsmith also does good business, making mugs (*kīzān*, singular *kūz*), primitive lamps, and other articles on the spot, using for this purpose old paraffin-oil and petrol tins.

A shoemaker is usually to be seen squatting at work in a spot on the outskirts of the market, with a number of shoes ready for sale on the ground by his side (Fig. 96). He has an iron anvil in front of him, similar to that used by the brass- and copper-smiths, described in the first chapter (p. 32). Near by may be seated sellers of musical instruments, such as the pipe (*nāi*), the *zummāreh*,[1] and the

[1] Double pipe with a drone.

drum (*darābukkeh*), etc., while at a short distance the tattooer may be engaged in decorating the hand of some youth.[1]

Various entertainers attend most of the larger markets, such as a conjurer, a reciter of legends, musicians accompanied by a male dancer, to say nothing of the fortune-teller, who, seated in a small tent, usually attracts a considerable number of people. He makes a series of holes in sand spread on a handkerchief upon the ground in front of him, and by certain methods of counting these deducts his conclusions. The conjurers are really very clever.

It will thus be seen that business on market-days is pleasantly combined with pleasure.

Conversation is general and loud, sounding to the unaccustomed European ear like violent quarrelling.

When the warmer weather begins the traders erect rough booths, looking like primitive umbrellas, under which they can take shelter from the heat. Both time and patience are required to effect a purchase, for the seller of an article asks quite double the price he will accept. Arguing and gesticulating, the trader and would-be purchaser wrangle over the article until the price is adjusted to the satisfaction of both parties. Sometimes, if the trader is insistent, the would-be purchaser gets up from the ground and proceeds to walk away, whereupon the trader usually betrays a readiness to make further concession, and finally agrees to accept a lower price than that demanded.

In the hot season the water-carrier does good business, as heat, bargaining, and shouting make for thirst. He is usually paid not in money, so I was told, but by small presents of onions, tomatoes, or other delicacies.

I have observed that the people show praiseworthy consideration for the animals which they bring to the market. On their arrival one of the first things the men do is to provide their animals with fodder, and also water if such is obtainable. One year, when I was living in the fields near a village, the market was held close to my camp, and I particularly noticed this consideration for their beasts on the part of the peasants.

As the afternoon advances the traders begin to pack up the goods which have remained unpurchased, and those who have come from a distance load their baggage on their donkeys, and so depart to their several villages.

[1] See Chapter III.

CHAPTER X

AGRICULTURE AND HARVEST RITES

THE wealth and prosperity of Egypt is, and always has been, dependent upon the produce of the soil, and the peasants are before everything else agriculturalists, as is also indicated by the Egyptian Arabic word for peasant—*fellāḥ* (plural *fellāḥīn*), meaning one who digs or tills. The peasants, most of whom are quite illiterate, are remarkably clever agriculturalists, and every young boy is well versed in all that pertains to the cultivation of the soil. Their methods are, for the most part, very primitive, though, of course, the present system of storing water and of distributing it over various districts has been adopted comparatively recently, and to maintain it a number of highly trained engineers are required. This book is not concerned with these modern developments, which, indeed, lie beyond the scope of anthropology, but with the ordinary work in the fields, where ancient methods and ancient implements are still largely employed, and ancient customs are still observed.

The cultivated lands in Egypt lie along either bank of the river, without any apparent boundaries, for there are no hedges to divide the fields as in England. To the eye of the ordinary traveller there is nothing to indicate where one man's property ends and another's begins. The fields are broken up into small squares, separated from each other by ridges of earth and narrow trenches. When water is distributed over a given area it is conducted through the trenches into the square plots by making an opening through the ridges which surround them. When the plots have received their due allowance of water the openings are built up again and the stream is directed to another portion of the land.

The greater number of the peasants own or hire small plots which are marked off one from the other by boundary stones stuck into the ground at intervals of six feet or more. Many a village quarrel has arisen over these stones, the removal of a neighbour's landmark being a constant cause of disturbance. If a man, for instance, thinks he would like to add to his own property by stealing a portion of his neighbour's he will surreptitiously shift his boundary stones farther on to the adjoining land. This is, of course, quickly detected by the man whose land has been encroached upon, and a bitter dispute will follow, which may end in a violent quarrel.

The plough which is in common use at the present day is a primitive, but quite adequate, machine (Fig. 97). It is made entirely of wood, with the exception of the share, which is tipped with iron. It is generally drawn by oxen, but in Upper Egypt I have seen more than one plough with a camel and a donkey yoked together, a somewhat incongruous pair! The peasant follows on foot, guiding the plough, and usually singing as he works. Except during the inundation the work in the fields is incessant, for, owing to the very fertile soil, one crop can follow another in quick succession.

FIG. 97. A PLOUGH AS USED TO-DAY

The watering of the fields is very strenuous work, the commonest machine used for this purpose being the *shādūf* (see Fig. 13, right, and Fig. 108), a primitive water-hoist. It consists of two upright wooden posts, or pillars, made of mud and *būṣ*, connected by a horizontal bar, across which is slung another bar, or a stout branch of a tree, weighted at one end with mud and stones, while from the other end is suspended a leather or basket-work bucket. The man working the *shādūf* pulls down this bucket into the water (either river or canal), and, when it is full, allows the weighted end to raise it to the level of the land. He then pours the water into a prepared channel, through which it flows in the required direction.

If the land to be irrigated is much above water-level two or three of these *shawādīf* (plural of *shādūf*) are worked one above the other.

The men thus engaged usually sing at their task, some of their songs being very melancholy, and descriptive of their hard and laborious toil. One of them runs thus :

> *Shawādīf,*
> Their ropes are of palm-fibre
> And their pails are of goatskins.
> And it was in ancient times that *shawādīf* were
> invented
> By the blessed Ṣāliḥ Zabādi.

The ropes referred to are those by which the bucket is suspended from the end of the weighted branch which acts as a lever. The name of the supposed inventor is, of course, mythological.

The following is a lament on the hard labour involved in the working of a *shādūf* :

> Hast Thou resolved upon strangling me, O God ?
> Loosen the noose !
> No mother weeps [for me],
> No aunt,
> No sister ! [1]

Another method of raising the water is by means of a water-wheel round the circumference of which pottery jars are attached. Another small wheel with cogs is attached to the same axis as the larger wheel, and into it fit the cogs of a large horizontal wheel. When this is made to revolve the two vertical wheels are set in motion. A long pole is attached to the horizontal wheel, and to it an ox, cow, or buffalo, or even a camel, is yoked and driven round and round by a man or boy. The animal is usually blind-folded to prevent it from becoming giddy. The groaning and creaking of the turning water-wheel form, to my mind, a most soothing sound.[2] Yet another contrivance for raising the water to the level of the fields is the Archimedean screw, depicted in Fig. 98.

During harvest-time every available man, woman, and child is employed in the fields ; but before any of the corn is cut some of the villagers go into the fields and pluck the finest ears by hand. These are plaited into a special form, and this object, called the

[1] See H. Schaefer, *The Songs of an Egyptian Peasant*, translated by J H. Breasted (Leipzig, 1904), pp. 43 f.

[2] For excellent photographs of a *shādūf* and a water-wheel see *op. cit.*, pp. 45 and 107.

'bride of the corn' (*'arūset el-ḳamḥ*), is used as a charm. One may be suspended over the house-door as an antidote to the evil eye; another may be hung up in the room containing the stores of food, as a charm to ensure abundance. Many tradesmen hang such objects in their shop-windows, believing that this will bring them plenty of customers. Again, in some parts of Egypt the 'bride of the corn' is temporarily placed on the heaps of grain after the winnowing is completed, as a charm to secure a good harvest the following year. Sometimes the grain from these heads of corn is extracted and mixed with the next year's sowing. The 'bride' may be left hanging till it is replaced at the next harvest, or, again, it may be allowed to remain in its place until it falls to pieces (Fig. 99).

FIG. 98. THE ARCHIMEDEAN SCREW

Before the field is cut a certain number of people are given presents of corn by the owner. These gifts of the firstfruits are bestowed on some of the poorest people in the village, as well as on the barber, the *mueddin* (the man who chants the call to prayer from the mosque), the *zummāreh*-player, the carpenter, and the *fuḳahā*—the last-mentioned being poor men who recite the Ḳorān in mosques, in private houses, at funeral ceremonies, and at the periodical visits to the grave (see pp. 112, 114 f., 117 ff., and Fig. 100).

The corn is cut with a primitive sickle (Fig. 101), and is immediately tied up into small sheaves, which are carried to the threshing-floor on the backs of camels (Fig. 102). The threshing-floor is usually a bare place near the fields, and here the corn is piled up in great heaps.

The threshing is done with a sledge-like machine, called *nōrag*, drawn by oxen. It consists of a wooden frame, on which the driver sits, and solid iron wheels which are passed over and over the corn, breaking up the stalks and separating the grain from the husks (Fig. 103). The broken stalks are collected and packed into net sacks, which are carried off on the backs of donkeys (Fig. 104). The grain, which is, of course, still mixed up with chaff, is piled up in heaps ready for winnowing. This takes place out of doors, the grain being thrown up into the air with a large wooden fork or a wooden spade (Fig. 105). The wind carries off the chaff, the grain falling below in a heap (Fig. 106). A second process is necessary in order to clear the grain entirely of chaff, and so it is carefully sifted in large sieves. The grain is then piled up into heaps, over which palm-branches are sometimes placed to prevent the wind from blowing any of it away. The heaps are left standing all night, and late in the evening it is customary for the owner to place flat, round loaves of bread among the grain, these loaves being the perquisite of the man who, on the following morning, carries it to the owner's granaries.

FIG. 99. TWO 'BRIDES OF THE CORN,' THE UPPER ONE NEW, THE LOWER SOME YEARS OLD

The granaries are usually situated on the roofs of houses, and are made of clay or basket-work.[1]

It is the custom to pay all the harvesters in kind (Fig. 107), and

[1] See pp. 153 f., 158.

strings of women and children can be seen coming from the fields carrying their wages on their heads. The custom of paying in kind is a very ancient one, and is not confined to harvesters only. The village barber is also paid by his fellow-villagers in this way, with beans and corn, and those who thus remunerate him can

FIG. 100. A MUEDDIN RIDING HOME WITH HIS GIFT OF FIRSTFRUITS

demand his services for shaving and haircutting for a year. Only those, however, of his own village can pay the barber in this way; outsiders must pay him in cash. This rule applies also to the ferryman, who, when the fields belonging to a village lie on the opposite bank of a canal, conveys over the cattle and labourers every morning, and brings them back just before sunset (Fig. 108).

In some parts of Upper Egypt the following customs are observed in connexion with the cultivation of *dura* (maize) only. A *dura*-field is irrigated by means of a water-wheel or a *shādūf* ten times, and when the water has been conveyed to the fields for the last time the owner, or one of his family, brings to the field *faṭīr* (a kind of sweet pastry), or *kunāfeh* (fine macaroni), or *rashteh* (macaroni cooked in milk). He then stands on one of the pillars of the water-wheel or *shādūf* and cries to his neighbours in the field, "Come and eat," firing his gun at the same time. Such firing takes place regularly at weddings, or on any joyous occasion. After the food has been eaten the owner of the field plucks some of the heads of the *dura*-plants and places them on one of the empty food plates. This he presents to whichever member of his family brought the food. He then returns to the field and plucks four heads of *dura*, which are fastened on the foreheads of the two oxen or buffaloes which worked the water-wheel. The animals are then driven home, and all who see them will know by the heads of *dura* decorating their foreheads that the irrigation of their owner's field of *dura* is finished.

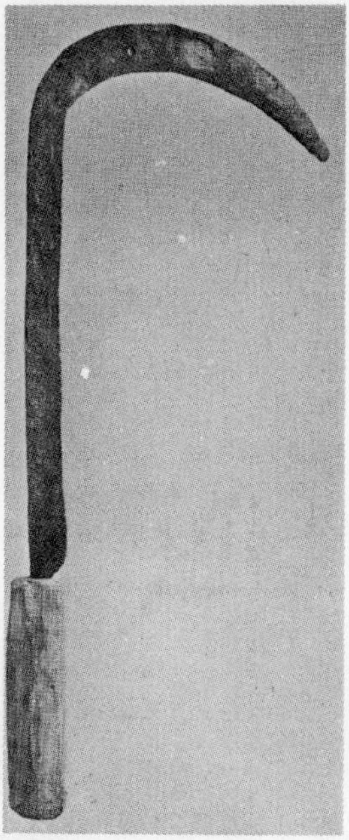

FIG. 101. A SICKLE

When a *shādūf* is used for raising the water the owner plucks a head of *dura* for each *shādūf* that has been used for irrigating his field. The *dura* is attached to the arms (or levers) of the *shawādīf* which, like the cattle, are brought home thus decorated with the maize.

The last time of irrigating a field of *dura* is called *el-fiṭāmeh*, which means the act of weaning. The same name is given to the last occasion on which a mother suckles her child.

In many of the provinces of Upper Egypt, when the *dura* or wheat or barley has been threshed the heaps of grain are left standing on the threshing-floor all night. But before sunset, when the work is completed, the owner of the grain brings some food to the threshing-floor, either *faṭīr*, *kunāfeh*, or *rashteh*, or cooked meat. He stands up on one of the heaps of grain and calls out to his

FIG. 102. CARRYING CORN TO THE THRESHING-FLOOR

friends, " Come and eat," and he fires off his gun as a sign of joy. When his friends have eaten he places some of the food that is over

FIG. 103. THRESHING WITH THE NŌRAG

around and in the heaps of grain. This, it is believed, will bring a blessing and a plentiful supply of the grain; also, so the peasants

FIG. 104. CARRYING AWAY THE STRAW

believe, it will satisfy the *ʿafārīt*, who will eat some of the food thus placed for them. If the owner neglected to do this the *ʿafārīt* would take some of the grain.

FIG. 105. HARVESTING-FORK

This custom, as well as that mentioned before, of placing bread among the heaps of winnowed grain suggests a belief, at some period, in a corn-goddess, to whom offerings had to be made. So far as I have yet discovered there is no trace of such a belief left in the minds of the peasants, but these ceremonies certainly suggest the possibility of an earlier belief in some fertility or earth-goddess, and the name given to the last time of irrigating a field (i.e., *el-fiṭāmeh*) bears out this idea.

FIG. 106. WINNOWING

FIG. 107. A HARVESTER WITH HIS WAGES IN THE FORM OF A SHEAF OF CORN

FIG. 108. A FERRY-BOAT

In the chapter dealing with survivals it will be seen that some of these harvest customs can be definitely dated back to very early times in the history of the country.

I have stated above that harvesters are usually paid in kind instead of in cash, and that the women and young girls carry these wages home on their heads. The methods of threshing and winnowing the corn received as wages are more primitive than those already described in this chapter. The threshing is done by beating

FIG. 109. THRESHING WITH A STICK

with a stick (Fig. 109), and this process is often, though not always, carried out by the women. When threshed the corn is usually placed in a large, round tin bath, and the winnowing is done by simply taking up the grain in the hands and throwing it into the air (Fig. 110). The chaff is blown away by the wind, the grain falling down again into the bath. It then goes through a second process of winnowing with a sieve.

The grain, when required for use, is ground in primitive hand-mills, and "two women . . . grinding at the mill" is quite a common sight in Egyptian villages (Fig. 111). The stones from which these hand-mills are made are obtained, so I was informed, from the desert, and are chipped into the desired shape. The flour is very coarse after this grinding, and, moreover, after it has fallen down round the grinding stones on to the dirty ground it can hardly be called pure or clean! Fortunately there is in most villages at

FIG. 110. WOMAN WINNOWING WITH THE HANDS

FIG. 111. A HAND-MILL

least one mill worked by steam, and the women take their flour there to be ground for a second time. During this process many of the impurities are removed from the flour.

The native bread has a good deal of *dura* mixed with the wheaten flour, but it is quite good to eat when fresh, and if you can choose your bakeress! It is certainly far more satisfying than the white bread eaten in England, and the fact that the most nourishing properties are not extracted from the flour may account for the beautiful teeth which are so noticeable among most Egyptians of all classes.

CHAPTER XI

MAGICIANS AND MAGIC

FROM the earliest times Egypt has been celebrated for its magicians, and accounts of their marvellous achievements have been preserved to us not only in ancient Egyptian records, but in the Bible and in the works of several of the classical writers. Furthermore, many of the tales in the famous collection of stories known as *The Arabian Nights* show what wonder-working powers were attributed to magicians in medieval Egypt. In modern Egypt also magicians abound—in fact, one or more are to be found in almost every village, and they are believed to possess exactly the same powers as did their predecessors in antiquity and in the Middle Ages.

FIG. 112. A CELEBRATED SHEIKH AND MAGICIAN

The modern Egyptian magician, who may be of either sex, is appealed to in all kinds of emergencies. Sometimes his fame has spread far beyond the confines of his own village, and urgent calls for help from distant parts of the country may cause him to travel far afield. I do not think that it is customary for female magicians to go beyond their own or neighbouring villages, but I have known more than one of the male sex whose 'practice' extended over many provinces.

Owing to his knowledge of spells and charms, which may be

employed for evil no less than for beneficent purposes, the magician is greatly feared as well as respected by the villagers. In order to propitiate him they offer him presents of grain, prepared food, and other desirable commodities, for there is always lurking in the peasant's mind the fear that he may unintentionally arouse the displeasure of the magician, who might thus on his own account devise evil against him, or at any rate be more easily induced to do so by an enemy of the unwitting offender.

FIG. 113. THE WOMAN WHO IS POSSESSED BY THE SHEIKH MUḤAMMED

There is a female magician of my acquaintance who is possessed by a certain sheikh Muḥammed (Fig. 113). This sheikh has never lived on the earth, but is a member of one of the communities of supernatural beings who are supposed to live "beneath the earth." This sheikh is always with the woman—*i.e.*, clothed with her body. She calls to him to draw his attention when she is requested to exercise her powers. For instance, if a sick person, whether child or adult, is brought to her she is supposed to be able, by the aid of the sheikh who possesses her, to say if the sick person will live or die. She is much sought after for spells and charms, and the sheikh advises her in each case which to employ. In fact, he is said to go beneath the earth to write the spell or charm in question, which he brings to her when it is completed, and which she passes on to the person who has come to her for treatment and advice. At such times this woman is *called* the Sheikh Muḥammed, and is supposed to assume his sex and character.

One of my village women friends who was suffering from a pain in her head went with me one day to consult this magician, and to ask to be given a cure. The house into which we entered was soon packed to overflowing, the very window being blocked with sightseers. The floor and the walls of the room were of mud, but a fairly clean mat was secured for me to sit on, the magician and her patient squatting close by me. The former took the kerchief from off her patient's head, folded it cornerwise, and measured it from corner to corner with the span of her hand. She then knotted it and sat on it. Suddenly her whole body began to shake violently, and she uttered curious noises. This indicated that the sheikh was assisting her and making his presence felt. Her face now underwent a remarkable change of expression, and her voice, attitude, and whole behaviour became distinctly masculine, and everybody present addressed her as the Sheikh Muḥammed. She told her patient that she was to visit a certain sheikh's well, which was situated some miles away from her village. The sick woman asked if she might not go to the well of a sheikh in the magician's own village, but this request was peremptorily refused. It was, she said, necessary that the well mentioned before should be visited. This event happened during Ramaḍān, the month of the Muslim fast, and the magician told the woman that she was to come to see her again on the day of the 'Little Festival' (which immediately follows Ramaḍān) and that then she would give her a charm to wear.

The magician kept up her manly impersonation even after the *séance* was over, and she presently declared, much to the joy and amusement of the villagers, that she had fallen in love with me and wished to marry me! This ridiculous speech was believed to come from the Sheikh Muḥammed who possessed her and whom she impersonated, at any rate for the time being. She would not be satisfied until I consented to be photographed with her!

Another female magician of my acquaintance (Fig. 114) is also somewhat renowned within her village circle. This woman's husband is dead, and she lives with two of her sons. One room in their house is set aside for her use only; no one else must ever enter it, except the people from beneath the earth, with whom she is supposed to be in close and intimate relationship, and for whom there is always a supply of food and a *ḳulleh* full of water in her room. When she takes a meal she does so in this apartment, and she will not eat with other people. She has five familiars who live beneath the earth, and through them she gets into touch with the other subterranean supernatural beings, including *ʿafārīt*. One of these familiars is called Zedimāl; another, a son of Zedimāl, is called

Mu'awwad; another is a man called el-Akhras (the dumb one), while two others are women, one of whom bears the name of el-Ḥaggeh. The last-named is the most important of all, but she never comes up above ground, and Zedimāl is her servant.

This magician, I learned, must always be very clean both in her person and in her clothes. If she wears a single garment that is dirty the male familiar, el-Akhras, comes up from beneath the earth and possesses her. He seizes her so that she falls on to the ground, shaking all over, and is unable to eat or move. On such occasions her sons will sit down near her, begging her to tell them what is the matter. Then Zedimāl comes up (I was not told how she was brought up) and stops all the anger. The magician must at once remove the dirty garment and put on clean clothes. There are only two colours, besides black, that she may wear—green and red. When I went to Egypt last autumn I took her a silk handkerchief. I chose a purple one, thinking that that colour would be a suitable one for a widow, but this had to be changed for one of the two colours permitted to her.

FIG. 114. THE FEMALE MAGICIAN WHO HAS FIVE FAMILIARS

A *ṣulḥeh* [1] is a sort of peace-making feast, and it is sometimes held by people who have appeased the sheikh or sheikheh by whom they may be possessed. When a man wants a *ṣulḥeh* this woman magician dresses in men's clothes and wears a silk scarf such as is worn by the men, and carries in her hand a stick with a silver knob. If it is a woman who requires the *ṣulḥeh* the magician wears her own clothes. This ceremony is described later (p. 199). When I last saw this magician there was trouble between el-Akhras, her male familiar, and his *ukht*,[2] for each person beneath the earth has an *ukht*. El-Akhras wanted to have a *ṣulḥeh*,

[1] *Ṣulḥ* = peace; *ṣālaḥ* = to make peace with.

[2] See pp. 74 ff.

sharing it with his *ukht*, but the latter was angry and refused, saying that she was greater than he, and must have the sacrifice of a ram to herself, demanding also that her *ṣulḥeh* should come first. The magician could not then afford to buy two rams for the double sacrifice, so matters were delayed, and nothing could be done while I was in Egypt.

This female magician is called in to help and give charms and advice on all manner of occasions. If a woman is suffering from sheikh-possession she will consult the magician as to why the sheikh is thus troubling her. A woman whom I have known for some years was afflicted in this way, and the magician was called in to advise. I was present at the time and witnessed the whole ceremony. The magician, having heard the woman's account of her trouble, went into a corner of the room and was covered all over with a blanket. After muttering to herself for some time she suddenly clapped her hands and began a conversation with her familiar Zedimāl. Salutations were passed between Zedimāl and all those present in the room, including myself, and then the magician asked why the sheikh was troubling the woman. It was explained that the sheikh demanded a pair of gold earrings, which the woman he possessed was to wear, and also a new *gallabīyeh* (dress), yellow in colour, also to be worn by the woman. If these were obtained the sheikh would be appeased. The husband of this woman was a poor man, but the gold earrings and the new dress had to be bought, and would be paid for by degrees. Shortly after this I was in the village again and inquired how the woman was. I was informed that the earrings and dress had been purchased, but that she was still troubled, though not to the same extent. She had again inquired of the magician, and I believe the sheikh had demanded more, but I never heard all the details!

In a small village in Upper Egypt there are two magicians, one a Copt, the other a Muslim. They are both clever, and both are in great demand, their fame having spread far beyond their native province. They are friends of mine, and have told me a number of the devices and charms used by them on various occasions. An inscribed charm obtained from magicians is usually enclosed in a small leather case, and hung by a cord of plaited leather or a string round the neck or waist of the person for whom it has been prescribed (Fig. 115). The following information was obtained from the two men mentioned above.

When a magician is called in to find hidden treasure he goes at night to the ground where the treasure is said to be hidden, and he sweeps the whole plot to get rid of impurities, afterward sprinkling it with water. When this is done he lights a fire in which he burns some of the feathers of a hoopoo. The whole ceremony is repeated two or three nights in succession. On the third night the magician cuts a cross with a knife the whole length and breadth of the selected site. On the knife are inscribed the letters of the King of *alif*, these letters representing the servants of the King. (I should explain here that each letter of the alphabet, of which *alif* is the first, is said to have a king attached to it.) The magician now brings branches from four different trees—*i.e.*, olive, pomegranate, apricot, and tamarisk (*ṭarfā*). These four branches are stuck into each outer point of the cross, and are brought together at the upper ends like a tent. Then he takes a branch from a young palm-tree that has not yet borne any fruit. The length of this palm-branch must measure from the magician's elbow to the tips of his fingers, plus the length of his hand. The upper ends of the four branches mentioned above having been tied together, the branch from the palm-tree is tied horizontally across them, its leaves being stripped off, leaving only the mid-rib. On either side of this mid-rib the magician writes the letters belonging to the two kings of fire, water, air, and dust—for each of these has two kings, one an *ʿafrīt*, the other a heavenly being. Then he will watch the branch to see in which direction it will bend. If it bends toward the right he will shift all the four branches which are stuck in the ground in that direction—*i.e.*, toward the right—and again watch the horizontal mid-rib. He will repeat this process until he gets to a spot where the mid-rib of the palm-branch remains absolutely horizontal and motionless, when he knows he has arrived at the exact spot under which the treasure lies concealed.

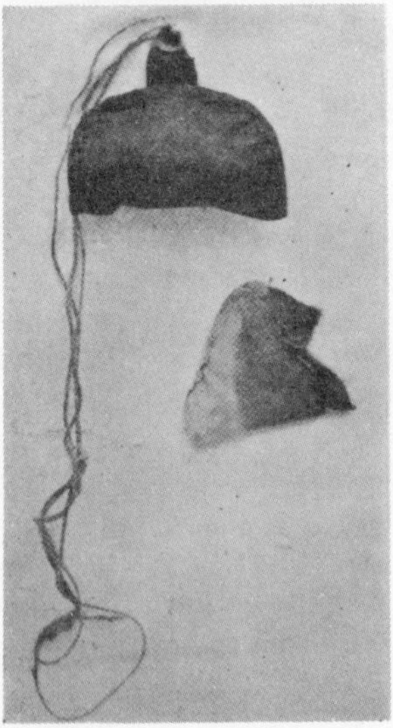

FIG. 115. CHARMS WORN BY A WOMAN TO KEEP HER HUSBAND'S LOVE

The following is another method of finding hidden treasure. In this case a priest acted as magician, and the exact spot where the treasure lay hidden was known.

On the outskirts of a certain village in Upper Egypt there is a very large stone. It lies on the ground and is covered with water for a great part of the year—probably water left from the inundation. Under this stone treasure of great value is believed to be buried The stone is said to extend some distance underground, its base being some yards below the surface. A cock is supposed to be the guardian of this treasure, and it sometimes appears to certain of the villagers, crows two or three times, and then disappears.

A Coptic priest in the neighbourhood owns a book in which is entered a list of all the buried treasures in that province, where such hidden hoards are believed to be numerous. Among others in this book was noted the description and locality of the hidden treasure in question, and he determined to see if he could get it. Accordingly, at midnight he went to the stone, taking his book with him, for in it were written the proper incantations to be recited on such an occasion. He also took incense with him, which he burned in a dish, meanwhile reciting the incantations prescribed in his book. Suddenly the great stone broke in two, the two halves banging together and making a sound like the roar of a lion. This terrific noise disturbed all the inhabitants of the village near by, who came out to see what was the matter. The priest was so afraid of being discovered that he climbed up a tall palm-tree not far from the spot and remained there till dawn, when he ventured to climb down and return to his house.

I was told that, as soon as the priest ceased burning the incense and reciting the incantations, both acts having come to an abrupt conclusion when he fled in terror to the tree, the two halves of the stone joined together again, and not the slightest trace of a crack is now visible.

The people say that it would be useless for anyone to attempt to dig up the treasure, for the deeper you dig the lower the stone goes into the earth.

There is a large number of stories current all over the country about hidden treasure, and I have been told of the existence of more than one book containing a list of places where treasure is to be found.

It is the custom of many of the countryfolk to hide their money underground, either in their houses or outside, and I know of more than one very rich man who refuses to put his money in a bank, but prefers to bury it. Such people, of course, though wealthy, are entirely without education, beyond a knowledge of reading and writing. Perhaps they may confide the secret as to where the money is buried to a brother or wife, but sometimes they die without telling anyone where it is concealed. I have been told by one or two officials that such stores of money have been accidentally discovered from time to time, and these discoveries are quite enough to account for the large number of stories about hidden treasure which are current all over the country.

As I have already stated, and as I propose to show in the following paragraphs, the magicians' powers are sometimes employed for sinister purposes.

If a man wants to make his wife hate him so that he may easily divorce her he calls in the aid of a magician, who will proceed as follows. He takes an egg which was laid on a Wednesday, and on the shell of it he writes certain magic letters, which are supposed to form the name of the King of the Tombs. He then takes the egg and buries it in a tomb, but on no account must anyone know which tomb it is. For Christians it would be the tomb of a Christian, for Muslims that of a Muslim. By the time that the magician has returned from depositing the egg in its hiding-place the charm has already begun to work. The egg must always be left where he placed it. Should anyone discover its secret hiding-place and remove it the charm loses its effect, and the woman would again love her husband.

If a man wishes to procure the death of a man whom he regards as his enemy he will go to a magician, who acts in the following way. He takes a hen and kills it, keeping the blood in some vessel. He then obtains an egg laid by a hen that has black feathers only, and on it he writes this magic square (Fig. 116) with the blood of the hen he has killed. He burns some incense, holding the egg over the fumes, with the inscribed side downward, repeating the following incantation three times: "In the Name of God, the Compassionate, the Merciful. By the Name of God, the Mighty King and Majesty. Possessor of Possessions, the Throne and Seat, the Heavens and Earth. Blessèd be God, Lord of the World, Lord of all power and transcendent might. Light of Light and Spirit of Spirits. All Glorious, Holy Lord of Angels and the Spirit, praise

Him, the Highest. Take charge, Angel Gabrāīl, of the illness [presumably in the sense of 'make it your charge to make him ill'] of so and so, the son of so and so [mentioning the mother's name]. Quickly, now!" The egg is then hidden in a tomb.

I am informed that this is a very interesting charm: black typifying evil, blood attracting spirits, and a tomb being the haunt of ghoulish spirits.[1]

It may be mentioned here that in all these charms, spells, and incantations it is necessary to write the name of the *mother* of the person whom it concerns. If the father's name is inserted instead the charm is abortive.

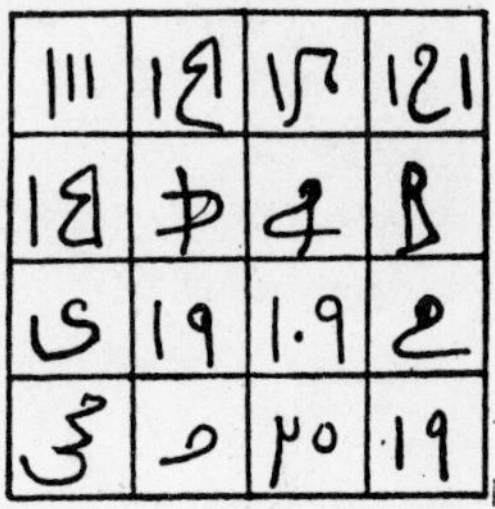

FIG. 116. A MAGIC SQUARE

The events related in the following story are, so my informant strongly maintains, perfectly true.

In a small village in Upper Egypt there lived a man and his wife, the latter being very good-looking. One day a certain *ḳāḍi*[2] who was visiting the village in question saw her, and, falling in love with her on the spot, desired her as his wife. Knowing that she was already married, his only plan was to get rid of her husband, and so he determined to drive the unfortunate man mad. To accomplish this he induced a magician to write a charm on a piece of paper, which he tied to an inner branch high up on a palm-tree, where it could not easily be seen. The reason for his thus tying the charm to a palm-branch is the idea that, as the branches of the tree are blown this way and that in the wind in apparent confusion, so the brain of the man against whom the spell was concocted would be tortured and confused. Possibly the woman's husband got to know what had been done, but anyhow the poor man lost his reason. He tore off his clothes, tied a rope round his waist, and spoke at times in an unknown tongue.

"You must say," so he told the village boys who congregated around him, "'*Kee ree bra ra kee ree bru.*'"

He would also constantly mutter, "Kamaleh [his wife's name] went to the east, Kamaleh went to the east," repeating it over and

[1] I am indebted to Mr E. S. Thomas for this information.

[2] The word means 'judge,' as has been already explained, but it is also, as in this instance, a title given to a man who draws up marriage contracts, hears divorce cases in villages, and so on.

over again. Finding that he got no better, his wife divorced him, whereupon the *ḳāḍi* asked for her in marriage, and was accepted. Meanwhile, the poor husband wandered aimlessly about, saying that he was king of his native village. He collected *būṣ*—dry *dura* (maize) stalks—each stalk of which he thought was a gun. With these he armed himself and the young lads of the village, and told them that he was their king, and that they must follow him to fight against the other villages. On the day of the weekly market he would repair to the market-place, seize large pieces of meat hung up for sale, and eat them raw. He would also pounce upon the fish which the fishermen had caught in the pond adjoining the village. At last the ʿ*omdeh*, or headman, of the village, finding that the poor fellow had become a disturbing element in the place, wrote to headquarters about him, and he was removed to an asylum. Here he died, but up to the last the one sensible word he was constantly uttering was his wife's name. The events recorded still form a common topic of conversation in the madman's native village.

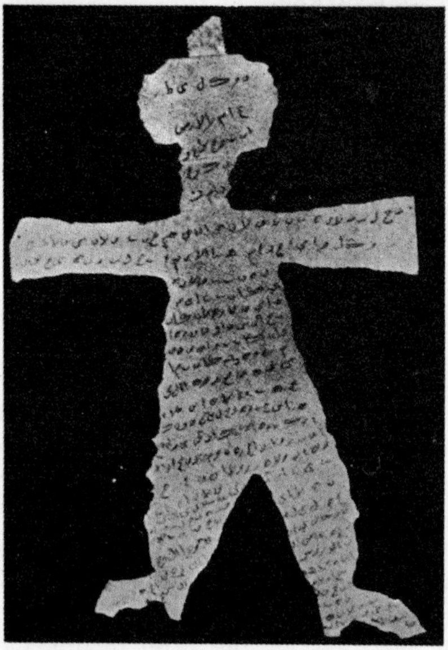

FIG. 117. CHARM TO DRAW A MAN OR WOMAN FROM A DISTANCE

I myself have seen the *ḳāḍi* who played such a prominent and cruel part in this bit of village history, and the poor madman's wife whom he married figures in the following account of how a woman can be drawn from a distance.

To bring a man or woman from a distance the magician proceeds as follows. He takes four branches of a pomegranate-tree and sticks them into the ground, tying them together at the top. He then makes a paper figure of a man or woman, and writes a charm on it (Fig. 117). The figure shown in the accompanying photograph was made and inscribed for me by the Coptic magician already mentioned. Though in theory the figure is supposed to differ for the two sexes, in practice this rule does not always hold, for the figure in my possession is said to represent both sexes equally well. Having completed the writing on the paper figure, he hangs it from the centre of the branches by a red silken cord, places burning incense below it, and begins to recite the incantation supposed to be written on the figure.

I should explain here that there are said to be seven kings beneath the earth, three of whom are more famous than the others. These three are called Ṭarish, Ḳasūra, and Zoba, the last having four heads. Their names are written on the figure. The other four kings are called Mīyemūn, Baraḳān, el-Aḥmar (the red one), el-Abyāḍ (the white one).

The translation of the charm runs thus: "O King Ṭarish, O King Ḳasūra, O King Zoba who hast the four heads! Go on, three great kings of the underworld, and give your orders to your servants to bring so and so, the son or daughter of so and so [mentioning the mother's name]. If he [or she] is sitting make him [or her] stand up, and snatch him [or her] up, and mount him [or her] on a horse, and fly with him [or her] through the air, till you arrive at my house." [1]

A man of my acquaintance who knew this Coptic magician well was at one time very sceptical of his professed powers, and was inclined to think that he simply deceived the people with rather clever chicanery. The magician was well aware of this, and, on meeting him in the village one day, spoke to him and told him that he knew he had no faith in his magic. He then offered to demonstrate his powers, if the man would come with him then and there to his house. This he consented to do, and the magician conducted him into his private room, where he proceeded to act in the manner described above. He first called up an *'afrīt*, whom he ordered to bring before him the woman who had married the *ḳāḍi*. The *'afrīt* was, I suppose, either one of these kings or one of their messengers. My acquaintance declares that he saw the *'afrīt* quite plainly. After a minute or two the woman whom the magician had summoned appeared before them, and the man told me that he noticed that her dress was covered with flour. Presently the

[1] The actual writing on this figure is a jumble of letters. The translation given is what the magician told me should be written on it. No doubt constant careless copying has led to this meaningless inscription.

magician dismissed her and she vanished. The woman had been brought from a village about three miles off, and, on inquiry, my acquaintance found that, at the time when she had been brought before them, she was making bread in her house, when her dress would, of course, be covered with flour! After this remarkable exhibition my acquaintance told me that he felt that the magician really had some extraordinary powers.

The object of one of the spells possessed by my magician friend is "to make a king or any governor merciful to his subjects, and to ensure his granting any request made to him." To make such a spell effective the following procedure is adopted. At sunrise the magician makes a fire of wood, or, perhaps, charcoal, or cow-dung,[1] but not of *bûṣ*. In this fire he will put two kinds of incense, ordinary frankincense and incense scented with musk. While the incense is burning the magician will repeat the names of the angels who are in the fourth heaven, and the name of their leader, seven times. The name of the leader of the angels in the fourth heaven is Kilīmya.

After he has finished this repetition he pronounces a formula beginning: "O angels, and leader of the angels of the fourth heaven! O Sun, which gives light all over the world!" Then he again addresses the sun, saying, "I pray you, O Sun, for the sake of the chief king [or governor, as the case may be, mentioning also his name and the name of his mother] that you may make his heart kind to so and so [*i.e.*, the suppliant]." Then the magician writes a charm and gives it to the petitioner.

The charm consists of a repetition of the names of the angels in the fourth heaven, and it must be worn under the left arm. Such charms are usually enclosed in a small leather case, which is suspended by a cord from the neck in such a way that it hangs underneath the arm.

If a man wishes to injure an enemy by making him unconscious he will go to a magician, who will tell him to bring some *ʿurûḳ el-fûweh* (roots of madder), the seeds of leeks, the fat of a crow, the fat of a tortoise (*fakrûn*),[2] and onion seeds. These ingredients, I am told, can be purchased at the shop of a village grocer. He must then light a fire and throw into it the five articles mentioned above. The smoke coming from this fire will make anyone who

[1] See pp. 154 f.
[2] Professor Margoliouth tells me that *fakrûn* is a Berber word, so possibly this particular magical receipt was brought into the country by Arabs or Moors.

smells it unconscious. Evidently the man induces his enemy to come to his house, and the latter, not knowing what has been prepared for him, becomes unconscious from the fumes before he has time to realize the trick played upon him. This method has been tried and has never failed, according to my informant.

In order to restore consciousness the urine of a man must be injected up the nostrils, which, I am told, is a sure restorative. Anyone who makes a fire of this kind must first take a mixture of *semn* (see p. 167) and olive oil, and stuff it up his nostrils to prevent himself also from being overcome by the fumes.

This device is likewise resorted to by people who are travelling across desolate and dangerous spots, where they are liable to meet wild animals. These, on sniffing the fumes from the fire, become unconscious, so that the travellers can pass them by in safety.

One day in 1926 when I was visiting a certain village in Middle Egypt one of my friends there, a very respectable and well-to-do man, came to see me and informed me that he had had several articles stolen from his house, and that he intended to call in the help of a magician who was clever at discovering thieves by means of divination. He invited me to attend the ceremony, which took place a few days later. The magician came from another village a few miles off, and was brought to me to be introduced. I ordered coffee and cigarettes, and after these refreshments had been partaken of we settled down to the business in hand. Some writing-paper was torn into small strips, and a different name, suggested in every case by my friend, was written on each. The magician produced a copy of the Ḳorān, and asked for an iron doorkey. One was brought, which he rejected, as he said it was not native-made. A suitable one, however, was found, and then the magician opened the book at a certain chapter, put in one of the inscribed slips of paper, and inserted the doorkey, leaving the handle of the key outside the book. This book and key were now bound together with string, in such a way as to prevent the key from moving. A pottery saucer containing a charcoal fire was then brought, into which the magician dropped incense. A third man who was present and the magician faced each other on either side of the burning incense, the Ḳorān being suspended by the key on the first finger of the right hand of each man (Fig. 118). The fumes from the incense rose around the Ḳorān, passages from which were recited by the magician. Presently the book began to move, and, according to the direction in which it turned, either to the right or left, the man whose name was inscribed on the piece of paper selected was guilty or not guilty. Several of these strips of paper were tested, and two or three people whose names were written thereon were detected as the thieves. The man whose things had been stolen told me that he had all along suspected these people, but, as

FIG. 118. DIVINATION CEREMONY WITH THE ḲORĀN TO DETECT A THIEF

they were related to his family, he did not like to prosecute them. They were the poorer members of the family, and were consequently very jealous of their richer relative. The magician employed on this occasion is renowned for his cleverness in such methods of divination, and no one would dream of doubting his decisions.

There is a form of black magic still practised in Egypt by means of human figures made of wax or clay. If a man desires to take his revenge on another who, he considers, has done him a grievous wrong he visits a magician and gets him to make a wax or clay figure (Fig. 119), supposed to represent the man he wishes to injure. If wax is used the figure is sometimes thrown into a fire, incantations being uttered by the magician at the same time. If clay is used the figure may be placed in water. As these figures disappear in the fire or water the man who is to be affected gradually dies. Such an extreme measure is very rarely resorted to—indeed, it would be exceedingly difficult to find a magician who would consent to carry it out, even with the promise of a large sum of money. There is supposed to be no cure for the man against whom such magic is worked; he is bound to die, as the figures cannot be rescued from the fire or the water.

FIG. 119. WAX FIGURES USED IN BLACK MAGIC

Such wax or clay figures are more commonly used to bring about rather less direful results in the people whom they are supposed to represent. Needles or pins are stuck into them, or, if these are not available, the sharp points of palm-leaves may be used instead. Wherever the pin or other sharp point is inserted into the figure the person who is represented will feel pain in the corresponding part of his body, until the pin is removed from the clay or wax figure. This pricking of the figure should always be done by the magician himself, who accompanies such actions with the recitation of magic spells. If the man who is being thus injured guesses what is causing him pain he will go to the magician and induce him by larger payments of money to remove the pin from the figure. The moment this is done the pain felt by the man ceases.

Similar practices have been resorted to up to quite recent times in more than one part of the British Isles, and are still current in many parts of the world, as the collection of such objects in the Pitt-Rivers Museum at Oxford well demonstrates.

I have already at the beginning of this chapter stated that some people are believed to be possessed by sheikhs, these sheikhs being among the many subterranean peoples whose existence is firmly believed in by the peasants. Such sheikhs may be good or bad; if the former they will assist the person they possess, if the latter they will require to be constantly appeased.

Possession may come suddenly, no one knows how. It is also

believed that if a woman gets a sudden fright she is particularly liable to become possessed. For instance, I was told that a woman coming after dark down the stairs which lead from the roof of a house to the ground floor, and carrying no light with her, may become frightened and fall, in which case a sheikh will come into her at once. She will realize what has happened and will ask the sheikh to tell her his name, whereupon he is believed to reply, "I am Sheikh so and so."

A man or woman may be possessed by several sheikhs of both sexes, and persons once possessed remain so till they die. As I have already explained above, a man or woman who is troubled by the sheikh who possesses them will consult a magician, who will inform them what the sheikh requires.

Sometimes it is necessary to have a ceremony called a *zār*—in fact, most people who are troubled with a sheikh either have such a performance at home or attend one which is being held in another person's house. When a *zār* is being held all the villagers know about it, for they hear the sound of the drum and smell the incense, and all those who are afflicted with this kind of possession will be attracted thither. The sheikhs "make them go," so I was told. Certain songs are sung by the conductor of a *zār* and his assistants. The meaning of the songs has, in some instances, been lost, and some of them may please one sheikh, but not another. Therefore, if a man is possessed by several sheikhs each in turn has to have the songs sung that please him.

One woman I know, after becoming possessed in this way, lost the use of both her legs, which swelled to an unusual size, and if she was moved she cried out with pain. Her brother, seeing her plight, arranged for her to have a *zār*, bringing the conductor and his assistants to his house with their musical instruments—a drum and tambourines. The performance, which was held in an inner room, having begun, the patient suddenly got up and began to dance, and the sheikh spoke through her.

Her brother and the people assembled there asked him what he wanted, to which he replied, "I want nothing."

"Why should you then make her unhappy?" the brother and his friends inquired, "and where do you come from? Are you an Egyptian or a Sudanese?"

He replied, "She was always sitting about and unhappy because her children died, and so I came into her."

So they again asked, "What do you want?"

This time the sheikh said, " I want silver anklets and nice clothes, and she must not be miserable."

After a week the ceremony called *ṣulḥeh* (p. 186) was celebrated, the procedure being as follows. A sheep is killed, and some of its blood is put on the dress of the woman who is possessed, the people singing and playing their musical instruments all the time. Seven candles are brought and placed round a large brass tray set in the centre of the room, either on the floor or on a stand. Seven kinds of sweetmeats, including dates, almonds, and raisins, are heaped up in the centre of the tray and covered with a bowl, on the top of which is placed one of the candles. All the seven candles are now lighted, and the people present, including the patient, eat, an extra supply being offered to the officiating magician, male or female. One of the people present hands the magician a five-piastre piece, which he dips in the blood of the sheep. At the *ṣulḥeh* held on behalf of the above-mentioned woman it was her brother who gave the money. The coin is wrapped in a piece of cotton stuff and given to the possessed man or woman, who will have it enclosed in a leather case and wear it always hung from the neck and passed under the left arm. This is a charm, and is supposed to be a present to the sheikh who possesses him or her. Such a charm is called a *lāzimeh* (an obligatory gift).

On one of the occasions when I was present at a *zār* a man came in, sat down for some time, and then went out. I was told afterward that his sheikh did not like the songs that were being sung, and so he could not remain in the room. When one of the possessed women who was present at this *zār* stood up and danced she began to bark like a dog, and her whole expression changed, her face becoming drawn and haggard. On another occasion a man became very violent, hurling himself about and striking out, so that it took three or four other men to hold him. When once this fit of excitement had passed his face assumed a calm and placid look.

Women on these occasions wear special ornaments (Fig. 120), if they can afford them, and must wear good clothes. People who are possessed by sheikhs are often supposed to be able to divine where a stolen article has been hidden. A young man of my acquaintance once lost a key. Thinking that one of his fellow-students had stolen it, he went to a man who was possessed, and, after giving him a small sum of money, asked him which of the students had stolen it. The man told him that none of them had done so, but that he had dropped it inside his trunk. He went back to the school, searched his trunk carefully, and found the key, as the man had told him he would.

The *zār* is not necessarily followed by the ceremony called the *ṣulḥeh*; this takes place when a sheikh has troubled a man or woman for some time, and at last becomes appeased. It is a form of peace-making between the sheikh and the person he possesses. If anyone is possessed by more than one sheikh it is not necessary to kill more than one sheep at the *ṣulḥeh*; one victim appeases them all.

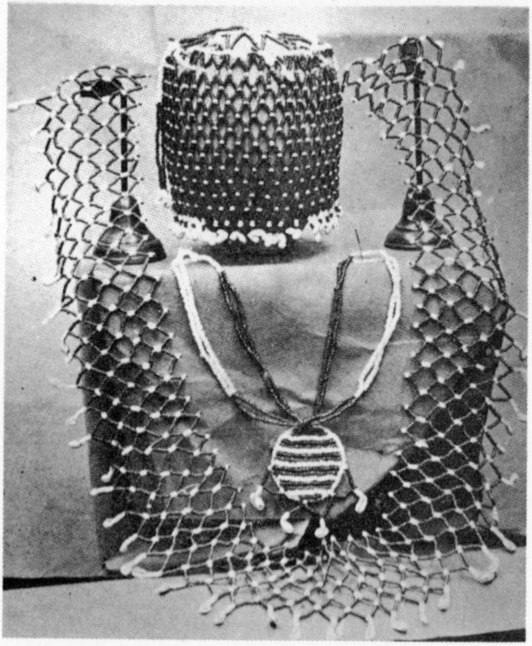

FIG. 120. ORNAMENTS—BELT, PENDANT, AND CAP—SOMETIMES WORN BY A WOMAN AT A ZĀR
The beads are green and white.

This belief, that it is possible to be thus possessed by a sheikh, is a very baneful one. The women who suppose themselves to be thus affected become exceedingly hysterical, and their husbands, for fear of the consequences, are put to great expense. The officials are quite rightly trying to put an end to the holding of the *zār*, but to suppress this ceremony completely will be difficult, as the beliefs associated with it are so deeply rooted in the peasants' minds.

CHAPTER XII

THE VILLAGE MEDICINE-MAN AND MEDICINE-WOMAN

THE village magician, whether male or female, often combines the practice of medicine with that of magic; indeed, it is difficult in many cases to distinguish the one from the other, so closely are they allied. Many of the cures are magic pure and simple, and when some herbal mixture is prescribed it is, more often than not, administered by the village 'doctor' to the accompaniment of the recitation of some magic spell. Without this addition many of the peasants would consider the medicine valueless so great is their belief in the efficacy of magic!

In a village where I have often resided for two or three months at a time there lives a woman who is renowned for her goodness. All her fellow-villagers have the greatest faith in her, and sick people beg her to come to them and cure them. She sits down or stands by the sufferer, and, holding a short length of dry maize-stalk, passes it round and round his or her head, repeating prayers and passages from the Ḳorān (Fig. 121). The stalk must then be either burned in a fire or thrown into running water. It is believed that the complaint passes into the stalk and is destroyed in the fire or carried away by the water. Twice over, when I was unwell, this woman was asked by one of my village friends to pay me a visit. On both occasions she acceded to the request, and, after she had finished her performance, the stalks were burned, and my friend declared that she soon noticed a decided improvement in my condition.

It can be readily understood that in these Egyptian villages, where dust and flies abound, and where the villagers themselves are so ignorant of hygiene, eye-troubles are very common. It is appalling to see how defective is the eyesight of many people of the peasant class and the amount of eye-disease, if not actual blindness, that prevails; and all this in spite of really excellent eye-hospitals controlled by the Government. Unfortunately, the seeds of disease are sown in childhood, and even babyhood. Until the women are less ignorant, and learn to realize the importance of keeping their babies clean, it will be difficult, if not impossible, for the doctors to combat the many eye-diseases that cause so much suffering to hundreds of the peasants. With conditions as they are, cures for sore and inflamed eyes are much in demand and are numerous. The following are some of the remedies for eye-trouble employed by the village medicine-man or medicine-woman.

FIG. 121. A MEDICINE-WOMAN PASSING A PIECE OF MAIZE-STALK ROUND A FEMALE PATIENT'S HEAD TO CURE HER OF ILLNESS

The medicine-woman whose methods of healing I described above has a great reputation as an eye-doctor. Those who suffer from inflamed eyes and swollen eyelids often resort to her for treatment. She takes a lump of sugar, and, turning back the inflamed eyelid, rubs it inside with the sugar. "Black blood" comes away after this operation, so I was told. She then takes a large onion, extracts the juice, and mixes with it some salt. This concoction she drops into the eyes of her patient. "It is very painful," my informant told me, but she added that it did a lot of good. While the woman is rubbing the inside of the eyelid with the lump of sugar her patients often stop up their ears with their fingers, as this is supposed to decrease the pain of the operation. For three days afterward the eye, or eyes, must be kept covered with a handkerchief, so that no air can get in. At the end of the three days the woman gives her patient a second dose of the onion juice and salt, and a few minutes later drops a mixture of *tūtia*[1] and honey under the lids. It is believed that after this the inflammation will quickly disappear.

In another village farther south there is also a woman who is regarded as an eye-specialist, and her knowledge of her art, together with one of the objects she employs, has been handed down in her family for two or three generations, so she told me. She has a large shell, called in Arabic *maḥāreh*, and a black stone called *ḥagar eṭ-ṭarfā* (stone of the tamarisk). She makes eye-medicine by first wetting the inner, concave surface of the shell, and then rubbing it with the stone (Fig. 122). She thus produces a white liquid which the peasants call 'milk.' They believe, as does the woman herself, that this 'milk' comes from the stone, whereas it comes, of course, from the powdering of the surface of the shell by rubbing the stone against it. The liquid is believed to be an excellent medicine for sore eyes, and people in her village who are suffering from that complaint visit the woman and get her to drop some of her medicament into their eyes. This eye-medicine is known in other parts of Egypt

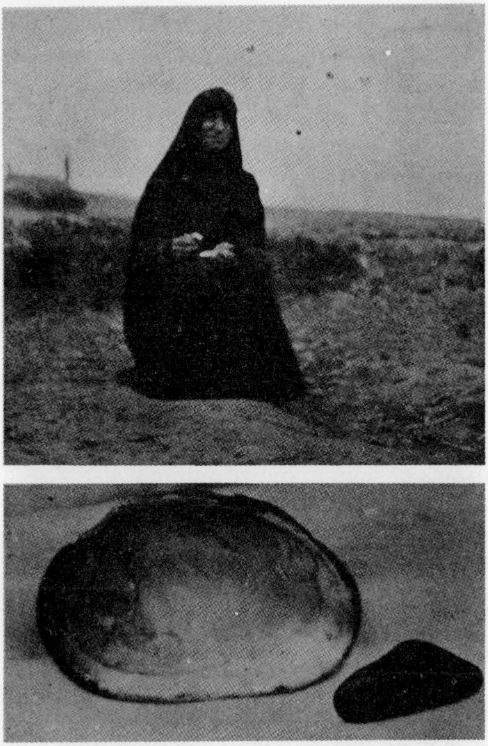

FIG. 122. THE FEMALE EYE-SPECIALIST HOLDING HER SHELL AND BLACK STONE, WHICH ARE SHOWN BELOW

[1] Sulphate of zinc.

as well, but the people make it and apply it themselves, without resorting to any medicine-man or -woman. The shells are found in the desert, so that when one is worn out it is not difficult to get a fresh supply. The stones used are also said to come from the desert.

A certain sheikh, who combined the profession of magician with that of a doctor, told me that he often prescribed the following cure for inflammation of the eyes. Some lotus-leaves are pounded in a mortar and then mixed with goat's milk. The eyelids are bathed with this preparation two or three times a day, when all the fever disappears, and the eyes soon recover. A remedy of his for an eye that is injured from a blow is to take some palm-leaves and, after thoroughly washing them, put them in a mortar and crush the juice out with a pestle. Some salt is mixed with this juice and the mixture dropped on to the injured eye. Three applications, so he says, effect a cure. The woman eye-doctor last mentioned has a different cure for an eye injured by violence. She rubs her shell with the stone as before, and, mixing the liquid with molasses, bathes the eye with this preparation.

If a man is suffering from sore or watery eyes he must get two drams of opium and two drams of the seeds of *er-rashād* (nasturtium). These he must grind up together and mix with the white of an egg. Placing the preparation upon a piece of cotton material, he applies it to his eye or eyes. This is the prescription of a Coptic magician, who says that it is an absolute cure.

The peasants quite realize the value of massage, and both a male and a female exponent of the art are to be found in many of the villages. Their services are employed in obstinate cases of constipation as well as for the curing of pain in the back and limbs. A man or woman who is suffering from a pain in the back is sometimes treated in the following way. The 'doctor' makes his patient lie on the ground, face downward, and ties his ankles together with a rope, while with another rope his hands are tied behind his back. The 'doctor' then places his foot on the exact spot in the patient's back where he feels the pain, and, grasping with both hands the ends of the ropes which tie the man's hands and ankles, draws them upward, his foot pressing down the spine. Probably a crack will soon be heard, or the patient himself will feel that something has gone into place again in his back, and he will be cured. A woman attends members of her own sex, and gives them the same somewhat drastic treatment.

A headache is sometimes cured in the following way. The magician in his capacity as medicine-man writes out a charm, which is hung on the patient's head over the spot where the pain is greatest. The charm must be written in a circle, and is, of course, in Arabic. Fig. 123 is an exact copy, only transliterated.

Sīdī Aḥmed el-Bedawī is one of the most celebrated sheikhs in Egypt. His tomb is at Ṭanṭa, where a great festival is held in his honour every year.

The following is a prescription for a disordered spleen. The magician fetches leaves of *el-atl* (tamarisk), pours red vinegar on them, and boils this mixture on the fire, afterward pressing it through a sieve. The patient must drink a coffee-cup of this medicine early in the morning, repeating the dose for seven days, during which time he must eat no solid food, but should drink soup made by boiling a fowl.

FIG. 123. CHARM TO CURE A HEADACHE

Distention of the stomach is a very common complaint among the peasants, due, of course, to acute indigestion. In some parts of Egypt a boiled crow is prescribed as a cure for this complaint, and the patient, I am told, quickly experiences relief after eating this most repulsive food. Another more reasonable cure is prescribed by a medicine-man of my acquaintance. A small quantity of flour is mixed with a little yeast early in the morning ; this must be left to rise in the sun till mid-day, when sufficient water is mixed with it to form a liquid. Soon after taking some of this preparation the patient must drink some soup made by boiling a fowl. The bowels will then act, and relief be soon experienced.

If a woman is suffering from prolonged labour, and birth is difficult, her relatives will call in the aid of a magician. He writes two charms, in the form of two magic squares, on two separate pieces of paper. One square is suspended by a string from the woman's waist, so that the inscribed paper hangs over her left hip. The other charm is burned, and while it is burning the magician repeats the inscription on it once, after which the child is immediately born. An exact copy of the charm to be hung on the woman is reproduced here (Fig. 124). There is no key to it, so I was told.

The inscription recited by the magician is from the hundred and fourteenth chapter[1] of the Ḳorān, of which the following is a translation:

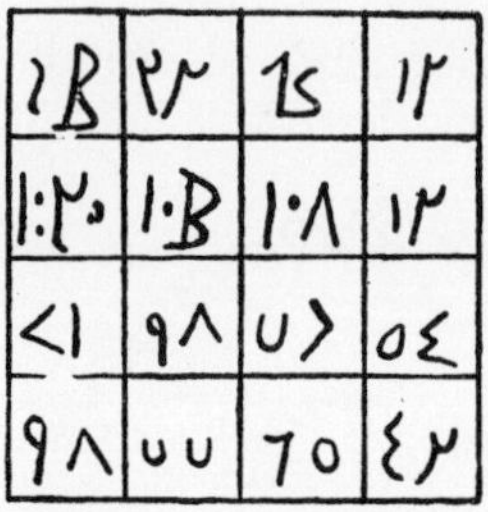

FIG. 124. THE CHARM TO BE SUSPENDED FROM THE WOMAN'S WAIST

"Say, I fly for refuge unto the Lord of men, the King of men, the God of men, that He may deliver me from the mischief of the whisperer who slyly withdraweth, who whispereth evil suggestions into the breasts of men [*i.e.*, the Devil]; from *ginn* and men." The magician then adds: "Make your servant so and so, the daughter of so and so [mother's name], bear quickly by the help of God Almighty."

Here is a cure for a headache: "Cure for a headache. Very excellent. The charm should be written on a piece of red leather and hung over the temple of the patient, and, whoever wears it, it [the headache] will certainly be removed by the will of God." These are the words of the medicine-man himself, translated as literally as possible from the Arabic. The inscription consists of nothing but letters, the first groups standing for Syrian names of God, and the others for the names of seven good sheikhs.

The following is a cure for fever. This prescription was given me by a sheikh who is renowned for his powers as a medicine-man, and he declares that by means of it he has cured many people. The sheikh takes four small pieces of paper, and on the first he writes "Hell is hot"; on the second "Hell is cold"; on the third "Hell is thirsty"; and on the fourth "Hell is hungry." All the letters of each word in these inscriptions must be well separated from each other. He then puts seven seeds of *kammūn iswid* (black cumin) on each piece of paper. Having done this, he takes a short, narrow strip of leather, which must be old, such as is used for making sieves for winnowing. This piece of leather must be divided into four portions, one for each paper. A candle like those used in Coptic churches is broken into four pieces, and

[1] One of those chapters of the Ḳorān which are often utilized as amulets.

added to the other articles on the papers. These papers are now rolled up with their contents, and each roll is tied round with spider's web. When an attack of fever comes on some olive oil is brought, and the patient must dip the first roll of paper in it. Then a fire is made in a pottery bowl, and the roll of paper is placed in it. As it burns the patient should let the fumes go up his or her clothes. If the patient is cured after this first burning of a roll he need not use the others. But if he has a return of the fever he must use the next roll, and so on, until he is cured.

All inscribed charms, so I was informed by the sheikh from whom I obtained the above information, should be written with a reed pen, a dry maize-stalk being generally used for this purpose. The reason he gave me for this rule is that the reed is made by the hand of God, while a metal pen is made by the hand of man.

The same sheikh wrote out for me a cure for a woman with "an issue of blood." A pure white plate must be brought, on the inner surface of which an inscription is written with black ink. Fresh water must then be put in the plate, and the patient must drink it. She will then be cured by the will of God Almighty. The ink with which the inscription is written comes off into the water, and the efficacy lies in the drinking of the inscribed sentences in this way.

A fortnight before I arrived at the sheikh's village he had cured a woman by this means. A literal translation of his prescription is as follows:

"A remedy which stops the flow of blood. Tried and true. You shall write it in a white plate, and it is washed out with water, and the woman shall drink it fasting before breakfast, and she shall be released from it [1] [*i.e.*, her illness] by the will of God most High. And this is what you write: 'Shalāsh, Shalāsh, Shinyūsh, Shinyūsh! Stop the blood for the sake of the Right [one of the names of God]. The blood shall be cut off from so and so, the daughter of so and so [mentioning the mother's name], for the sake of Damrurāg. Dry up, O blood, from the womb of so and so, the daughter of so and so [again mentioning the mother's name], as the sea dried up for Moses, and as Mary bore Jesus.'" [2]

Shalāsh and Shinyūsh are, so I was told, names of God in Syrian. Possibly they are very old words, and, on that account,

[1] Or cured.

[2] Evidently referring to a belief connected with the manner of the birth of Christ, which is, I understand, current among Muslims.

considered the more efficacious in an inscribed charm of this character. Names and words, evidently ancient, the meanings of which are now quite lost, often occur in modern Egyptian inscribed charms.

Here is a cure for dry scabs on the skin, given me by a Coptic magician. Early in the morning, before washing or eating, pass one finger over the front teeth and then rub it over the scabs. This should be repeated three, five, or seven times, accompanied by the repetition of the following words : " O dry scab, come into two pieces, and go to the skin of a dog."

A man whom I have known for several years was suffering from a dry scab on his left wrist, so he went to a doctor for a remedy, but the scab did not disappear. On returning to his village he spoke to the Coptic magician who also resided there, and told him about his complaint. The magician advised the treatment described above, and after carrying out these instructions the scab, so the man told me, quickly disappeared !

The following is another cure for the same complaint. Get a pod of lupine after the harvest, and after the seeds within it have been prepared for food. Then press the pod with one finger three, five, or seven times, repeating meanwhile the same words as in the previous cure. The lupine is prepared for food by frequent immersion in hot water ; the water is then drained off, and the lupines mixed with salt. They will then keep for a considerable time.

If a child has a cough the mother may go to a magician, who takes one of the narrow leaves off a palm-branch and writes a charm on it. He then rolls up the leaf, tying it with a string which is long enough to hang round the child's neck (Fig. 125). I have seen several children wearing these supposed cures for a cough, and I have one or two in my possession.

In Asyūṭ Province I was told that three leaves must be plucked from a palm-tree that has been inherited by the sick child's family from a relative, and that the following charms should be written on each leaf :

" Samkin, Samkin, Samkin.
Sam'akin, Sam'akin, Sam'akin.
Sam'ukin, Sam'ukin, Sam'ukin." [1]

" Go away, coughing, for the sake of the Mighty God, and leave as soon as you can."

[1] These are said to be Syrian names of God.

Each leaf should be rolled up separately, tied up with string, and hung round the child's neck. It is believed that as soon as the leaves dry the child's coughing will stop.

This prescription, given as a cure for a cough, is, so I was told by the sheikh who prescribed it, very old. Some seeds of the cotton-plant which have been dried over the fire are pounded up into a powder. The patient should take some of this dry, early in the morning and also at night.

FIG. 125. CHARM TO CURE A CHILD'S COUGH

There are a number of cures for various diseases which are well known to the people themselves, so that it is not always necessary to call in the aid of the 'doctor.' Among the large number which I have collected are the following.

Cure for a cough. A bunch of camel's hair is placed on the chest of the patient, and another bunch on the top of the head, the hair being first steeped in oil. Both bunches are kept in position by large handkerchiefs bound round the body and over the head. This is believed to make the patient perspire, after which the cough goes. This cure is used for children only.

A man who lives in a small Upper Egyptian village began, two or three years ago, to suffer from rheumatism in his legs. He got worse and worse, until he was so crippled that he was unable to walk. He consulted several doctors, so I was told, but they could do him no good. One day, when some of his friends came to see him, he told them how useless was all the medical treatment he had received. They therefore persuaded him to try the following remedy. Having made several cuts in both legs, he took some garlic and squeezed the juice of it over the cuts, rubbing it well in. The pain was awful, and the man wept from the agony. However, he persisted in the treatment every day for a fortnight. Each day a lot of pus came away—" yellow water " it was called when I was told about this remedy—and each day he got better, and the pain from the rheumatism less. The incisions were made once only, but the juice from the garlic was squeezed over the cuts every day. At the end of a fortnight, so I was told, the man was completely cured! I fancy that the peasants believe that the rheumatism, or, at any rate, the cause of it, comes away in what they call "the yellow water."

Sometimes a silk thread is drawn through the skin in the region of the stomach as a cure for a pain in that organ. The skin is picked up between the finger and thumb, and a needle threaded with silk is passed through it lengthways. The silk thread is then roughly tied and left in the skin for about six days. Then it is drawn slightly to the left or right, when it is probably found to be covered with pus. A day or two after it is drawn in the opposite direction, when more pus will be removed. This process is repeated on several successive days, until all signs of pus have disappeared. There is a raised scar left when the skin has healed. Sometimes a silk thread is drawn through the outer edge of the upper part of the ear as a cure for fever, in the case both of children and grown-up people. To cure pain in the side, stomach, or back a small plain ring is inserted in the upper edge of the ear.

A person suffering from a cough takes one of the strings which form the warp of a reed mat and places one end on the top of his head, holding it there, while the other end is passed round one of his toes, or is held on the ground by his feet. The string is then placed inside the wrappings of a person who has just died, and is thus carried to the grave. The cough of the living person disappears. The same remedy is employed for fever and shivering, only a knot must then be made near one end of the string.

As a cure for diarrhœa some leaves from a sycamore are dried in the oven, or in the sun if it is very hot. When dry the leaves are pounded into a powder, of which the patient takes two teaspoonfuls, mixed with a little sugar, every morning. It usually takes two days to effect a cure, though it may sometimes take a little longer.

As a cure for inflamed or sore eyes the dung of a black donkey (a male) is made hot in the fire, put in a piece of muslin, and then applied. This treatment must be repeated constantly, a fresh poultice being administered as soon as the first is cold, and so on till the eye is cured. After a time, according to my informant, a lot of water will come from the eye, and then it will be found that all the inflammation has disappeared.

The Arabs have a custom of attempting to cure sores, headaches, and other complaints by branding with red-hot nails. A man came to me on one occasion with a terrible skin disease on his hands and wrists. An Arab had burnt him in several places across both wrists, and these burns, having become septic, had, of course, made him much worse. I dressed his hands every day till I left the village, by which time he was much better.

A similar remedy is sometimes employed for fever or for nervous disorder. A fire of cow-dung (the ordinary household fuel) is lit, and some iron nails are placed in it till they are red-hot. The patient then squats on the ground with his arms tightly folded in front, and a man holds him securely in this attitude. Another man removes a nail from the fire, and with it burns one or two places on the back of the patient's neck. The nervous trouble supposed to be cured by this means is that caused by seeing an apparition in the fields at night or by some other alarming manifestation. One is inclined to speculate on the state of the patient's nerves *after* undergoing this exceedingly painful treatment!

The following is a cure for a broken bone. Some gum is obtained from an acacia-tree, and, after being pounded and passed through a fine sieve, is mixed with water. This mixture is spread on a piece of thick brown paper, which is then placed immediately over the injured part of the body. It is left in this position for a week, when it is removed, for by that time it is believed that the broken bone will have united again.

When visiting the market on market-day at one village I saw a man seated a short distance from the crowds of buyers and sellers. On approaching him I found that children suffering from very sore and inflamed eyes were being brought to him by their mothers. On examining the eyes of a child he remarked, "Yes, he has got them," and told the mother, who was sitting on the ground in front of him, to hold the child face downward. He then placed one hand on the back of the child's head, and with the other he gently rubbed its eyes (Fig. 126). Almost immediately numbers of tiny grubs fell from them on to the ground, where I saw them wriggling about. He did this with each child in turn, usually with the same result. I have seen him remove grubs from the eyes of children on more than one occasion, and I have never been able to detect any trickery. A friend of mine told me that he had been equally puzzled. I should mention that as he rubbed the child's eyes he repeated the *Fātiḥeh*, the first chapter of the Ḳorān.

Huskiness is supposed to be cured by the following curious performance. A boy who is well known to me was suffering from extreme huskiness of the voice. His relatives, finding that he got no better, sent for one of the village butchers. The boy was made

FIG. 126. THE 'EYE-DOCTOR' REMOVING GRUBS FROM A CHILD'S EYES

to lie down on a blanket spread on the ground, and the butcher pretended to cut his throat, placing the blunt edge of the knife against it, and saying, " In the name of God, the Compassionate, the Merciful," as he did so (Fig. 127). These words are also pronounced when an animal or even a fowl is killed for food. The relatives and friends present must be very careful not to repeat these words themselves, or the supposed cure would be useless. I saw the boy three or four days later, and remarked that he did not seem much better. His elder brother said it was because the butcher employed was too young. There was, however, a much older man who was very successful in effecting cures in this way, but he had not been available at the time.

The village barber is employed as surgeon by the peasants for most small operations. One of his specialities is blood-letting, which is regarded as a cure for persistent headache. The barber first shaves away the hair adjacent to the forehead, upon which he then makes a series of vertical cuts, extending from temple to

FIG. 127. THE BUTCHER PRETENDING TO CUT THE BOY'S THROAT TO CURE HIM OF HUSKINESS

temple. The patient bends over a basin in which the blood is caught, and when the bleeding has continued for two or three minutes the barber sponges the forehead with cold water, till the blood ceases to flow (Fig. 128). The peasants show wonderful pluck when undergoing this operation, which must be a very painful one, but they have great faith in the efficacy of this cure. The operation is probably highly beneficial in a hot country like Egypt, as it keeps the people from getting too full-blooded.

Coptic priests are often believed, both by Christians and Muslims, to possess the power of healing. If anyone is bitten by a mad dog a priest is called in to see the sufferer. He takes some of the hair of the mad dog, and, after rubbing the wound with spirit, places the hair on it and sets it alight. This must be done by a priest only, otherwise the person who was bitten will get hydrophobia.

The village ' doctor ' or ' surgeon ' is also called upon to treat

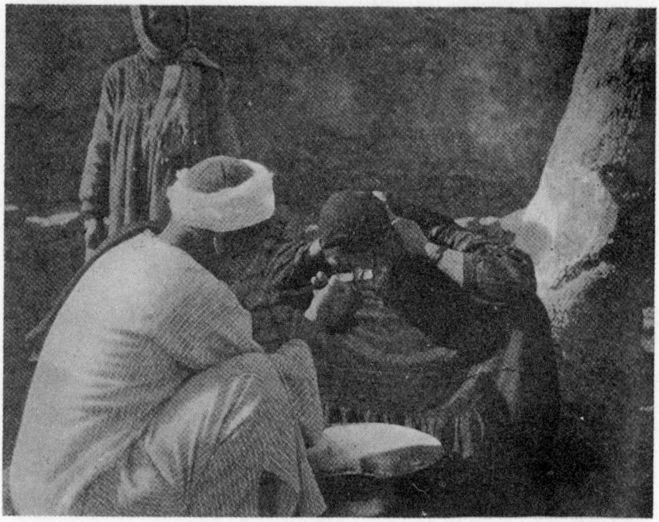

FIG. 128. SCRAPING THE BLOOD OFF THE FOREHEAD AFTER CUTTING IT AS A CURE FOR HEADACHE

animals when necessary. If an animal has a pain in one leg, for instance, it is branded with a red-hot nail on the part that is affected. When riding through the fields one day I saw a cow that had been branded on one of its legs, the marks forming a pattern (Fig. 130). On inquiry I was told that this had been done because the cow had had a pain in that part which was branded.

When travelling about Egypt it is my custom to take a large basket of medicines with me, and I do my best to cure simple cases of illness. Thanks to an excellent prescription given to me by a doctor friend of mine in England I have been able to cure some really appalling cases of inflammation of the eyes (Fig. 129). The peasants react in a remarkable way to simple cures, and many a

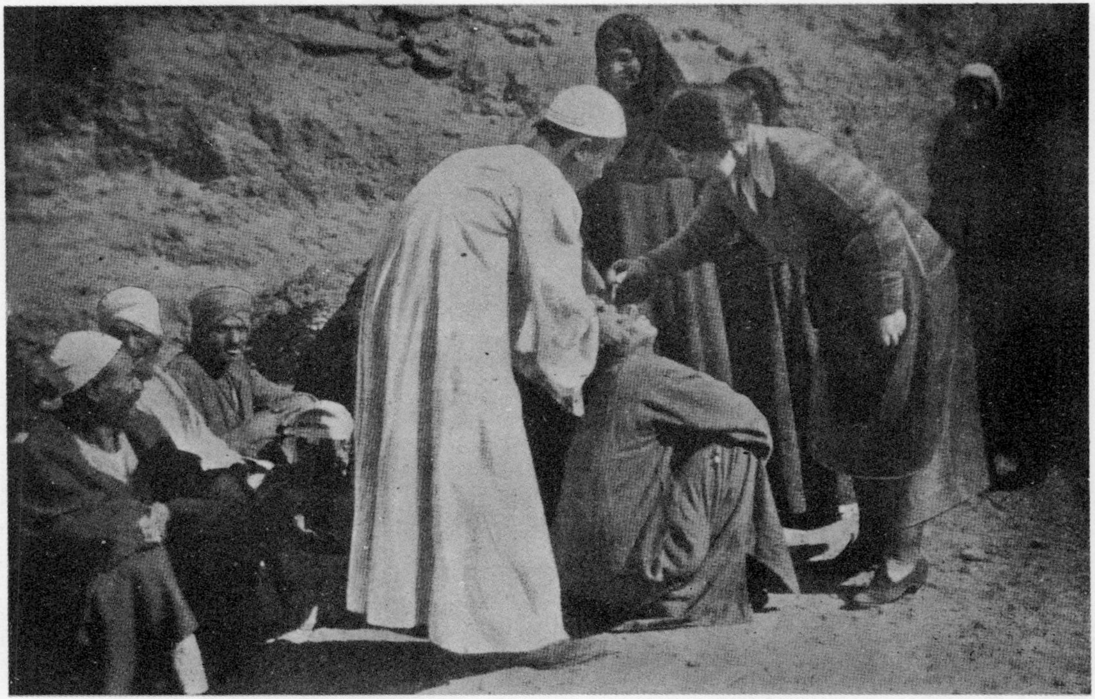

FIG. 129. ATTENDING TO THE EYES OF ONE OF MY PATIENTS

case of bad skin disease has been alleviated by application of boracic cream! Cascara also is largely in demand, and it is no exaggeration to say that I give away hundreds of these tabloids every year. Cases of fever likewise have recovered rapidly with judiciously administered doses of aspirin or quinine. This practice of mine has earned for me the name of the Sheikheh Shifā (the Sheikheh of Healing), and it is a title which I much appreciate and

FIG. 130. COW BRANDED AS A CURE FOR PAIN IN THE LEG

value, however undeserved it may be. I have been much touched by the gratitude shown me by many of my poor patients, and in some parts of Egypt there have been occasions when I have treated over a hundred of them a day (Fig. 131). It brings me into close touch with the people, and gives me opportunities of talking to the women about keeping their children clean and impressing on them the value of soap and water. I now make it a rule never to give medicine for any child who is brought to me in a dirty state. The mother has to go home and wash it first, and then bring it to me again. I am glad to say that they nearly always return with a very much cleaner infant.

Greater facilities for providing the peasants with adequate medical treatment are urgently needed in Egypt at the present time, and it is most encouraging to hear that the Government is now setting aside certain sums of money with a view to erecting more hospitals. Such a scheme deserves every encouragement and support.

FIG. 131. SOME OF MY PATIENTS

CHAPTER XIII

THE EVIL EYE AND OTHER SUPERSTITIONS

IN the preceding chapter I referred to the neglected condition of the children, partly due to the women's utter ignorance of hygiene and also to the fact that facilities for keeping themselves and their children clean are practically non-existent in Egyptian villages. My readers must bear in mind that all the water, for whatever purpose it may be required, has to be fetched by the women from the Nile, or a canal, or even some dirty pool, all of which may be situated at some distance from their homes. But the main reason for the children being so dirty is the belief in, and dread of, the evil eye, or eye of envy, which is to be found practically all over the world. It has not even died out in modern England, where, to my own knowledge, it exists in parts of the eastern counties, and it may possibly exist in other counties also. To the Egyptian peasants the fear of the evil eye is a very real terror from infancy to old age, and on that account it is considered unwise to let a child look too beautiful in case some one may cast the eye of envy over it. Certainly the dirt allowed to accumulate on some of these poor little specimens of humanity should afford a very effective protection against any and every evil eye!

To counteract this baneful influence innumerable methods are adopted, of which I will give a few examples.

If after a woman has received a visit from friends and neighbours her child shows signs of illness she immediately thinks that one of her guests has cast the evil eye on it. She accordingly cuts out a human figure in paper (Fig. 132), and then takes a pin, repeats the name of each of her late visitors in turn, pricking the paper figure at the mention of each name. When she has repeated all the names she sets the figure on fire, saying to her child, "Look at it, look at it!" When it is consumed, she takes a piece of alum, rubs it on the child's forehead, and then places it in a fire, over which she passes the child seven times. When the alum is burnt out, leaving only a charred substance, the mother takes it out of the fire and stamps on it. After this, it is believed, the injury done to the child by means of the evil eye has been effectually counteracted, and it will get well again.

Another means of averting the evil eye is to throw dust after a person who is suspected of having cast a baleful glance as he or she went by in the street or on the road. Or, again, a piece of the outer garment of the suspected person is secretly cut off with a sharp knife and is put in a pottery saucer containing burning incense. This is waved in front of the person affected, so that the smoke may pass over him and counteract the malign influence. Another method is to break a piece of pottery behind the back of the person who is believed to possess the evil eye.

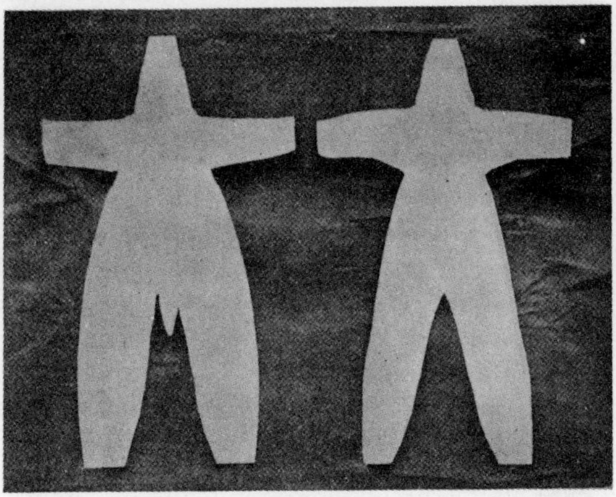

FIG. 132. PAPER FIGURES REPRESENTING A MAN (LEFT) AND A WOMAN (RIGHT), TO BE PRICKED WITH PINS AND THEN BURNT IN ORDER TO CURE A CHILD OF THE ILL EFFECTS OF THE EVIL EYE

Similar precautions are taken when animals are thought to have had the eye of envy cast upon them.

When I was residing in a small village in Middle Egypt the buffalo which produced my daily supplies of milk refused on more than one occasion to yield the necessary quantity for my morning meal. Its owners were convinced that this was due to the evil eye, so they put some fire in a pottery saucer, together with incense, and passed this seven times over the buffalo's head. Immediately after this the milk flowed, convincing them that they were right in their suspicion!

If a woman has a good-looking child, and visitors come to her house, she is careful to note if the child cries when they depart. If it does she then knows for certain that one or more of them has cast the evil eye over it. To counteract this she will take as many small lumps of salt as there were visitors, and throw them one by one on the fire, which leaps up into flame each time. As the flames burst forth so, she believes, will the evil eye burst, and all harm caused by it be taken away from the child. This is a common practice among both Copts and Muslims all over Egypt.

Again, if a woman, whether Copt or Muslim, has a baby that is constantly crying she believes that it has had the evil eye cast over it. In order to dispel the mischief done, the child's grandmother (either paternal or maternal), keeping it well away from her body, carries it to the *zīr* (see p. 137), round which she passes it seven times. As she does this she repeats seven times, "O angel of the water, take away the evil eye from this child." Water being very valuable in Egypt, it is believed that every vessel containing it possesses a guardian angel of the water, and this angel, it is thought, will remove the ill effects of the evil eye from the child.

When admiring a child or any other of your neighbour's possessions, it is the correct thing to say, "*Mā shā' Allāh*" ("What God willeth is") or "*Ṣalla 'a 'n-Nebi*" ("Bless the Prophet"), in order that your praise may not be taken for envy and that there may be no suspicion that you are casting the evil eye upon the object of your admiration.

The first year that I lived in an Egyptian village I fell ill two or three times with fever. The villagers had never come into close contact before with any Englishwoman, and so every article of my dress was noticed and commented on, as well as my eyes, the colour of my cheeks, and so on. When riding through the village many kindly and complimentary remarks were made: "See, she has the eyes of a cat"—a great compliment, to the minds of the villagers—"How beautiful is the colour of her cheeks!" etc. When I fell ill the second time my attendant, a most faithful and devoted man, was convinced that it was entirely due to some one having cast the evil eye upon me. He therefore harangued the villagers, and told them that they were, of course, quite right to admire me, and that all that they said was true, but that in future such remarks were not to be made without one at least of the protecting phrases mentioned above. The consequence was that the next time I went out riding I was followed by a whole concourse of people, men, women, and children, all ejaculating as I passed, "*Mā shā' Allāh, mā shā' Allāh ; ṣalla 'a 'n-Nebi, ṣalla 'a 'n-Nebi,*" as fast as they could speak.

Another year, when I was again visiting this village, I contracted a bad chill, accompanied by fever. Some of the village women insisted on seeing me, and, with many head-shakings, declared that it was the evil eye again, and in any case they must make the usual test to see. Alum was burned in a fire placed in a pottery saucer, and while it was burning it was carefully watched by my village friends. Alum, when thus being heated, forms a lot of little bubbles, which the peasants call 'eyes,' and the women watching this process remarked on the number of eyes that had been cast at me, and that it was no wonder I was ill. When the alum becomes a charred mass it is supposed to assume a male or female form. In this instance it assumed both, so it was decided that the harm done to me had been committed by both a man and a woman. Sometimes the alum, after being burned, is submitted to an old woman, who is supposed to be able to tell who the actual culprit is. After this test, in my case, several presents of incense were sent to me by my poor neighbours. The Coptic priest, then living in the desert monastery near by, also sent me some, which, he said, had been blessed in the church. All this incense was, at different times, burned in the room where I lay ill, the saucer in which it was burning being passed over me seven times. As I got decidedly better a day or two later it was, of course, credited to the incense, which had, so they believed, destroyed the harm done to me by the evil eye.

FIG. 133. NECKLACE WORN BY A YOUNG CHILD TO AVERT THE EVIL EYE

Blue beads, and necklaces made of them, are worn by women and children (Fig. 133) as protective charms against this supposed evil ; and animals are decorated with blue cotton tassels and strings of beads, with the same end in view. Red is also an effective charm, and I have often noticed, as a string of camels has passed by me in the cultivation or in the desert, that the leading animal is wearing red tassels or blue beads, or both, round its neck. The idea is, I suppose, that it is on the first camel that the eye would be cast. A pattern is sometimes cut in the hair on one or more of the legs of a camel. I was told that this is often done to keep the evil eye off that part of the animal's body. For if its legs are firm and well covered with flesh some one may cast the eye over it, and the camel will fall down.

A certain woman in Upper Egypt who was well known to possess the evil eye saw a very fine camel coming along one of the paths in the cultivation. "Oh," she said, "what a splendid camel!" whereupon the animal fell down and broke one of its legs. The truth of this story was vouched for by my informant, who declared that he saw the accident happen and heard what the woman said.

If a child under eight years of age is thin and delicate the mother, or, if her husband will not allow her to do so, a neighbour, will carry it to the bank of the Nile on the first day of the inundation, taking with her some dates and *kishk*.[1] She then stands at the edge of the water, holding the child in her arms, and makes it throw the dates and *kishk*, one by one, into the river. As the child throws in each article it must say to the water, "As you increase in depth, may I increase in strength!" After this the woman undresses the child and bathes it in the river. It is believed that the child will then grow steadily stronger. Angels are supposed to be in the water, and they, it is thought, will take the dates and the *kishk*, and, in return for these gifts, will remove the weakness from the child.

A child may suffer from a cough accompanied by gasping, as if it could hardly breathe. This may happen at any time until it has passed the age of seven years.[2] To cure it the mother, or grandmother (either paternal or maternal), or a woman friend, takes the child early in the morning to the enclosure (*zarībeh*) in which the sheep and goats are kept in the fields at night. She enters the *zarībeh* and hands the child over to the shepherd, who lays it on its back on the ground, and, taking a knife, places the blunt edge against the child's throat, pretending to cut it. The child will then start crying, whereupon the man will remove the knife and return the child to the woman who brought it.

Sheep are regarded as very gentle animals, and are supposed

[1] Small cakes, sometimes round like large marbles, and made of flour and milk.
[2] After this age the mother's *ḳarīneh* cannot injure it. For fuller information on this subject see pp. 71 ff.

on that account to be watched over by angels, who, on hearing the child cry, will drive away the mother's *ḳarīneh*, who has caused the illness by clutching at the child's throat.

If a boy or child under eight years of age cannot walk the mother believes that her *ḳarīneh* has sent an *ʿafrīt* into the child. To cure this infirmity she calls in a neighbour to help her. The mother seats the child on the ground, and places in its lap a number of dates and some *kishk*. The neighbour and child then go to the mosque, taking the dates and *kishk* with them. Friday is a favourite day for such a visit, and they arrange to arrive at noon, when the men are praying inside the building. The woman leaves the child seated outside the doorway, and herself retires to a short distance. When the people begin to come out of the mosque they see the dates and the *kishk* spread out on the child's dress, and they all scramble to get their share of them. This frightens the child, and it begins to scream. On hearing its cries the woman who brought it to the mosque goes and takes it up in her arms and carries it home.

It is believed that the screams of the frightened child will scare away the *ʿafrīt* in its legs, and that after this it will be able to walk.

Christians employ the same cure for their children who are similarly affected, and, be it noted, take them to the mosque, not to the church. An old acquaintance of mine, who is a Copt, told me that a child of his was at one time unable to walk, but that it could do so after thus visiting the village mosque. He added that he had taken the child to several doctors in Cairo and Asyūṭ, but that they had been unable to do it any good!

In a large town in Upper Egypt there are two mosques, in both of which there is an ancient pillar. People who are ill with jaundice go to either of these mosques and lick the pillar, and then, so I am informed, speedily recover. I visited one of the mosques and at once detected the ancient pillar, which stands in the main part of the building among the other pillars supporting the roof.

In Egypt, as in many other countries, hair-cuttings and -combings and nail-parings are carefully kept, for if anyone else obtained possession of them he would, by their means, be able to gain an influence over, and so injure, the original owners. Bones from which the meat has been eaten, skins of fruit, and the like are also, for the same reason, either carefully buried or burned in a fire.

If a man loves a woman and wants to marry her, and she has no affection for him, he asks a female friend to assist him in the following way. The friend visits the woman at a time when she is likely to be combing her hair. It is the custom for women to conceal all their hair-combings in the wall of one of the rooms, between the bricks. The friend notices where the woman puts her hair-combings, and, at the first opportunity, steals some of the hair when the owner is not present, and gives it to the man. He takes it to a magician, who measures the length of each hair by the span of his hand. The magician then writes a spell, and, going to a grave, puts the hair inside it, keeping the spot a secret, for no one must know where the hair is hidden. He puts the spell in his pocket, and on some pretext or other (he may ask her for a cup of coffee, for example) visits the house of the woman whose hair he has buried. While he is sitting in her house he will produce the paper on which he has written the spell, and tell her to wear it under her arm, stating that it will afford her excellent protection in the event of anyone else writing a spell against her to prevent her marrying. He thus persuades her to accept his spell, hinting that it may also bring her a good husband. The woman, of course, has no idea that the magician is in league with the man who wants to marry her. She accordingly accepts the spell, hangs it round her neck, and, immediately becoming madly in love with the man who is in love with her, is, of course, only too glad to marry him! This is a very common practice in many parts of Egypt.

It is also the custom to protect houses from the evil eye, and various decorations are employed for this purpose. Sometimes a plate or saucer is plastered into the wall just above the main entrance, or pieces of old carving, picked up from an ancient rubbish-mound, may be let into the masonry round about the door. The horns of sheep and other animals are also hung over the doorway as a charm to protect the house from the evil eye. A 'bride of the corn,' as already stated,[1] is hung over the front door for the same purpose. Inside the house, on the walls of the living-rooms, I have seen painted designs which the owner told me were put there to keep off the evil eye. Indeed, the devices resorted to for protecting houses, fields, animals, and people of all ages against this dreaded power are multitudinous, and to describe all those that I am acquainted with would require an entire book.

[1] See p. 172.

It is a common belief in Egypt, as, indeed, in some other countries also, that the soul can leave the body during sleep. It is therefore considered unsafe to wake anyone suddenly, for fear the soul should not have time to return to the body of the sleeper. Such awakening must be done very slowly, so as to give the soul ample time to return. I am not quite clear as to what happens if the soul does not get back in time; probably the sleeper's personality changes, or he becomes imbecile.

There is a strong belief among the peasants that the dead can appear to the living, speak with them, and issue commands. The strength of this belief can be seen in connexion with the sheikh cult, discussed in Chapter XV. There are a number of ghost stories current in the country, the ghost being usually regarded as the dead man's *ʿafrīt*, which, as will be seen in the following chapter, is not the soul, but a separate entity. The two following ghost stories may interest my readers, the second ghost having only just begun to 'walk' a week or so before I arrived at the dead man's village.

The engine which controls the machinery for irrigating the fields of the rich *ʿomdeh* (headman) of a certain village is worked by steam, and the boiler is covered with a large sheet of iron. The steam is shut off late every evening, at about seven-thirty, and is turned on again at daybreak. To turn it on a man has to stand on the sheet of iron above the reservoir. One day the son of the assistant engineer made a mistake, saying that he had turned on the steam when he had not done so. The consequence was that more was generated than the boiler could contain, and it promptly exploded. An unfortunate man who was standing on the iron sheet was crushed against the ceiling and killed instantly. One night later a man who was sleeping in the engine-room with some of his fellow-workmen began to call out. His companions were aroused from sleep by his cries, and asked him what was the matter. He told them that he had seen the man who had been killed, and that he was wailing and crying "*Akh! akh! akh!*" ("Alas! alas! alas!"), and also had tried to poke out his (the speaker's) eyes with two of his fingers. Since this incident a great explosion is heard in the engine-room every night at twelve o'clock. The first time it was heard the guards and other people thought that there had been another accident, but, when they went to look, nothing had occurred, and the engine was not working. The explosion is heard regularly every midnight, but no attention is now paid to it, as everybody has got quite accustomed to it.

Very shortly before my visit to the village in which the above-mentioned events took place a man was murdered in the adjacent fields, and not long after my arrival the following incident occurred. A woman was walking from this village to another not a great distance off, carrying bread and eggs to two of her grandsons who were at school there. She was alone, and as she approached the spot where the murder had taken place she saw a man who seemed to be ill, and who kept on crying, "*Akh! akh! Yā abūi! Yā abūi!*" ("Alas! alas! O my father! O my father!"). She went up to him and caught hold of his hands, raised him up, and then walked on with him, trying to comfort him. But after walking a short distance with her the man suddenly disappeared. She thereupon was terrified, and wept with fear. A man who was on his way to the same village overtook her, and, seeing her distress, asked her what was the matter. She told him about the stranger whom she had found and had tried to comfort and who had so mysteriously vanished. The man told her not to be frightened, that it was nothing, and that the apparition had appeared to him in the same way. It is generally supposed that this mysterious weeping apparition is the ghost (or *ʿafrīt*) of the man who had been murdered.

CHAPTER XIV

ʿAFĀRĪT

AMONG the various supernatural beings who figure conspicuously in the life of Egyptian peasants are the *ʿafārīt* (singular *ʿafrīt*). This word is usually translated in dictionaries 'devils' or 'demons,' as distinct from the *ginn*, who are, properly speaking, the good spirits.[1] The peasants, however, so I have found, employ the words *ginn* and *ʿafārīt* indiscriminately, the latter word being more commonly used. The *ʿafārīt* are believed to be made of fire, and to have been created many thousands of years before Adam. They may be the chosen assistants of people of evil intent who wish to harm others; they may also, of their own accord, enter into anyone who is doing something wrong, thereby laying himself open to such possession. They are sometimes quite harmless, and will do no injury to a human being unless they are interfered with.

The *ʿafārīt* are supposed to live under the earth, where they form an organized society, with a king at their head. They haunt, so it is believed, springs and wells in uninhabited regions, such as the desert, and the narrow paths which wind about through the cultivation. There are other places, even on high roads, which are known by those versed in such matters to 'belong,' as they say, to *ʿafārīt*.

On a recent visit to Egypt a charming Rest-house with a good garden was generously placed at my disposal by the Egyptian Government (Fig. 134). It was my custom, when the weather was hot, to sit out in the garden every evening, where some of my village friends would join me, drink coffee, and have a chat. Among them was a small dealer in antiquities, who had a considerable knowledge of the folklore of the people. He told me one evening in the course of conversation that the road which ran past my house had, some years back, been much haunted by *ʿafārīt*, and that a portion of the

[1] See E. W. Lane, *The Manners and Customs of the Modern Egyptians* (London, 1871), vol. i, pp. 283 ff., and also his translation of *The Arabian Nights* (London, 1883), vol. i, pp. 26 f. (notes to Introduction).

ground facing the house on which a mosque has lately been erected, had especially belonged to them. They were, of course, driven from this spot when the mosque was built, and since the introduction of motors and telephones, to which they strongly object, the road also had been made uninhabitable for them. They have therefore taken refuge in the Rest-house garden, where several people claim to have seen them. Three such appearances occurred during my residence.

One night, while my guard was enjoying a peaceful sleep, he

FIG. 134. THE REST-HOUSE AND ITS HAUNTED GARDEN

suddenly awoke in terror and saw towering above him a huge figure in the form of a man, which remained standing thus for a minute or two and then vanished. On another occasion the same guard saw an ʿ*afrīt*, in the form of a dog, run round the garden, pass the windows of the Government offices overlooking it, and then vanish. About a week later, as my servant was crossing the garden on his way from the house to the kitchen, carrying a lighted lamp in his hand, the light was suddenly put out, though there was no wind, and presently he saw a shadow run along in the same direction as that taken by the dog. This, he said, when he recounted to me his adventure, was an ʿ*afrīt*.

The *ʿafārīt* are, as I have said, supposed to be made of fire, so they are naturally found in their native element. Therefore, before extinguishing, or casting anything into, a fire it is usual to say "In the name of God, the Compassionate, the Merciful," thus giving the *ʿafrīt* who may be in the fire time to withdraw. Also, before pouring water or other liquid on to the ground many people say "*Dastūr*" ("Permission") or "*Dastūr yā mubārakīn*" ("Permission, O blessèd ones"), in case there may be *ʿafārīt* near by. For should there be *ʿafārīt* in the fire at the moment that it was put out, or should the water touch them when poured on to the ground, they would take revenge on the person who had not duly warned them of what he or she was going to do.

FIG. 135. A MAGICIAN OF MY ACQUAINTANCE

Before beginning to eat, and also before removing any food from the room in which the household stores are kept, both Muslims and Copts will say "In the name of God, the Compassionate, the Merciful." This, I am told, is to prevent the *ʿafārīt* from taking any of the food. Copts will sometimes say "In the name of the Cross," and will make the sign of the Cross over the food, for the same purpose. Again, a woman will make use of one of these two phrases before beginning to mix the flour for making bread.

A magician is supposed to be able to control *ʿafārīt* and to make them appear before him. He can also issue orders to their king, which the latter has to obey. The magician calls up the *ʿafārīt* from below the earth by reciting incantations, burning incense the while, and sometimes pouring out a libation of water (see p. 193).

People who are afflicted by *ʿafārīt* regularly apply for assistance to magicians, who are often men of benevolent character, and who, when their petitioners are poor, will exercise their magic powers on behalf of the sufferers without exacting a fee.

The *ʿafārīt* may appear of their own will to ordinary individuals, sometimes in human form, but more usually in the shape of an animal, such as a dog, a cat, or a donkey. Again, they may be seen by animals when invisible to man. Therefore when a donkey refuses to pass a certain spot in the desert or cultivation his rider knows that an *ʿafrīt* bars the way, and he usually has to dismount and forcibly lead his ass past the danger zone.[1]

Some magicians are supposed to be married to female *ʿafārīt*, and to have children by them. This is a belief to be found, not only in Egypt, but in other countries also. A man thus married will never disclose the fact, but it becomes known among his relatives, who sometimes, looking for him in the place where he sleeps at night, will find that he has disappeared. They then suppose that he has gone to his wife "beneath the earth," but they will not dare speak of the matter to him. This is believed of a magician who is well known to me, and who lives in a small village in Upper Egypt. His relatives have constantly urged him to marry, since the Egyptian peasants consider it a disgrace for a man to remain a bachelor. This magician has always refused to take to himself a wife, and has turned a deaf ear to the entreaties of his family. Accordingly, they now believe that he has an *ʿafrīteh* (feminine form of *ʿafrīt*) as his wife, as sometimes he is not found sleeping on his mat at night. Since he is a Copt he cannot take a human being as a second wife, as a Muslim would be able to do in similar circumstances. Such a supernatural wife helps her husband in all his work as a magician; indeed, his powers are often attributed entirely to the assistance he receives from his wife beneath the earth.

Most magicians possess books, usually manuscripts written by themselves, containing numbers of incantations for repetition, directions as to the performance of the accompanying rites, and also charms in the form of magic squares. These spells may have been in use in the magician's family for several generations, and handed down orally from father to son, but in more recent times committed to paper, now that the knowledge of writing is commoner among the villagers.

The Coptic magician mentioned above has several such manu-

[1] *Cf.* the story of Balaam and his ass.

scripts, one of which he designates the "Book of Adam." He has with great labour collected and written out magical cures and protections for those troubled by *'afārīt*, and these form the contents of one of the books. He learnt his art, so he told me, from another magician, who was not a member of his family, but under whom he served a long apprenticeship.

During my sojourn in Egypt I have been given many accounts of the wonderful cures wrought by magicians on people possessed by *'afārīt*. I wrote the details down when they were given to me, and some of them may be interesting to my readers. The names of the people concerned, and the villages in which they live, are suppressed, in deference to their feelings; indeed, it would be a breach of confidence to divulge them. Such happenings are not usually discussed with foreigners, and were related to me only because I am regarded by the villagers as a trustworthy friend.

A young man in Upper Egypt became very angry with his wife one night while she was sitting in front of the fire cooking the evening meal. In his anger he took a pottery water-bottle (a *ḳulleh*) and struck her with it. In doing this he broke the bottle, and the water and some of the pieces of pottery fell into the fire, extinguishing it. The next moment he heard a voice saying to him, "You have broken the head of one of my children, so I will come into you [*i.e.*, possess you]." The man thereupon became mad, and began to tear his own face, and strike all those who came near him. Some of his relatives, seeing his terrible condition, proceeded to bind his hands behind his back and tie his feet together at the ankles, to prevent him doing further harm to himself or anyone else; but he continued to cry out and to speak meaningless words. His relatives took him to one doctor after another, but they could do him no good, and he continued in the same condition of violent madness.

At last, when he had remained in this state for three months, they went to see a certain sheikh. This man is a magician, and of a charitable character, and they begged him to cure the unfortunate man, pleading at the same time his poverty. The sheikh, who possesses (for he is still alive) many books of incantations and charms such as those mentioned above, listened sympathetically to their pleading, and consented to visit the sufferer, but he told them that they must first bring him a small piece of one of the garments belonging to the madman. They went home and returned shortly with a piece of the material demanded, on which the sheikh wrote some magic words. After doing this he told the anxious relatives that the man was possessed by an ʿ*afrīt*, and thereupon, according to his promise, accompanied them to the madman's house.

Here he found the patient lying on the ground covered with a blanket, with his hands tied behind his back and his feet bound together at the ankles with strong cords. The sheikh then started to burn incense in a dish and to read some of the incantations from one of his books. Whereupon the madman tore asunder the cords which bound him, and began to strike out right and left. When the sheikh asked him why he behaved in this way the ʿ*afrīt*, speaking through the madman, replied, "You have an unclean woman in the room." [1] On hearing this the sheikh was very angry, for no unclean woman must ever be present on such an occasion. So he ordered all the people, and there were many present, to leave the room, with the exception of a few of the man's male relatives. Crowds always collect on the slightest excuse in all Egyptian villages, offering conflicting advice at the top of their voices. On such an occasion as this of the sheikh's visit to the madman the room where the patient lay would have been packed with sympathizers and eager sightseers.

When the crowd had been banished from the room the madman became quiet, and the sheikh continued to burn incense and to recite magic sentences. The sheikh finally told the ʿ*afrīt* to leave the man, but he replied (of course speaking through the man), "From what part of his body shall I leave him? May I come out through one of his eyes, which will then become blind, as a punishment for his breaking the head of one of my children?" The sheikh replied that he would not permit him to do this, but that he was to come out of the big toe of one foot. The sheikh then placed a *ḳulleh* on the ground, and said to the ʿ*afrīt*, "I shall know that you have left the man if you knock over this *ḳulleh*."

Presently, as he continued reading his incantations, the sheikh saw a few drops of blood fly from the man's big toe toward the *ḳulleh*, which was immediately flung with a crash against the wall. The madman then sat up and said, "Where am I? And who are you?" After a while he recognized all his relatives, whom he had not known during the whole period of his madness. They

[1] A menstruous woman is always regarded as unclean.

asked him where he had been, to which he replied, "I have been among the *ʿafārīt*."

Since that day he has been perfectly sane, and is now living happily in his native village.

The following is another case related to me in 1923, the incident occurring, so I was told, in 1920. In a town in Upper Egypt there dwells a somewhat celebrated Coptic magician, whom we will call the Sheikh B. He is known to be married to an *ʿafrīteh*, because he disappears every night, but neither his wife nor her children—for the people have discovered that she has offspring by the sheikh—are ever seen. They may come up above ground sometimes while people are talking about them, but they remain invisible.

The upper story of a certain house in this town was occupied by a Coptic clerk employed in a large business firm, while in the lower story lived a man whose wife had no children. The husband of this woman, distressed at having no offspring, begged the Sheikh B to come and see his wife, hoping that he might be able to give her some charm or read some incantation which would cure her barrenness. Accordingly, one evening, at a late hour, the magician arrived.

The occupant of the upper story was in the habit of praying every night and morning. On the evening on which the Sheikh B arrived this man was reciting some of the Psalms of David in a loud voice. On hearing these recitations the Sheikh B cried out, "Oh, make this man stop reading, for he is interrupting me!" Some of the people who had assembled to see the sheikh went up to beg the man to stop reciting. However, he paid no attention to their request, and read through all the Psalms, repeating them in a loud voice, so that they could easily be heard in the rooms beneath him.

The Sheikh B then cried out to him, "Oh, stop reciting these Psalms, you have burnt one of my sons"; for the sheikh had brought up many *ʿafārīt* from under the earth, including his own sons, so that he might consult them as to what should be done for the childless woman.

Finally the clerk went to bed; but as soon as he had laid himself down he felt that there were people in the room, and suddenly found himself being lifted off the bed. He opened his eyes, and saw four small *ʿafārīt*, dressed in quaint coats and trousers of many colours, and wearing tall, peaked hats. Two of them held him by the feet, and two held his head. He immediately crossed himself, and said, "In the name of the Father, the Son, and the Holy Ghost." At the mention of these sacred names the *ʿafārīt* dropped him on the floor and disappeared.

I was told that the Sheikh B's anger was aroused because the man, by his recitation of the Psalms, had stopped his communications with the *ʿafārīt*; and so, in order to punish him, he sent the four *ʿafārīt* to frighten him. Since that date the Sheikh B has refused to enter that house.

FIG. 136. A COPTIC CHOIR-BOY

The following story tells how a naughty boy was punished by an *ʿafrīt*. It should be explained here that it is the custom among the Copts for men and boys to gather together every evening during the month of *Kiyahk*, which begins on December 9 or 10, to recite from memory special prayers and passages from the Bible in Coptic. Thus engaged they remain in the church till daybreak, when the priest comes for the service. Coptic boys acquire a smattering of the ancient language when at the school of the *ʿarīf*, the title of the officiant who leads the singing in the church.

On one such occasion the boy just alluded to was in the church with a number of his companions, taking part in the recitations. He left the church for a few minutes, and on his way back saw a very fine donkey standing in the open space in front of the church. The sight of this donkey proving to be irresistible to him, he immediately mounted it, and, digging his heels into its sides, urged it to go faster and faster round and round the open space. Suddenly the donkey began to grow taller and taller, till it reached the height of about five metres It then suddenly vanished, and the boy fell to the ground, where a stone struck one of his eyes and destroyed the sight. The boy then knew that the donkey was really an *ʿafrīt* which had assumed animal form, and presently he heard it saying, " Don't come here again. If you do I will injure you ! "

Up to the present time the boy, who is now a grown man, has never dared to return to this church for fear of the *ʿafrīt*. He told my informant this story himself, and swears to the truth of it.

The *ʿafārīt*, as I have already explained, sometimes leave their subterranean home and come above ground. It is therefore considered dangerous to stamp on the ground, to strike it with a stick, or to throw anything violently on it. Such acts should be especially avoided at night, when the *ʿafārīt* are believed to come up in large numbers. If a man, therefore, has to walk some distance at night he is glad if he can get a fisherman to accompany him, for he believes that then no *ʿafrīt* will come near him. The *ʿafārīt* are afraid of fishermen and of their nets, and when they see these men throwing their nets they run away in terror. One woman told me that the *ʿafārīt* fear that they may get caught in the nets.

A few days after I had left a certain village in Upper Egypt a boy who was employed by the *ʿomdeh* (headman of the village) was in the building containing the machinery installed by the *ʿomdeh* for pumping up water for irrigating his fields. It was at night, and for some reason or other the boy happened to stamp on the ground with his feet. Soon after he lay down to sleep, but was aroused by an *ʿafrīt* who tried to pluck out his eyes. The boy cried out, " Oh, leave me, and forgive me ! " But the *ʿafrīt* refused, saying that when he had stamped on the ground he had injured the head of one of his children. The boy cried out, and then, being a Copt, crossed himself, whereupon the *ʿafrīt* disappeared.

That *ʿafārīt* are capable of kindly actions is shown in the following belief. A boy who is still uncircumcised may be mysteriously carried away when sleeping beside his mother at night. He will be brought back to his sleeping-place on the same night, and on the following morning his mother will find that he has been circumcised, the operation having been much better done than if it had been performed by the village barber; moreover, the wound will be found to have already healed. In such a case it is believed that the boy has a good *ḳarīn* who has brought good *ʿafārīt* to perform this painful operation painlessly.

Before people take up residence in a newly built house, or complete a well for a water-wheel, or use new machinery for irrigation or grinding corn, an ox or a sheep, or, if the people are poor, a fowl, must be killed on the threshold of the house, or close to the engine, or inside the well before the water-level is reached. This is done in case these spots may be haunted by *ʿafārīt*, who will trouble the owners if not first appeased by the blood of a sacrifice.

Within a year three people were killed by the irrigation machinery

FIG. 137. THE MOTHER OF THE BOY WHO WAS KILLED WAILING OUTSIDE THE ʿOMDEH'S ENGINE-HOUSE

belonging to the *ʿomdeh* of the village mentioned on p. 235 (see also Fig. 137). One, a woman, was killed not long before I arrived there, a boy was caught in the machinery and killed during my visit, and a man was killed in a similar way just after I had left. This *ʿomdeh* had made no sacrifice before using the engine, so a number of the villagers went to him and demanded that he should kill an ox on the spot. This he did, about a month after I had gone, and some of the blood of the animal was sprinkled on the engine. Apparently this has appeased the *ʿafārīt*, for I have heard of no accidents since the sacrifice was made!

There is an old Copt in that village, considerably over ninety years of age, who used to be a village guard. He told a friend of mine that he knew that the ground on which the *ʿomdeh's* engine now stands used to be the haunt of *ʿafārīt*, for, when doing patrols at night round the outskirts of the village, he had sometimes seen on that spot a plough pulled by oxen and driven by a man, or sometimes a threshing-machine with the oxen and their driver, all made of fire. As this guard approached them he would cross himself, whereupon the *ʿafārīt* who had assumed these forms would disappear.

If a woman fears that *ʿafārīt* are in her house she puts a *ḳulleh* of water on the floor of one of the rooms, and near it she places some bread and salt, leaving them in this position during the night. This protects the whole house, and effectually prevents any *ʿafārīt* from entering it.

Nightmare and sleepwalking are supposed to be caused by *ʿafārīt*, and if a child suffers from either of these complaints it is a sign that an *ʿafrīt* has entered its body. This may have happened because the child has done something wrong; perhaps, so it was suggested to me, it had plucked some of the ears of corn from a field belonging to a neighbour. If a Coptic child sleepwalks or has nightmare its parents call in a priest, who tells them to bring seven *ḳanādīl* (old-fashioned saucer-lamps, with floating wicks). The priest then asks for a jar of water, and prays seven special prayers, burning incense meanwhile in a censer. As he finishes one prayer he puts out one lamp, after a second prayer a second lamp, and so on, till all the prayers are said and all the lamps extinguished. He now tells the parents to place the jar of water on the roof of the house, where it must remain for one night. On the following morning the child is bathed in the water, after which, it is believed, he will be cured.

Among the Muslims if a child is affected in this way the parents go to a magician, who writes a charm of protection for the child to wear.

In addition to his soul (*rōḥ*) every human being is believed to possess an *ʿafrīt* which leaves his body at death. In certain circumstances it may be a menace to any person who comes near it. Animals also have an *ʿafrīt*. This belief especially attracted my attention recently. A little dog which had been badly injured took refuge in the bathroom of my house. My servant told me that he was sure it could not live, and that, before it died, he must remove it, or its *ʿafrīt* would for ever haunt the house. As it was a hopeless case I gave my servant a revolver and told him to shoot the dog. This he did, but he first took it away to a more distant spot.

While I was in Egypt in 1925 a poor man who came to trade in the village in which I was staying was drowned. He had gone to the Baḥr el-Yūsuf canal to perform his ablutions before his morning prayers, but the water was deeper than he thought, and he was unable to swim. No one was near at the time, it being very early in the morning. As he did not return people went down to the canal to look for him, and found his clothes on the bank. A large crowd collected, but nothing was done till early in the afternoon. The officials had been informed of the accident, but no doubt more pressing business detained them, and in any case they had to come from some distance. I went down and mixed with the crowd. The man's wife, mother, and little son were standing close to the water's edge, accompanied by numbers of sympathizers. The women were gesticulating and wailing, as they always do after a death, and were waving the blue and black handkerchiefs used on such occasions. "O my father! O camel of the house!"[1] they cried. A boat was manned by two or three men with a line, to which large fishing-hooks were attached, by means of which they hoped to hook up the body. They had been searching one portion of the canal in this way for some time, with no result, when I suggested that they should try another part, in the direction of which the current was flowing. They followed my advice, and very soon found the body. It was placed on the shore and immediately surrounded by a large crowd, which, after some time, dispersed, and then I saw the mother and wife of the dead man, one seated at the head and the other at the feet. I was strongly reminded of the ancient representations of Isis and Nephthys bewailing the dead Osiris. After this accident I was told by some of the villagers that no woman would go alone to fill her water-jar at that spot for fear of the drowned man's *ʿafrīt*, which would always remain in the water. It might be a good *ʿafrīt*, and then it would do no injury; but—who could tell?—it might be bad!

A few years ago some women in a neighbouring village had gone

[1] The camel, being a beast of burden and a means of livelihood among the peasants, typifies the breadwinner of the family.

to the Gīzeh canal to fill their water-jars. One of them, thinking it would be pleasant to have a bathe, for the weather was very hot, took off her clothes and went right into the water, dancing about with her water-jar on her head. Suddenly she cried out and started wailing, as she felt that she was being drawn under the water. No one made any effort to save her, as they said that an *ʿafrīt* of some drowned person had caught her by her hair and was dragging her down. They believed that if one of them attempted to save her he or she would probably be caught also—and, besides, the *ʿafrīt* wanted her and must have her!

CHAPTER XV

MUSLIM SHEIKHS AND COPTIC SAINTS

THE Egyptian peasants venerate a number of holy men and women to whom miraculous powers have been ascribed, either during their lifetime or after their death Such a holy person is given the title of sheikh. The word sheikh means literally an old man, and a man who is advanced in years is often addressed as Sheikh so and so as a term of respect. The word also signifies the head of an Arab tribe, the leading man in a village, and, finally, a learned man (*i.e.*, one learned in the sacred writings).

Certain of these holy men and women are venerated all over the country, the cults connected with them having become part of the general popular religion. But, besides these greater personages, there are innumerable local saints, who, however, often draw their devotees from localities beyond the boundaries of their villages.

However great may be the veneration paid to a saint in his lifetime, the honour he receives after his death is far greater. Among the Muslims it is the custom to erect over the grave of such a person a small whitewashed building, crowned with a dome, the outer and inner walls being usually decorated with line-drawings in colours and with inscriptions consisting of passages from the Ḳorān (see Figs. 139, 140). In many cases it is customary to provide a 'servant' (Fig. 138), or sometimes a number of 'servants,' whose salary is paid out of an endowment in land or money, augmented by the donations of those who visit the tomb. This man, or it may be a woman, is known as "the servant of the sheikh," and the office may descend from father to son. Besides the land surrounding the tomb, the sacred precincts may include a well, the water of which is supposed to be endowed with miraculous properties.

Sometimes a stone, or a heap of stones, or a tree or clump of trees, alone mark the last resting-place of a departed sheikh, but when there is a domed tomb a tree or trees are usually associated with it. However, a tomb is not usually built until the dead sheikh appears to some one and demands such a building.

Most Muslim sheikhs of any standing have two or more tombs, or other burial sites, associated with them. This does not mean that the body of the sheikh is actually buried in any one of these sites, though there are many cases where this is so. A dead sheikh may appear to some man in a dream, or even when he is awake, and tell him to build a tomb on such and such a spot, and may even personally conduct him thither. It may happen that the inhabitants of a village possessing a venerated sheikh have been guilty of misconduct, or have offended the holy man by neglecting to pay him the respect which he considers his due. In such a case, it is believed, the sheikh will appear to a man in a distant village and instruct him to build another tomb. The new tomb often becomes more popular and is visited by a larger number of people than the older building. Thus a sheikh whose original tomb is in Lower Egypt may also be associated with a tomb or tombs far south in Upper Egypt.

FIG. 138. THE 'SERVANT' OF THE SHEIKH SAYID

Candles, or money with which to buy them, form a favourite offering. Such lights are kept burning every night in some sheikhs' tombs ; in others they are perhaps burned on one night only in the week, usually a Friday. A number of votive offerings are generally found hanging on a cord or cords stretched across the interior of the building. The gifts display great variety, including glass and bead bracelets, bunches of human hair, handkerchiefs, first-fruits of the cornfields, and so on. Each one registers an answered prayer, for the people flock in crowds to these tombs on certain days of the week—usually Thursdays or Fridays—generally to make some special request, or with the object of being freed from some disease, which they believe the sheikh can cure. A childless woman, or persons possessed by *ʿafārīt*, will come to beg the sheikh to intercede for them. Indeed, the performances of certain rites at the tomb may in themselves effect a cure.

Having removed his or her shoes before entering the building, the visitor then walks from left to right round the catafalque erected beneath the dome three, five, or seven times, reciting meanwhile special passages from the Ḳorān. These perambulations accomplished, the servant of the sheikh takes a broom, kept for this special purpose, and carefully brushes out all the footprints in the interior of the building.

Sick animals are also brought by their owners to a sheikh's tomb, round which they are driven seven times.

In one of the provinces of Upper Egypt, on the lower desert, stands the domed tomb of the sheikh Ḥasan ʿAli (Fig. 139). It is surrounded by a low mud-brick wall, which encloses a few small trees, a well, and two or three graves, wherein relatives of the dead sheikh lie buried. Pots of *ṣabr* (aloes) also decorate the sacred spot, for this plant is believed to bring happiness to the dead. The building is whitewashed, and is decorated with line-drawings in red and blue, illustrating the pilgrimage to Mecca. The surrounding desert is covered with the graves of more ordinary folk. These are marked by heaps of sand, into which are stuck branches of palm-trees, for palm-branches, like the aloe-plants, are believed to be the means of conveying happiness to the dead who lie beneath.

The sheikh Ḥasan ʿAli was only eighteen years old when he died, but from his earliest years he was noted for his piety. He was educated at a small school in his native village, and, as soon as he had learned to read, he spent all his leisure moments studying the Ḳorān. When he died he was buried in an ordinary grave in the lower desert among his dead fellow-villagers. However, one day, when old ʿAli (his father) was squatting on a *maṣṭabeh* (see p. 32), with his head resting on his hand, his dead son appeared before him and caught hold of him by the wrist, saying, "I am very angry."

His father said, "Why are you angry, my son?"

The boy replied, " Because you have not built me a large tomb, and if you do not do so now I will go away to another village."

" O my beloved son," said his father, " to-morrow morning I will begin to build a fine tomb for you."

Young ʿAli held a paper in his hand, and he now presented this to his father, telling him that on it were written full directions for the building of the tomb, together with a specification of the exact

FIG. 139. DOMED TOMB OF THE SHEIKH ḤASAN ʿALI

spot where it was to be built and also as to where would be found a well of water, the locality of which was hitherto unknown.

The tomb was built with all speed, the workmen following the instructions written on the paper presented to old ʿAli by his son. A well was sunk on the spot indicated, and the water from it is excellent. The father states most emphatically that he was wide awake when his son appeared to him. When I questioned old ʿAli as to what he had done with the paper he told me that it had been lost by the workmen !

A small model of a boat is hung up in the sheikh Ḥasan ʿAli's tomb, as in the tombs of many sheikhs, the boat being called the sheikh's ferry-boat.

The mother of this sheikh, who was very devoted to her son, did not survive him for many years. I was present at her funeral, which was attended by a large crowd of friends and relatives. She was buried in a grave near the tomb of her saintly son.

The sheikh ʿAbdu 'l-Laṭīf lived in a small village in Middle Egypt, where some of his family still reside. An old man, the son of the sheikh's paternal uncle, is well known to me.[1] The sheikh ʿAbdu 'l-Laṭīf was, in his lifetime, looked upon as a *walī*.[2] Insanity is the usual qualification for this high standing among the Muslim saints of Egypt, persons thus afflicted being regarded as the favourites of God. The sheikh had a habit of entering the houses of the people at night, after the doors had been locked, and while the evening meal was being cooked; for locked doors formed no barriers to the egress or ingress of this holy man. On entering he would immediately eat up all the food; meat, bread, and vegetables, no matter how large the quantity, would all be devoured on the spot. Any glass bottles that happened to be lying about might be included in this repast, for these he would bite up and swallow without drawing any blood. There was only one thing he feared, and that was water. If anyone threw a few drops of water at him he would run away in terror, as fast as his legs could carry him. My informant remembered him well, and he told me that on one occasion the sheikh entered his house after the entrance door had been securely locked and ate up all the food, including soup prepared for the evening meal.

When the sheikh died hundreds of people attended his funeral, and, being a very good man, he made his bearers walk quickly to the grave.[3] Above it has been erected the usual domed tomb; it is situated near that of the venerated sheikh Umbārak (Fig. 140) for whom a *mūlid*, or festival, is held once every year.[4]

One year, on the occasion of this festival, a man climbed on to the outside of the tomb of the sheikh ʿAbdu 'l-Laṭīf without first removing his shoes. Some of the people standing round remonstrated with him for this act of irreverence, but he replied, "Who is the sheikh ʿAbdu 'l-Laṭīf? He is nobody!" and refused to climb down or to take off his shoes. However, when he wanted

[1] At the moment of writing this I received a letter from Egypt telling me of this old man's death. He is the same man who divorced his wife by the triple divorce, described in Chapter V, pp. 95 f.

[2] *Walī* means 'friend' (*i.e.*, of God), and a Muslim saint is commonly so designated.

[3] See Chapter VII, p. 113.

[4] See Chapter XVI, pp. 252 ff.

to climb down and join the festive crowds he found that he could not move, and that, when he tried to do so, his limbs were rigid and his whole body paralysed. On seeing the plight of the wretched man cries to the sheikh were immediately raised. People came with drums and tambourines, others sang and clapped their hands in rhythmic accompaniment to the music, till at last, after about two hours of such intercession, the man regained his power of locomotion, and so was able to move away.

FIG. 140. TOMB OF THE SHEIKH UMBĀRAK

The external mural decorations are to be noted.

Some time after this exhibition of his power the sheikh ʿAbdu 'l-Laṭīf appeared to a man in a village a few miles distant, telling him to build him a tomb there. The people of this village went in triumph to the sheikh's native place and exultantly told the inhabitants that their sheikh had now come to them.

The original tomb still exists, but it is in a very dilapidated state, and no doubt in course of time it will wholly disappear, unless something happens to revive the veneration formerly paid to the holy man in his native village. Meanwhile, the people of the village where ʿAbdu 'l-Laṭīf's later resting-place is built hold a *mūlid* every year in honour of their acquired sheikh.

During the sheikh ʿAbdu 'l-Laṭīf's lifetime he was visited on one occasion by the sheikh Sulimān, who resided in a village some miles distant. Wherever he went the sheikh Sulimān was always accompanied by his faithful servant. On the occasion of this visit the two sheikhs conversed together in an unknown language. This roused the curiosity of the sheikh Sulimān's servant, who after the interview asked his master what they had been talking about. The sheikh told him that ʿAbdu 'l-Laṭīf had remonstrated with him for coming to his village and had bade him remain in his own neighbourhood. Doubtless jealousy was at the root of this ill-feeling.

A few days later the servant noticed very early in the morning that his master's fingers were all burned at the tips. He immediately questioned him as to the cause of this injury, and the sheikh told him that it was his custom to go every night to all the sheikhs' tombs in the neighbourhood and light candles for them, and that while he was engaged in this pious work his fingers were burned.

The sheikh Sulimān is now dead, but his piety is still remembered. He is buried in his native village, but six other tombs are erected to his memory in various parts of the country. Moreover, the inhabitants of his village hold a *mūlid* every year in his honour.

In one of the provinces in Upper Egypt, close to the desert hills, lived the sheikheh Ṣulūḥ. This woman had, during her lifetime, a great reputation for holiness, and people flocked to her, in times of difficulty, from all quarters. Her skin was very dark from constant exposure to the sun, and her head, on which she wore no veil, was covered with a crop of hair, thick and long like the wool of a sheep ; from beneath her brows peered dark, sharp-looking eyes. Her clothes were scanty, consisting merely of a piece of linen rag and a sort of coat. She remained out in this desert solitude all day, and at night, so I was told, slept alone " in the mountain." As I have explained, the people call the often precipitous high-desert hills the mountain (*el-gebel*), so she probably took shelter in one of the natural or artificial caves which exist in great numbers in the hillsides.

On one occasion, when a number of men and women had come to consult her, one of the former asked her what had become of his most valuable camel, which he had lost. The sheikheh at once told him the exact hour in which this loss had occurred, and informed him that one of his sons had stolen it and had sold it to a man in another village in the same province. She then told him the name of the man who had bought it, and said that if he went to the house of the purchaser he would be able to recover his lost property.

I was told that this information proved to be true, and the man eventually got back the camel which he had lost.

Another man then came forward, and when he had presented the sheikheh with a small sum of money she told him his name and the name of his village, though he was quite unknown to her. She also informed him that he had three sons and one daughter—a perfectly correct statement—and said, moreover, that on his return home he would find that his daughter was ill, this information also proving to be true.

This woman died two or three years ago, and crowds flocked to her funeral, men of all ranks coming to do her honour.

A certain Sheikh Ṣabr is buried in a small village in Middle Egypt, and a tree only marked his resting-place. This tree, which was large and very old, was blown down in 1926. I inquired if a tomb would now be built over the grave, but I was informed that probably no such building would be erected until the sheikh had appeared to some one and commanded him to build for him a domed tomb. I had visited this village on several occasions before the disaster occurred to the sacred tree, and was fortunate enough to secure some good photographs of it. The tree stood at the end of the village, and devotees who came to beg the sheikh to intercede for them so that they might obtain some special benefit, or who wished to be cured of headache or other ailments, would knock a nail into the trunk and then usually twist some of their hair round the nail. A cure, so it was believed, would follow this act. The nails must be virgin-nails—*i.e.*, not used before—and must be of native manufacture. Childless women also visited the tree to be cured of their barrenness. The sheikh Ṣabr is very highly venerated, and a *mūlid*, described on p. 256, is held in his honour once a year.

All these sheikhs were poor men, and the veneration shown to them is due to the virtues they displayed and to their supposed miraculous powers. The high esteem in which they hold their local saints is really good for the peasants, as it sets them some standard of conduct, and gives them a higher ideal of life than mere moneymaking and material success.

Coptic saints receive the appellation Māri (Saint), and many of the beliefs and ceremonies associated with them are similar to those connected with the Muslim sheikhs.

A Coptic saint is usually buried within the precincts of a monastery or church, which may be dedicated to him. A popular saint may be honoured by the dedication of numerous monasteries and churches to his memory, in all of which he is equally venerated.

Sometimes the same saint may be claimed by Muslims and Copts alike, in which case the grave is often situated in an open space, possibly under the shadow of a tree or trees, the lower branches of which are covered with votive offerings contributed by the followers of both religions. With the Christians as well as with the Muslims candles are a favourite form of votive offering, and when the saint is claimed by the adherents of both faiths their candles may be seen burning side by side.

Many years ago, on a spot in the cultivation in Upper Egypt where a church dedicated to Māri Mīna el-ʿAgayebi now stands, there was a square plot of *ḥalfa*-grass. This site was claimed by the Muslims as the burial-place of a sheikh. There was a very poor man who lived in the town adjoining these fields and who acted as *farrāsh*[1] at the sugar factory in the same town. One night while he was sleeping he felt some one give him a kick. This naturally aroused him, and he saw standing beside him a man whose face and form were of great beauty, and who was clothed in white garments. This man told the poor *farrāsh* that he was Māri Mīna el-ʿAgayebi, that he wished him to build a church, and that he would himself indicate the spot on which he wished it to be erected. The saint told the *farrāsh* that he had called him to do this work instead of a rich man, as the latter would boast that by his riches he had built the church, whereas the saint himself would supply the poor man with all that he needed for the erection of the sacred building.

Māri Mīna then led the *farrāsh* to the patch of *ḥalfa*-grass in the fields, and told him to measure two metres from the edge of the *ḥalfa*-grass toward the east and two metres from the edge of the *ḥalfa*-grass toward the west. Then he was to dig the whole plot thus measured out to a depth of two and a half metres. When

[1] Literally, sweeper—the title given to servants employed by the Government to keep the Rest-houses clean, also to men employed in other public buildings in the same capacity.

he had done this he would first find a very deep well, and westward from this he would find a large quantity of bricks, enough for the building of the church ; while to the east he would find piles of white lime to be used in the construction of the building. To the east again of the lime, if he dug down to the depth of half a metre, he would find a heap of money, sufficient to pay for the entire building of the church, including the wages of the workmen employed. The saint told the *farrāsh* that he was to start at once to build the church, and that if he disobeyed his orders he would be killed. Then Māri Mīna el-ʿAgayebi vanished.

The *farrāsh* set to work to dig up the plot indicated, and found everything as the saint had told him, including the well, which he discovered first.

The church still stands on this spot, but the old *farrāsh* who built it has, of course, been dead for a long time, and since his day the building has been enlarged by one of the Coptic bishops. The well is still to be seen within the precincts of the church.

Māri Mīna el-ʿAgayebi is a very popular Coptic saint, and he is venerated not only by the Christians, but also by many of the Muslims, who have, so I was told, the greatest faith in him, and who often appeal to him for aid in time of need.

Egladiūs el-ʿAzab is a saint of great repute. Several churches in Egypt are dedicated to him, and his body lies with those of four other saints in a special edifice set apart for them in a large town in Upper Egypt. The bodies of these five holy men are still in a good state of preservation, though they have all been dead for a long period of time. Each body lies in a coffin. Egladiūs el-ʿAzab was very young when he died, having been killed, so I was told, by the Arabs because he was a Christian. He wears a wide ribbon of gold across his breast, and a gold earring in one ear. A special festival is held every year in his honour, for the due celebration of which the people make large quantities of bread, and bring cattle, which are slaughtered at the churches. The bread and meat are distributed among the poor, who flock in great numbers on these occasions to all the churches dedicated to him.

In a certain village in Asyūṭ Province there is a Coptic church dedicated to Māri Egladiūs el-ʿAzab. A man who lives close to the sacred building was, on one occasion, entertaining a Muslim friend who had arrived from another province. While they were engaged in conversation together the talk turned on to the subject of sheikhs, and the Muslim remarked that the Copts had no real saints, but that what they believed about their so-called saints was all rubbish. To this his host replied, "That is not so; we have a celebrated saint to whom the church close by is dedicated." But his guest scoffed at him.

At night, when the Muslim was sleeping in a room in the upper story of the house—his host sleeping on the ground floor—a young man appeared before him, and touched him to wake him from his slumbers. This uninvited guest then seized the Muslim by the throat and asked him how he dared to speak of the Coptic saints in the scornful way he had done.

Meanwhile, the host, hearing his guest choking, and crying out, "Leave me, leave me! I am wrong, I am wrong!" rushed up, thinking that he was being attacked by thieves. When he arrived on the scene he found his guest weeping, so he asked him what was the matter. The Muslim then told him of his unexpected visitor, and described his appearance. From the description the host knew that the mysterious person was the great saint himself. So loud had been the cries of the terrified Muslim that the whole neighbourhood had heard him.

On the following morning the now repentant Muslim repaired to the church dedicated to Māri Egladiūs el-ʿAzab, and, with shoes hanging round his neck, knelt before the altar and prayed to the saint, saying, "Pardon me, pardon me, pardon me!" After this he left the church.

Since this visitation of the saint the Muslim, who still remains a follower of Islām, sends every year a gift of wax for the manufacture of candles used in the services held in the church, together with a present of incense.

It must be explained here that it is the custom all over Egypt, when a Copt or a Muslim has committed a wrong against a saint or sheikh, for him to repair to the church or mosque and borrow a pair of shoes such as are worn by the poor *fellāḥīn*. These shoes are suspended by a cord round the neck of the penitent, who must wear them in this way as he kneels before the altar, or *ḳibleh*,[1] as the case may be. As he kneels he must repeat the words "Pardon me," seven, five, or three times, the number of repetitions being decided by the priest or *imām* present in the church or mosque. When this act of repentance is finished the man goes out and returns

[1] The prayer-niche turned toward Mecca.

the shoes to the original owner. The shoes must always be those of a very poor *fellāḥ* who is in wretched circumstances, thus indicating the attitude of mind of the penitent man in the presence of the saint or sheikh whom he has wronged.

With regard to the offering of wax, it may be of interest to explain that the candles used in religious ceremonies in the Coptic church are always made by the priest himself or else by the servant who is responsible for the cleaning of the church.

CHAPTER XVI

SOME ANNUAL FESTIVALS

THE *Mūlid en-Nebi*, the annual celebration of the birthday of the Prophet, is of course the most important of all the festivals held in honour of Muslim saints. However, I shall content myself here with a description of some of the annual *mawālid* (plural of *mūlid*) held in honour of local village saints which I have attended myself during my six years' sojourn in Egypt.

The sheikh Umbārak is buried in a village in Middle Egypt, and a whitewashed domed building has been erected above his grave. One or two of the outside walls of his tomb are, as is customary, decorated with pictures descriptive of the pilgrimage to Mecca,[1] roughly sketched in red and blue paint, the remainder being inscribed with passages from the Ḳorān. Around the dome are small, what might almost be called clerestory windows, in each of which a lighted candle is placed every night. There is a female 'servant' attached to this sheikh, who is supposed to keep the tomb in order, receive the donations of devotees, and light the candles every evening. One wonders how she manages to carry out this work satisfactorily, as she is quite blind!

The *mūlid* held in honour of the sheikh Umbārak takes place in April and begins early in the afternoon, on the morning of which day similar festivals are inaugurated in certain neighbouring villages in honour of their own particular sheikhs.

At about two o'clock a large crowd collected in the vicinity of the sheikh's tomb, several people, chiefly women, seating themselves around it. The blind servant received donations from the faithful on behalf of the sheikh, part of the time having the sheikh's flag wrapped around her (Fig. 141). As the donors presented their gifts they recited the *Fātiḥah* in low and rapid tones. In the road which ran past the burial-ground, and in the adjacent palm-grove, the holiday-makers engaged in friendly conversation or indulged in various amusements (Fig. 142); and along the roadside booths

[1] See p. 245, Fig. 140.

had been erected, wherein butchers and vendors of sweetmeats, toys, and other wares plied their trade, to all appearance doing excellent business (Fig. 143).

Eggs dyed a bright cerise or yellow are a special feature of all these *mawālid*, and those who sold them attracted a considerable number of customers. These coloured eggs, which are also sold on the Coptic Easter Monday, are used for two games, which are played as follows. In one game two boys or men take part, each grasping an egg in his hand. One of them knocks his egg against that of his opponent, and the man whose egg is not cracked is regarded as the winner and takes the cracked egg of his adversary. In the other game several eggs are arranged in a row on the ground, and a number of men sit at a certain distance away from them. Each in turn rolls an egg toward the row of eggs facing him, and the man who first succeeds in cracking one of them wins the lot. These games are played by large numbers of people at all *mawālid*, but never by women and girls. Coloured eggs are used for games, in many cases similar to these, in various parts of Europe, especially in the Balkan states. Again, in some of the Northern counties of England coloured eggs are still used in a game played on Easter Monday which closely resembles the second Egyptian game.

FIG. 141. FEMALE 'SERVANT' OF THE SHEIKH UMBĀRAK, WRAPPED IN THE SHEIKH'S FLAG ON THE DAY OF HIS MŪLID

There were other attractions at this *mūlid* of the sheikh Umbārak. In the palm-grove a conjurer in one part and a poet

FIG. 142. MŪLID OF THE SHEIKH UMBĀRAK: SCENE IN THE PALM-GROVE

FIG. 143. VENDORS' BOOTHS AT A SHEIKH'S MŪLID

(*cf.* p. 266, Fig. 152) in another had collected large and interested audiences. The poet was accompanied in his recitations by a woman—and sometimes by two or three men as well—who beat a single-membrane drum. Peep-shows also contributed to the amusement, the pictures shown usually representing favourite national saints and heroes and heroines. Lastly, roughly made little cars hung on wheels, which turned round and round on a horizontal axis, were much patronized by the children (Fig. 144).

A special sheikh of this district, later to conduct the *zikr* (see

FIG. 144. SWINGS, WHEELS WITH HANGING CARS, AND OTHER AMUSEMENTS AT A SHEIKH'S MŪLID

below) in honour of the sainted Umbārak, paraded through the crowd on a donkey, preceded by three men carrying large banners decorated with various designs and inscriptions, and by musicians playing on cymbals and a double-membrane drum. One of the banners belonged to the sheikh Umbārak, but the others came from the tombs of sheikhs in neighbouring villages. Such banners are always carried in procession on the occasion of a *mūlid*, and the men who bear them advance with dancing steps instead of an ordinary walk.

It should be mentioned here that a *zikr* is a kind of religious dance performed by men and older boys only; the women and girls never take part in it. A detailed description of it is given later on.

In spite of the heat, millions of flies, and clouds of dust, the festival of the sheikh Umbārak was conducted with the utmost good humour, and the behaviour of the crowds was perfect. It came to an end at about seven o'clock.

On the following day the annual *mūlid* of the sheikh Ṣabr was celebrated at his village, which is most picturesquely situated on the bank of the Yūsuf Canal. As I have stated in Chapter XV, this sheikh is much venerated, not only in his own village, but in villages for many miles around. I have been present at his *mūlid* on two or three occasions, and each time large crowds have assembled to do him honour.

The festival begins in the morning at about eleven o'clock, and a number of people joined me as I rode through the fields on my way to the village. Upon these occasions a brisk trade is always carried on, and piles of brightly coloured sweets are exposed for sale, together with toys, cheap ornaments, dates, and other delicacies. The vendors seat themselves under rough booths, which they erect on the spot, and under which they can take shelter from the fierce rays of the sun.

When I arrived a large *zikr* was taking place under the shade of the branches of the sacred tree. It was executed by a number of men forming a circle round the sheikh who conducted this religious exercise. The men swayed rhythmically from side to side, nodded their heads, or bent backward and forward as they pronounced the name of Allāh over and over again. The presiding sheikh beat time by clapping his hands, while now and then a *fiḳīh* would chant passages from the Ḳorān. The ceremony was conducted with great earnestness and solemnity, but some of the performers became so worked up with religious fervour that from time to time they leaped into the air, and finally fell on the ground from exhaustion.

Close to where this religious performance was taking place was to be found the usual large wheel, with its hanging seats. Here the children had congregated, all of them clamouring for a ride, as they are to be seen doing about the whirligigs and swings provided at the fairs in England.

At another spot a poet had collected a large audience, which listened with evident enjoyment while he gave his recitations to the accompanying beats of two tambourines and a shallow, single-membrane drum (*cf.* p. 266, Fig. 152).

The banners were much in evidence at this festival, and I

managed to secure a good photograph of them and of their bearers as they stood grouped under the sheikh's tree together with a few musicians and the inevitable crowd (Fig. 145).

These *mawālid*, when well conducted, are quite harmless, and are one of the very few pleasurable excitements enjoyed by the peasants. Most of those at which I have been present have been quite orderly, but much depends on the officer in charge of the district in which

FIG. 145. SHEIKH'S BANNERS AND THEIR BEARERS

they are being held. If he is neglectful, and does not see that order is kept and objectionable shows prohibited, the festivals can degenerate into anything but wholesome recreation for the people.

The modern Egyptian *mawālid* show striking resemblances to English fairs, especially as celebrated during the Middle Ages and on into the seventeenth century. These too were associated in every case with a saint, and also with trading. Our modern fairs, though often still named after the saints in whose honour they were originally held, have now lost their religious significance.

A monastery in Middle Egypt situated on the high-desert edge, which at this spot approaches close to the Yūsuf Canal, is one of a number dedicated to Māri Girgis, our St George (Fig. 146). The cliff on which the monastery is built towers up above the canal, while behind the building, and outside its surrounding walls, lie two fairly large cemeteries, one Christian and the other Muslim. The present building stands on an ancient site, and many of the old walls of the church and religious houses around it are of great thickness. A considerable portion of the old walls which surround the whole settlement still remain intact, and stories are told of the miraculous powers attributed to them. This monastery, as the massive character of the ancient walls indicates, must have served

FIG. 146. A MONASTERY DEDICATED TO ST GEORGE

as a stronghold for the Christians, who built it when religious wars raged between them and the Muslims. One or two pillars preserved in the more modern church are, so I was told, relics from an ancient building which has perished.

The annual festival held here in honour of St George attracts a great number of people, who flock to the monastery from considerable distances. It is interesting to observe that the crowds which congregate within the monastery precincts are composed of quite as many Muslims as Christians. Except for the fact that there was no *zikr*, the proceedings were much the same as those of the Muslim festivals described above. The same trading went on, and similar musical and other entertainments were provided. This *mūlid* continues for a week, and during the last few days horse-racing and displays of fancy riding take place. Many of the visitors remain for the whole week, engaging rooms for themselves beforehand if they are not lucky enough to have friends in the neighbourhood with whom they can stay. Certain proceedings which I witnessed at this festival, happily absent from most of the village *mawālid* for Muslim sheikhs which I have attended, would, I fear, have met with the strong disapproval of the good St George!

Ramaḍān is the month of the Muslim fast. From an hour before sunrise till after sunset no food must be eaten by the faithful, and, what is a severer privation in a hot, dry climate like that of Egypt, not a drop of water must pass their lips. I am always filled with admiration for the courageous and cheerful way in which the poor *fellāḥīn* endure this most trying penance, carrying on their tasks with the same light-heartedness that they are wont to display at all times. It is a very serious strain on the fortitude of all those who have to work, and it is especially trying to those officials who observe the fast strictly, and yet whose duties oblige them to travel on tours of inspection or for the investigation of crimes.

On the day following the termination of Ramaḍān, *el-ʿĪd eṣ-Ṣughaiyar* (Little Festival) is held. It is a day of great rejoicing and is observed as a public holiday, for the trying fast is over at last. Friends visit each other to express their good wishes, and all classes endeavour to show special hospitality in honour of the occasion. The poor are never forgotten on this day of rejoicing, and gifts of money and food are distributed by those who are in more fortunate circumstances.

On this day the dead also are held in remembrance and most families repair to the cemeteries early in the morning, the women carrying baskets on their heads containing bread, dates, and other sweet things, which are distributed in the names of their dead relatives among the poor (Fig. 147). Palm-branches are laid on the graves, or are broken into shorter lengths and stuck upright in front of the tombs. *Fuḳahā* (see p. 172) are always present on these occasions, as most people engage them to recite by the graves, paying them for their services with gifts from their baskets, and sometimes with money also. The rest of the day is given up to festivities, which are continued for two days more.

El-ʿĪd el-Kibīr (the Great Festival, held in commemoration of the sacrifice of Isaac) follows forty days later, and a public holiday of three or four days' duration is observed. Quantities of grain are given as gifts to the poorer folk by those who possess land. Such suppliants are constantly arriving to receive their donations during the whole of the first day of this festival, while coffee, sweets, and cakes are distributed to other friends who come to pay visits of congratulation. Prayers are offered in the mosques, which are filled with worshippers. On the first day of this festival all who can afford it sacrifice a ram (thus calling to mind the ram substituted for Isaac) outside the house, and sprinkle some of its blood on the house-door.[1]

FIG. 147. A CEMETERY CROWDED WITH VISITORS ON THE DAY OF THE LITTLE FESTIVAL

Once when visiting the house of some of my village friends I found that not only was such a sacrifice in prospect, but another ram was also to be killed for the following reason. The woman's only son had been very ill some two or three years before, and in her despair she had made a vow to some sheikh that if her son recovered she would kill a ram as a thank-offering on the first day of *el-ʿĪd el-Kibīr* every year for the rest of her life (Fig. 148). The blood of this animal, however, was not sprinkled on the door.

Again on this festival the cemeteries are visited by crowds of people, many carrying palm-branches to be placed on the graves.

[1] *Cf.* the ancient Semitic custom of sprinkling blood on the doorposts, exemplified in one of the ceremonies of the Jewish Passover.

Gifts of food are distributed by the visitors in the names of their dead ; in fact, the funerary customs observed at this festival are identical with those connected with *el-ʿĪd eṣ-Ṣughaiyar*.

The first day of *Khamasīn*, which falls in April and is called *Shemm en-Nesīm* (the Smelling of the Zephyr), is observed in the following way. Early in the morning a bunch of onions, or a single onion, is hung up above the house-door. The owners of the house, more especially the women, may smell the onions before

FIG. 148. RAM TO BE SACRIFICED AT THE GREAT FESTIVAL IN ACCOMPLISHMENT OF A VOW

The mother who made the vow stands beside the animal.

hanging them up. I was told that in some parts of Upper Egypt the onions, after being hung up, are squeezed or beaten with a stick, so that the juice from them may fall on the threshold. I have also been told that this custom is observed because it is believed to make people strong. I have heard, moreover, that in other parts of the country on the night before the festival people hang a bunch of onions over the places where they sleep. Early on the following morning each person on rising immediately takes his or her bunch of onions, smells it, and then throws it over his shoulder, after which he walks out of the house without looking back. My informant said it is believed that all evils are thus thrown away. I have not as yet come across this custom myself.

On this day most of the people rise very early and go into the fields, spending the entire day out of doors. The men, at any rate in Fayūm Province, usually bathe in the Yūsuf Canal, the water of which is supposed to possess special *barakeh* on this occasion.[1]

On *Yōm Sabt en-Nūr*—the Sabbath, or Saturday, of the Light—people of both sexes and of all ages put into their eyes a small

FIG. 149. PALM-BRANCHES PLAITED INTO VARIOUS SHAPES, USED IN A COPTIC CHURCH ON PALM SUNDAY

quantity of powder made from the placenta of a cat dried and pounded.[2] It is believed to make the eyes beautiful. To be told that you have the eyes of a cat is a great compliment (see p. 220).

On the Coptic Palm Sunday it is the custom to plait the leaves of palm-branches, without their being removed from the mid-rib, into a variety of forms, many of which are very intricate. Sometimes a round loaf of Eucharistic bread is enclosed within the plaited leaves. These palm-branches are taken to the church for the service held on this occasion. The illustration (Fig. 149) shows a group of men holding their palms, which they had taken to the church belonging to a Coptic monastery in the desert close

[1] See p. 33. [2] *Cf.* E. W. Lane, *op. cit.*, vol. ii, p. 223.

to el-Lāhūn, in Fayūm Province. I photographed them in the monastery precincts after the service had taken place.

The festival of the Epiphany is celebrated by the Copts on either January 18 or 19. On the previous evening the men usually bathe in the Nile, holy water from a church having been poured into the river first. In some places a priest comes to the house of a Copt bringing a supply of holy water with him and also a small silver cross. A number of prayers are recited, and the *Kyrie Eleison* is repeated forty-one times, these repetitions being counted by means of a Coptic rosary, which contains forty-one beads. The whole assembly is then sprinkled with the holy water. This is a substitute for the bathing in the Nile.

On the following day, called *Yōm el-Ghiṭās*, all the Copts repair to the cemeteries to visit the graves of their dead relatives. This visit is called *eṭ-Ṭala*ʿ, and many of the rites are similar to those observed by the Muslims at their *Tala*ʿ. The following is an account of what I have myself witnessed at this ceremony, and is typical of all these celebrations in the country parts of Egypt.

The first thing to catch the eye on arriving at the Coptic cemetery was a large group of women indulging in a curious dance close to some of the graves. It was very similar to the dance after a death described in the chapter on funerary customs, and consisted of a stamping, circular movement, the women being closely packed together the whole time

The cemetery was crowded, and visitors on camels, donkeys, or on foot were constantly arriving. Others, having paid their tribute to the dead, were departing, wending their way to the various villages in the cultivated area. All this time the wailing never ceased. It was, to my mind, the most pathetic sound I had ever heard. The monastery made a picturesque background for the whole scene. Moreover, its walls afforded a welcome shelter from the sun for the horses, donkeys, and camels that were tethered beneath them.

The groups of mourners varied in size, some being quite large and consisting of about twenty people, possiblymore. Occasionally a woman could be seen wailing in solitary grief. I noticed one such woman talking to her dead husband through a small hole pierced at one end of the tomb. Coloured silk handkerchiefs, similar to those used at all the funerary ceremonies of the Muslims, were in evidence. The graves, especially those with no superstructure, were covered for the occasion with a rug, called *kisweh*,[1] generally of a striped woven material, such as is often placed on the floor or on a *maṣṭabeh* for a guest to sit on. The women made no change in their dress for this occasion, but in most cases their hands, arms, and faces were dyed blue as a sign of mourning.

FIG. 150. WIFE, ACCOMPANIED BY WAILING WOMEN, AT THE GRAVE OF HER DEAD HUSBAND ON THE FESTIVAL OF YŌM EL-GHIṬĀS

The superstructures over the graves show very little variation in form in this cemetery. They are rectangular structures with barrel-vaulted roofs. Many of them were covered with white paint, with simple designs in blue or red; in some cases both colours were used for decoration on a single tomb. Sometimes a text from the Bible was inscribed in Arabic, in red or blue paint, along one side of the monument, a cross being frequently either painted or incised at one end.

At one grave there was a number of women, their faces and hands streaked with blue dye, each one holding a silk handkerchief, either mauve or green in colour, with which they gently stroked and patted the grave as they wailed in piteous tones, "Still young, O

[1] The same word is used for the covering of the catafalque in a sheikh's tomb. See p. 242.

my brother!" evidently addressing the dead. By another grave there was a large concourse of people, some seated higher up on an adjacent tomb (Fig. 150). Here a widow was bewailing her dead husband in the following words: "Come and get up! See the weariness [or sorrow] of me and of my children. See how your eldest son[1] has wearied me, and how your brother has oppressed me. You have left me alone with young children. Who will feed them, and who will clothe them?" After this harangue the wailers took up their part, smiting their hands together and striking their cheeks to the rythmic beats of a shallow, single-membrane drum, called *nadam*. When the wailers ceased the widow again started her lament, other women sometimes joining in as a sort of chorus. Passing friends stopped and endeavoured to console her; and one of her young children, who was seated near her, embraced her from time to time. The grave was covered with a *kisweh*, and the *nadam* was bedaubed with blue dye. The widow held two handkerchiefs knotted together, one in each hand, and with these she alternately wiped the tears from her cheeks and patted the grave.

FIG. 151. FEMALE SWEET-SELLER WITH HER TRADE-SIGN

[1] Probably the son by a former wife.

Meanwhile, in another part of the cemetery a Coptic priest was going from grave to grave, censing both the mourners and the tombs, in return for which service he was sometimes presented with additional incense or with a certain amount of grain. Grain

FIG. 152. A POET RECITING ON THE FESTIVAL OF YŌM EL-GHIṬĀS

thus collected is, so I was told, generally distributed afterward to the poor. Water-carriers were busy plying their trade, or occasionally offering a free drink in the name of a dead relative. A sweet-seller was also advertising her wares [1] by means of a tin rattle similar to those bought as children's toys, fixed on to the top of a long stick, which was twisted with a thick sugary substance (Fig. 151). Close to the cemetery a market was in full swing,

[1] I am told that it is a man who usually sells sweets in this way; it is very rare for a woman to engage in such a trade.

where, besides various foods set out for sale, rattles and other toys, as well as small tin cups, could be bought for children. The cups were hung round with small, heart-shaped pieces of tin, which jingled against the sides. Such cups are bought and presented to the children by their parents in memory of this day's ceremony. On another part of the ground a professional poet was entertaining a large crowd. On seeing me, and on my presenting him with a small sum of money, he started reciting a poem in my honour, of which the only words to be distinguished were those with which he wound up the oration: "God will that you return safely." He very cleverly twirled on one of his fingers a drum, resembling in shape the *nadam* used by the wailing women, and in it he collected money from the bystanders (Fig. 152). His attendant was provided with a similar instrument, on which he beat an accompaniment to the poet's recitations.

Gifts of bread, either in the form of flat loaves or sometimes of rings, as well as dates and sweets, are often distributed to the poor at this festival in the name of a dead relative.

The festival lasts till sunset. All who have remained in the cemetery up to this time then return homeward, the women wailing as they go. Often, even after they have reached their homes, they continue their demonstrations of grief, striking their faces and beating their hands together as they have done at the graveside. On such occasions their neighbours will come to condole with them. As night falls the wailing ceases, and the next day work goes on as usual.

CHAPTER XVII

THE VILLAGE STORY-TELLER AND HIS TALES

THE modern Egyptian peasants are as fond of stories as were their ancestors in the days of Herodotus. Since few of the older people can read or write they have largely to depend for such entertainment on the public recitations of story-tellers. Most villages possess at least one story-teller, who, as a rule, has some trade with which he is engaged during the day. In the evening the male villagers are in the habit of congregating in one another's houses, or in some shop or *café*. To such a gathering the story-teller is a welcome addition, and he tells his tales in return for very small sums of money presented to him by members of his audience. The story-teller may have taken years to collect his tales, or he may have inherited them from his forbears. The peasant is an excellent *raconteur*, possessed of great imagination, very dramatic, and entirely free from self-consciousness.

Among my village friends are two or three story-tellers, and from them I have collected and written down a large number of tales. Some were related to me in my brother's desert camp the first year I was in Egypt. I would appoint a day for the story-teller to visit me, and, as the hour approached, I would see him and the schoolmaster who came with him to assist me in my translations of the stories riding across the lower desert on donkeys. On their arrival coffee was brought, and, when they had partaken of this refreshment, the story-teller seated himself cross-legged on the ground, drew his robe around him, and, after some minutes' reflection, began one of his tales.

One of my story-teller friends, a cheery person, was a dyer by trade, as, indeed, was made evident by the state of his hands, which were stained almost as dark a blue as his cotton clothes. When he was a young boy he was apprenticed to a firm of dyers, and he would listen to stories told to his fellow-workmen as they plied their task. Having a retentive memory, he stored up all these tales, which he now relates to the people of his village in the evening. He also tells his tales to his customers, who often wait while he is dying the cloth which they have brought him. Thus some tedious hours of waiting are pleasantly whiled away.

When he first came to me he was somewhat shy, but after a while, seeing that I was really interested, he would start off without hesitation. Sometimes he would consult the schoolmaster as to what he thought would be most to my taste, giving him a short epitome of two or three stories. Then, when a suitable one was chosen, he would go ahead without further delay. Several stories were recited at a sitting, and occasionally I was writing them down for three or four hours on end. Our servants would often stand near, listening in breathless attention as the plot developed.

FIG. 153. STORY-TELLER, WHO IS ALSO A WATER-CARRIER BY TRADE

The next year I engaged another man, who was a water-carrier by trade (Fig. 153). I was then living in tents near an out-of-the-way village in Upper Egypt, and the *'omdeh* (headman of the village) kindly placed his reception-room at my disposal. Wealthier villagers would drop in from time to time and take a seat at a respectful distance from me, while humbler folk stood at the doorway, or squatted on the threshold, all alike listening enthralled, and from time to time uttering ejaculations of appreciation.

I was assured that these tales had never been committed to writing, but had been handed down orally. It may interest my readers to peruse the following, selected from a large number in my possession.

THE FELLĀḤĪN OF UPPER EGYPT

The Work of Women is better than that of Men; or, the Ideas of Women are Superior to those of Men

Once upon a time a judge had a wife who was always telling him that he invariably gave judgment in favour of men and never of women. To this accusation the judge replied, " Oh, my dear wife, I think that women are very inferior to men; they are always in need of our help."

As the judge continued to pay no attention to what his wife said, she became angry with him, and said to herself, " I will find a way in which to punish my husband."

So one day the wife told her husband to buy some meat and a melon for dinner. After she had prepared these things a friend came, and she offered *him* the meat for his dinner and cooked some lentils for her husband's meal, to take the place of the meat which she had given to her friend. She then cut out the inside of the melon and poured water inside the rind, which had been left whole. She brought also some fish and put them inside the melon-rind in the water.

When her husband came to take his dinner as usual she brought him the lentils.

He was much surprised when he saw this, and said to her, " What is the matter? I bought meat, not lentils."

So she said to him, " This is all that you bought; you must eat it." So he ate.

After he had eaten the lentils she took a knife and began to cut the melon into pieces, and then started laughing. Her husband said, " What is the matter with you?" She replied, " My dear husband, you must come and see the fish which are in this melon."

The man was very surprised to see such a curious thing, and he went outside his house, where there were some people sitting, and said to them, "I have bought a melon inside which there are fish. I shall invite you to eat some of these fish to-morrow."

The next day he sent out his invitations to the people who had promised to dine with him on the fish. When the guests arrived he said to his wife, " Bring the fish!" So she came forward and said, " O my husband, do fish live in melons? What is the matter with you? O people, you must perceive that the judge has become mad!" So they took him to the asylum and made some one else judge in his place.

When they asked the poor man every day the names of the days of the week he repeated them correctly, but when they asked him, " Where do fish live?" he replied, " Fish live in melons."

One day the woman went to visit her husband and said to him, " When they ask you ' Where do fish live?' you must say, ' They live in water, in ponds and rivers and lakes.' " Then they let him go free, and when he arrived at his house the people came to salute him.

One night his wife said, " I can make you judge again and make the other judge mad ! " She then told him that he must go to the market and buy some milk. So he went and bought it. Then she said, " We are going to invite the new judge to eat with us, and I am going to tell you something that you must say. When I hang a bag of skin filled with milk on your neck, I shall milk you, and you must make a noise such as buffaloes make." So her husband said, " Very well, I will do so."

The woman invited the new judge, and when he came to the house she began to laugh, saying, " I am going to milk my husband, but I am ashamed to do this before you ! " The judge replied, " Are husbands milked ? " to which she answered, " Yes, they give good milk, and you are going to see it for yourself."

Then the woman called her husband and began to milk him from the skin which was concealed under his clothing. The new judge was very much astonished when he saw this, especially when he ate the food which she had prepared with the milk. After he had eaten he asked the wife, " How can a husband give milk ? " to which she answered, " If you wish to be milked you must go to a street which leads to the market, and then you must take off all your clothes and begin to eat grass. When anyone speaks to you do not reply, but make a noise like a buffalo. After that you will give good milk."

So he went and carried out her instructions. While he was thus engaged the inhabitants of the town passed by and saw what he was doing. " What is the matter with you, O our judge ? " they asked. He did not answer them, but made a noise like a buffalo. Then they said that the judge had become mad, and they took him to the asylum and brought the old judge and restored him to his position.

The Two Shoes of Ḥenēn

Once upon a time there was a shoemaker whose name was Ḥenēn. An Arab came to him and wished to buy a pair of shoes, but they did not agree about the price, and quarrelled with each other, and Ḥenēn was much annoyed and desired to take his revenge on the Arab.

So when Ḥenēn learnt that the Arab was going to cross the desert he took a pair of shoes and went along the road on which he knew the Arab would go. As he went he put one of the shoes on the ground ; the other shoe he placed on the road a mile away from the first. Then he hid himself in a tree near where the second shoe lay.

When the Arab passed by the first shoe he said to himself that it was like Ḥenēn's shoe, and he left it on the ground and did not take it. He then went on his way till he found the second shoe a mile distant from the first. Whereupon he said to himself, " I must leave the camel here and go back to take the first shoe."

So he went back. And after he had turned back, leaving his camel, Ḥenēn came down the tree and led the camel off to his house. When the Arab returned to the place where he had left his camel he found it had disappeared, so he took the pair of shoes and went to his house. When he arrived there his family said to him, "What have you brought?" He replied, "I have brought back the two shoes of Ḥenēn instead of the camel."

And this proverb, "I have returned with the two shoes of Ḥenēn," is quoted when anyone returns with small things in exchange for large ones.

The Shah of Persia and his Daughter

Once upon a time the Shah of Persia had a wife who gave birth to a very beautiful girl, and then died.

After many years the Shah said to his vizier, "I wish to marry again. I have two pairs of gold bracelets, and whichever woman can fit these bracelets on her wrists shall be my wife."

So the vizier called an old woman and told her to look for a girl on whom the bracelets could be fitted. The old woman sought for such a girl, but the only one she could find was the daughter of the Shah. She informed the Shah of this, so he sent for his daughter and asked her if she wished to marry him. The girl replied, "Very well, my father, I will marry you if you can pay my price." So the Shah asked his daughter what her price would be. The girl replied, "I want you to make for me a large golden cow."

So the goldsmiths came, and the daughter made a drawing of the cow, which she represented as having an empty belly. After the goldsmiths had made the cow she ordered them to make a lock in the belly of the cow. So the goldsmiths did as they were told.

Three days later the girl took water and bread with her and entered the belly of the golden cow and locked herself into it, for she was very much ashamed at the thought of a marriage with her father.

When the Shah sent a message to her to come and be married to him they sought for her everywhere, but could not find her.

The Shah, as he could not find her, waited for three months. Then his viziers aid to him, "What is the use of the golden cow which you caused to be made? We must sell it." So they offered it for sale, and the King of India bought it and took it to his house. At midnight, while he was sleeping, the girl who was in the belly of the golden cow came out to look for food and water, for the bread and water which she had taken with her were finished. While she was looking for food the King saw her and was much astonished, for she was the most beautiful girl he had ever seen. So he took hold of her and said, "Who are you? Are you a fairy or a human being?" The girl replied, "I am a human being; I am the daughter of the King of Persia." And she told him all that had happened.

Then he said to her, "I will marry you instead of one of my cousins. But I am about to travel to another country, for I have work to do there. While I am absent you must stay in the belly of the cow lest perchance one of the daughters of my uncle should hear of you and kill you. I will tell my mother to bring you food for every meal and to place it before the cow. When she departs, you can come out and eat as you wish."

Before he left the King brought his mother to see the cow and said to her, "Act kindly with the cow, as you act with me." So his mother said, "Will the cow eat?" He replied, "Oh, it will eat, and you must put food before her for every meal, and leave the room as soon as you can, shutting the door behind you, or the cow will take cold and die." And he went on his way.

At midday the King's mother cooked meat and took it with a jar of water and put it in front of the cow, and left the room quickly and locked the door. After a while the girl came out of the cow and ate a good meal. Half an hour later the mother of the King returned to see what had happened, and found that the food had been eaten and the water drunk, and she said, "I must believe my son, for the cow has eaten the food which I placed in front of her."

Now the three daughters of the King's uncle saw that the King did not wish to take one of them to wife, and they said, "Surely he has found something inside the golden cow, and we must discover what it is." A day later the youngest girl went to the King's mother and asked her to give her the cow, so that her sisters might see it. But the King's mother refused. The next day the eldest girl went to the mother of the King and asked her for the cow. And the mother did not refuse this time, for, she said to herself, "It will be a shame to refuse twice." And she gave the cow to the girl, saying, "You must offer it food at every meal." And the girl said, "Very well," and took it to her home.

At midnight they brought the cow to a special place and made a fire under its belly to melt the gold. When the girl inside the cow felt the heat she came out, whereupon the three girls took hold of her and began to beat her severely, exclaiming, "Ah, you are going to marry, are you? We will kill you." So they made a box and put her inside it and locked it and threw it into the sea.

At daybreak they returned with the cow to the King's house. Then the King's mother cooked food and put it in front of it. And after a while she went again to see what had happened. But she found that the cow had not eaten its food as usual. So she began to cry, fearing her son the King.

Next day the King returned home, and he asked his mother about the golden cow. His mother said, "I did my best with it." At supper they put food in front of the cow, and the King stood by to see the girl. But she did not come.

So he ordered some of his servants to boil a big cauldron full of water and had his mother brought to him, and he said, " I will put you in this boiling water if you do not tell me what has happened to my cow." So she told all that had happened.

Then the King resolved to kill the daughter who had taken the cow from his house. First he married her. The next day he struck her severely and bade her tell him what she had done with his cow. So she told him all that had happened. Then he took a sword and cut off her head, and also cut her body up into pieces. He then put the flesh in a basket and threw it inside the house of her parents and hanged her head on the door of their house.

Now a certain fisherman came at daybreak to the place where the box had been cast into the sea, and threw in his hook to catch fish. Finding that it was very hard to draw in his line, he took his clothes off and dived into the sea and found a big box. So he took it out and went to his house, where he opened it and found in it a very beautiful girl.

The girl asked him about his business, and the fisherman said to her, " I am a poor fisherman, and I have no business at all except fishing." So she told him that she was going to weave him beautiful clothes, and that he could sell these clothes and live on the proceeds.

One day she made a beautiful cloth, weaving into it an account of all her adventures, and then bade him go and sell it to the King of India. When the King saw it and read the writing which was on it he was very glad, and said to the fisherman, " If you will bring me the lady who made this cloth I will give you a great sum of money as a reward." So the fisherman went back and told the girl all that had happened to him. Then the girl was very happy and said, " Very well, you must take me with you." So the fisherman took her to the King of India, who, when he saw her, kissed her many times, and wept. And he gave the man a great sum of money as he had promised.

And he made a feast for forty days, and when this was ended he married the Princess of Persia.

The Story of a Brick-maker

Once upon a time the wife of a brick-maker said, " O God, give me a boy like a camel ! " So God heard her prayer and gave her a son like a camel.

The king of the city had seven beautiful daughters, and they went to see this boy who resembled a camel.

When they had departed the boy said to his mother, " I want to take the youngest daughter of the King as my wife." But his mother said,

" O my son, you are a camel. How can you marry the daughter of a king ? " Then he said, " Never mind. I am going to give you a golden tray and also cups of gold, and you must go to the house of the King and enter it and give them to the King's wife. If one of the doorkeepers speaks to you give him some money, but do not speak to anyone at all."

So the woman took the tray with the golden cups and entered the palace of the King, and placed them before his wife, and then went away without speaking a word.

The next day the camel gave his mother a beautiful table with golden dishes upon it, and said, " Go to the palace of the King and place these before his wife, but do not speak."

When the King came and saw these beautiful things he said to his wife, " If the woman comes again you must ask her what she wants."

So when the woman arrived on the third day the wife of the King said to her, " What do you want ? " And she said, " I want your youngest daughter to be the wife of my son, the camel."

When the King came and heard this he was very much astonished, and he called his vizier and said to him, " How can I give my daughter to a camel ? We must consult together on this matter for a while."

Then the vizier said to the King, " I think that the camel must be a rich and noble man, for he sends you such precious things, the like of which your Majesty does not possess. I think he must be very rich and that you may give your consent. But first you must name a high price for your daughter ; if he agrees well and good, we will give her to him ; but if he refuses it will be better for you to deny him his request."

So, when the mother went again to the palace she was told that the King approved of her request, but as a war had broken out between the King and another country and he needed money and arms he required that the son should bring one hundred camels loaded with guns and rifles as the price of his daughter's hand.

Then the mother went home and said to her son, " O my son, the King has asked me for such and such things, and you cannot possibly obtain them, for we are very poor. Your father is only a brick-maker, and we live in a cottage made of *būṣ*.[1] Whence can we get these things ?"

But the camel said, " Fear not, O my mother. Stay here till I come back." Then he went out and brought a rope and hung it in the doorway of his cottage, and told his mother to take an end of the rope in her hand and to walk to the King's palace. So his mother took hold of the rope and started on her way.

As she went along a number of camels, over two hundred in number, loaded with guns and rifles, followed, and when she reached the King's palace she offered them to the vizier. Then the vizier told the King that the mother of the camel had brought more than two hundred camels,

[1] Dried *dura*-stalks.

"and," he continued, "I think, therefore, that we should give her your daughter to be her son's wife."

The King followed this counsel, and sent a message to the camel that he was ready to give him his young daughter. So the camel caused a notice to appear in the papers that he was about to marry the King's daughter, and he invited some of his friends and gave them a supper. After supper they went to the King's palace and brought the bride to the camel's house.

Then the camel placed a sword between him and his bride, and said to her, "I am going to show you a secret thing." Then he took off his skin, and, behold! he was a very beautiful fairy prince with golden hair.

At daybreak the mother of the bride made some nice biscuits for her daughter and also prepared a dish of macaroni, suspecting that the camel would eat it instead of straw. When she came to her daughter to offer her these things, she asked her about the camel. The daughter said, "It is a camel, my mother, not a human being," and did not tell her mother what she had seen at night.

Before the camel went out he brought his wife a gold tray on which were golden dishes full of delicious food, and he ordered her to offer her mother some breakfast, which she was to take to the King's palace.

When the King saw these precious things he was much astonished, and said to his vizier, "Surely this camel is a very rich man; he always offers us precious things which we do not possess."

On the seventh day after the marriage, as is the custom to the present day, the King and his wife took some beautiful presents to offer to their daughter. When they reached the place they found that the cottage was burned down and that no one was to be seen. But the camel had taken his wife, his mother, and his father and had gone to a distant place, where, after he had prayed to God, a beautiful palace, built of gold and silver bricks and surrounded with flowers, arose upon the spot. The palace, also, was protected by a large number of soldiers. Then the camel took off his skin and became the prince of these parts.

After a while the King and his vizier wandered about, dressed as Arabs, trying to find the King's daughter. One day they were passing near the palace when they were observed by the Prince, who ordered one of his soldiers to bring in these strange men, who, he said, doubtless were thieves. And they were cast into prison.

After three days had passed the men were brought before the Prince, and he asked, "Where were you going?" The King and his vizier replied, "We have a daughter whom we married to a camel, and we are trying to find her." The Prince asked, "How can a camel marry a girl?" And the King answered, "I gave him my daughter."

While they were thus speaking the King's daughter looked out of a window, and her father saw her and recognized her, but he could not speak because he was in the presence of a prince.

Then the Prince said to the King, " I am the camel who took your daughter, but now I am a prince, and God made me what you see me."

So the King was full of joy, and the Prince became king in his stead. And that's all !

The King and the Story-teller

Once upon a time there was a king who had a story-teller. And this story-teller had a son and two daughters. Three years after the birth of the youngest child the story-teller died, but before his death he said to his son, " My son, if a poor man comes and wishes to marry one of your sisters give one to him if he is a noble and honest man. But if a rich man comes and asks for one of them, and he is not an honourable man, do not grant his request."

Now one day an Arab, who was an honourable man, came to the boy and asked him for one of his sisters. The boy said, " Very well, I will consider the matter, and will give you an answer in two days' time."

During the two days he made inquiries as to the man's character among the members of his tribe. They told him that the Arab was a thoroughly good man, but that he had no house and was living in a tent. So the boy went to the man and said, " I will give you one of my sisters, but first take £1000 and build a good house here." And after the house was built the boy gave the Arab more money to buy the furniture, and also some camels.

Three days later the marriage was celebrated, and the bridegroom made a great feast for the Arabs with the camels, which he had killed.

Next a rich man came and asked the boy if he might marry the other sister. The boy replied once again, " I will send you an answer in two days' time." As a result of his inquiries he learned that the man was very rich, but not honourable.

However, he said to himself, " Nevertheless, I will give my sister to him ; I will then see what will happen." So he gave the girl to the rich man, thus disobeying his father's wishes.

A week later the boy wrote a letter to the King to whom his father had been story-teller and asked that he might be taken into the royal service. When he read it the King said, " Let the boy come here, for he is the son of my story-teller."

After a while the boy returned to his own home and said to his mother, " O my mother, my father, before he died, told me never to do good things to human beings, but to be kind and do good things to dogs. He also said that I must make friends of dogs, not of human beings."

Now the King had a fierce dog, and the boy was in the habit of giving this dog a fine pie every morning. The King had also a small gazelle, of which he was very fond. One day the boy asked the keeper of the gazelle to accept some money from him and to give him the gazelle in exchange. So the boy took the gazelle and put it in a special place and brought a keeper to look after it. The next morning the King made inquiries for his gazelle, which had disappeared. A poor man, who was living near the house in which the gazelle was kept by the boy, went to the King and told him that his gazelle was in the house of a person whom the son of the story-teller had engaged to look after it.

So the King called the keeper to him and said, " I will cut off your head if you do not tell me about the man who stole my gazelle." On hearing this the man was very frightened, and said, "This boy [pointing to the son of the King's story-teller] who is sitting beside you brought it to me one day and ordered me to look after it." So the King said to the boy, " Why have you treated me in this way? Your father was a faithful man. I will tell my fierce dog to eat you."

Then they brought the dog to eat the boy. And when the dog came it began to jump and spring up at the boy, and licked his hands and played with him, and was overjoyed to be with him. When the King saw this he was very much astonished, and said, "What have you done to my dog?" The boy said, " I have done nothing at all, but my father told me to be always kind to dogs." Then the King forgave him.

But a week later the boy wished to test the words which his father had spoken to him. So he stole the gazelle a second time, and put it in a house in the city, and brought a man whom he ordered to look after it. The King was very angry when he heard that his gazelle was again lost. Three days later a man came and said to him, " O King, live for ever! I know the man who took the gazelle. He is the boy who is sitting beside you."

Then the King said to the boy, " Surely I will cut off your head in a week's time." But the boy begged the King to allow him to return to his own house in order that he might see his mother and his two sisters. And the King allowed him to go.

When the boy went back to his home he took some presents and went to the house of his sister who had married the Arab, and he told her and her husband about all that had happened to him. Then the Arab wept bitterly and said, " Surely I will ask the King to cut off my head instead of yours." But the boy said, " Never. I will not consent to such a thing," and left him.

A day later the boy went to the house of his other sister, who had married the rich man, and told her and her husband all that had happened. Then the husband said to the boy, "You are very bad, and your father and mother are also very bad. Why did you steal the King's gazelle? You deserve the punishment."

So the boy left him and went back to his mother's house. Three days later he returned to the King's palace as he had promised, and his rich brother-in-law and his Arab brother-in-law followed him. When they reached the palace the Arab came forward and said to the King, "O King, live for ever! you must cut off my head instead of this boy's." But the rich man said nothing.

Then the boy said to the King, "O King, live for ever! I will repeat three sayings to you before you cut off my head." And the King gave him leave.

So the boy began to speak, and he said, "My father gave me three pieces of advice, and I wished to test them. And the first is, 'You must do good to dogs, not to human beings'; the second is, 'Give your sisters to poor but honourable men'; and the third is, 'Do not give your sisters to rich and dishonourable men.' So I made a practice of giving a pie every morning to your fierce dog, and I stole your gazelle. Then you threw me to the dog to be eaten by him, but your dog remembered the kindness I had shown him, and he would not harm me, but licked my hands and played with me. The second saying I tested by giving one of my sisters to this poor, honourable man, and he came forward just now and wished to give his life for mine. The third I tested by giving my other sister to this rich and dishonourable man, and he blamed me much and never did me one good turn. Therefore I am between your hands, and it is for you to do with me as you wish."

Then the King said to the boy, "You are very clever." And he pardoned him and gave him a post of honour in his palace.

The Cat and the Rat

Once upon a time there was a rat that was very hungry. And while he was searching for food a cat met him. So he hid himself behind a pillar. And the cat said to him, "O rat, let us go and look after the hens." To which the rat replied, "My father told me never to trust or associate with one's enemy." Then the cat said to the rat, "My dear, I am a pilgrim, and I am wearing a large rosary, and I have made a vow to God that I will never injure any rat, and I pray all day long."

So the rat went to tell his mother what the cat had said. But his mother said, "O my son, do not go with your enemy, for your father told you never to do so." But the rat said, "O my mother, he is a pilgrim, and he has a large rosary hung over his neck, by which he counts his prayers." So his mother said, "Very well, you can go."

He then set off, and said to the cat, "It is all right, I will accompany you." Three days later the cat became very hungry, so he killed the rat and ate it.

The moral of this story is, Do not trust or associate with your enemy.

CHAPTER XVIII

ANCIENT EGYPTIAN ANALOGIES

I WISH to make it quite clear that in this chapter I am by no means supplying a full list of the ancient analogies with which I am acquainted. My intention is merely to give the reader some idea of the importance of this particular branch of my research. In my strictly scientific account of the *fellāḥīn*, to which I have referred in the Preface, the question of survivals will be dealt with very fully.

As I am shortly publishing a book which deals exclusively with Coptic saints and Muslim sheikhs, to be followed later by a book on modern Egyptian medicine-men and their remedies, I am here omitting all references to the numerous and important survivals connected with the cults of those saints and sheikhs, and I am only just touching on the resemblances of the modern to the ancient magico-medical prescriptions.

An ancient Egyptian town and village must have presented much the same appearance as an Upper Egyptian town and village of to-day.[1] Then as now (pp. 27 f.) the better sort of house had one or more upper stories,[2] was doubtless often whitewashed or colour-washed,[3] and had a staircase probably (as is now frequently the case) of brick, leading from floor to floor and on to the roof, where were erected exactly the same mud granaries (p. 28) as are to be seen there nowadays (see Fig. 154).

On the roof of an ancient as of a modern house were often placed two *malāḳif* (singular *malḳaf*),[4] the ventilators by means of which the north and south wind are conveyed into the house during the hot weather.

[1] See A. M. Blackman, *Luxor and its Temples* (London, 1923), p. 4; T. E. Peet and C. L. Woolley, *The City of Akhenaten*, Part I (London, 1923), p. 54 and note 1.

[2] A. Wiedemann, *Das alte Ägypten* (Heidelberg, 1920), p. 168; A. Erman and H. Ranke, *Aegypten und aegyptisches Leben im Altertum* (Tübingen, 1923), pp. 190 ff.; W. Wreszinski, *Atlas zur altaegyptischen Kulturgeschichte* (Leipzig, 1923), Pl. 60*a*.

[3] Nina de Garis Davies, *The Tombs of Two Officials of Tuthmosis the Fourth* (London, 1923), Pl. XXXIV, p. 30.

[4] A. Erman and H. Ranke, *op. cit.*, pp. 205 f.; A. Wiedemann, *op. cit.*, p. 168; N. de Garis Davies, *op. cit.*, p. 30.

The poorer classes lived in tumbledown dwellings similar to those in which they live at the present time, as can be seen from the clay models of such houses dating from the Herakleopolitan Period (*c.* 2445–2160 B.C.).[1] Houses exactly like those of the respectable but not well-to-do *fellāḥīn* have recently been found at el-ʿAmarneh.[2]

The portico, so marked a feature of the better type of modern

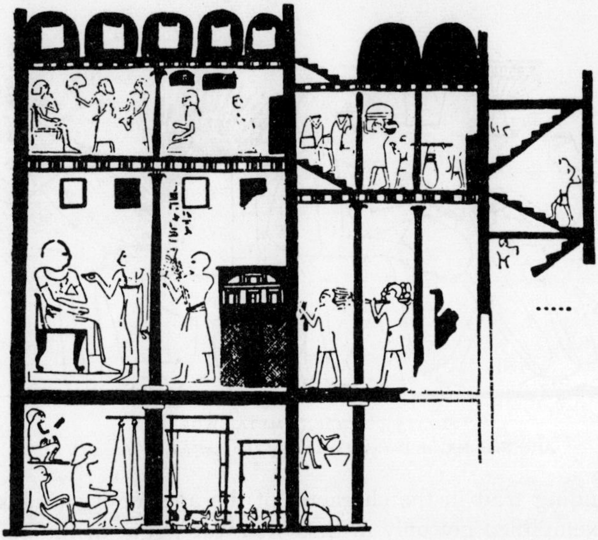

FIG. 154. AN ANCIENT EGYPTIAN TWO-STORIED HOUSE
After A. M. Blackman, *Luxor and its Temples*, p. 3.

house (*cf.* p. 228, Fig. 134), especially the country house or house enclosed in a garden, was no less a feature of the ancient mansions also, as can be seen from numerous representations of such belonging to different periods.[3]

The *maṣṭabeh* outside the house-door (p. 32) was probably no less frequent in an ancient than it is in a modern Egyptian town

[1] H. Schaefer and W. Andrae, *Die Kunst des alten Orients* (Berlin, 1925), p. 267; W. Wreszinski, *op. cit.*, Pl. 48*b*, 2.

[2] T. E. Peet and C. L. Woolley, *op. cit.*, pp. 55 ff.; see also W. Wreszinski, *op. cit.*, Pl. 48*b*, 4.

[3] See, for example, J. Capart, *L'art égyptien*, vol. i, "L'architecture" (Brussels, 1922), Pl. 11*b*; A. Erman and H. Ranke, *op. cit.*, p. 207; H. E. Winlock, "The Egyptian Expedition, 1918–1920," Part II of *The Bulletin of the Metropolitan Museum of Art, New York*, December, 1920, pp. 24 f.

or village.[1] Doubtless, too, the ancient craftsmen were to be seen at work in the open shops as are their descendants to-day; and here it is to be noted that a support, somewhat resembling that upon which the modern coppersmith rests his vessel in order to hammer it into shape (p. 32), is depicted in numerous New Kingdom paintings of metal-workers plying their tasks [2] (Fig. 155).

I have spoken (p. 23) of the light-heartedness of the modern Egyptians. This, as my brother has pointed out to me, was an

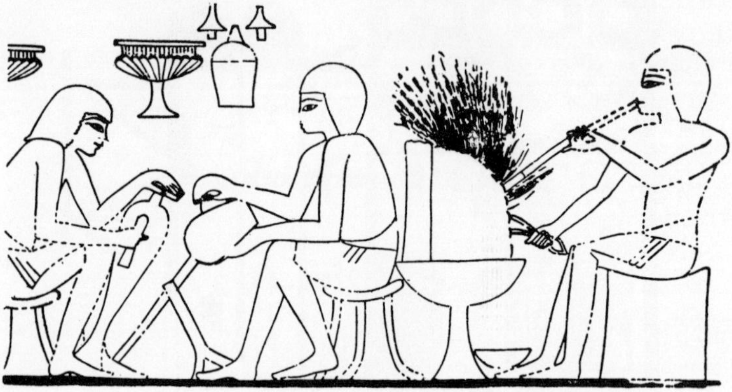

FIG. 155. ANCIENT METAL-WORKERS
After Nina de Garis Davies, *The Tomb of Two Sculptors at Thebes*, Pl. XI.

outstanding trait in the character of the ancient Egyptians, as is well exemplified not only in their literature,[3] but in the paintings and sculptures which adorn the tomb-chapels of the wealthy, and which depict feasting, sport,[4] pastimes, and daily life in general. The Egyptians devoted all this labour and expenditure to the construction and decoration of their Houses of Eternity not because they were always morbidly brooding over death, but because they hated death and loved life and all that life stands for.[5]

I have pointed out on pp. 38 f. that it is to her brother that a

[1] See A. M. Blackman, *op. cit.*, p. 4.

[2] *E.g.* W. Wreszinski, *op. cit.*, Pls. 36, 59*a*, 228, 241, 242, 317.

[3] See A. Erman, *The Literature of the Ancient Egyptians*, translated by A. M. Blackman (London, 1927), especially pp. 36 ff., 133, 242 ff., 251 ff.; W. Spiegelberg, *The Credibility of Herodotus' Account of Egypt*, translated by A. M. Blackman (Oxford, 1927), p. 29.

[4] *Cf.* A. H. Gardiner, *Journal of Egyptian Archæology*, vol. ix, pp. 9, 12 and note 4, 15 and note 9; A. Erman, *op. cit.*, pp. 119, 122, 125.

[5] On this subject see especially A. H. Gardiner, " Life and Death (Egyptian)," in Hastings, *Encyclopædia of Religion and Ethics*, vol. viii, pp. 19 ff.

woman has recourse when trouble arises between her and her husband. This is evidently a deeply rooted custom, for in the *Complaints of the Peasant*, a literary work of the Herakleopolitan Period (*c.* 2445–2160 B.C.), the peasant flatteringly describes the High Steward Rensi, to whom all his nine petitions are addressed, as " the brother of her that is put away."[1] Unfaithfulness in a wife was evidently punished with death in ancient[2] as it is in modern Egypt. Within the last year or two a case came to my knowledge of an unchaste girl being burned to death by her father and other male relatives, an act that may be compared with the burning of the faithless wife of the chief lector Ubaoner in one of the stories in *King Kheops and the Magicians*.[3]

The love of son for mother, of which I have spoken on p. 45, was evidently as strong in ancient Egyptian families as it is to-day. The following injunction of the sage Anii to his son in respect of his mother bears a striking resemblance to what my friend (p. 45) said to me about his own mother :

> Double the bread that thou givest to thy mother, and carry her as she carried [thee]. She had a heavy load in thee, and never left it to me. When thou wast born after thy months, she carried thee yet again about her neck, and for three years her breast was in thy mouth. She was not disgusted at thy dung, she was not disgusted, and said not : " What do I ? " She put thee to school, when thou hadst been taught to write, and daily she stood there . . . with bread and beer from her house. When thou art a young man and takest to thee a wife and art settled in thine house, keep before thee how thy mother gave birth to thee, and how she brought thee up further in all manner of ways. May she not do thee harm nor lift up her hands to God, and may he not hear her cry.[4]

The modern Egyptian women closely resemble their ancestors in their love of personal adornment, though, to be sure, the jewellery of to-day, particularly the earrings and bracelets, are less massive than they were, at least in the Eighteenth and Nineteenth Dynasties. The bead collars worn by many of the modern peasant women are very much like those that the women are depicted as wearing in paintings and reliefs of all periods.

Tattooing (pp. 50 ff.) may have been practised in the predynastic age.[5] But that this method of personal adornment was

[1] A. Erman, *op. cit.*, p. 119.
[2] *Ibid.*, pp. 38, 161 and note 3.
[3] *Ibid.*, p. 38.
[4] *Ibid.*, p. 239 ; see also A. M. Blackman, *Luxor and its Temples*, pp. 25 f.
[5] J. Capart, *Primitive Art in Egypt* (London, 1905), pp. 23, 30.

in vogue in Egypt during the Middle Kingdom (2160–1788 B.C.) is definitely proved by a blue faience figure of a girl dating from the Eleventh to Thirteenth Dynasty and by the mummies of two girls dating from the Eleventh Dynasty. Both the mummies and the faience figure have tattoo marks on the body and the limbs.[1]

Either locks of false hair fastened on, or whole wigs, were commonly used by the ancient Egyptian women.[2] The long plaits of hair worn by the modern peasant women (p. 56) can certainly be matched in ancient times;[3] Professor Petrie found a long plait of hair and a false fringe even in a First-Dynasty royal tomb at Abydos.[4] We have no indication, however, that the plaits served the same utilitarian purposes that they often serve nowadays (see p. 56)! It is to be observed that the wooden combs used to-day in dressing the hair (p. 56, Fig. 26) are very like the ancient ones (Fig. 156).

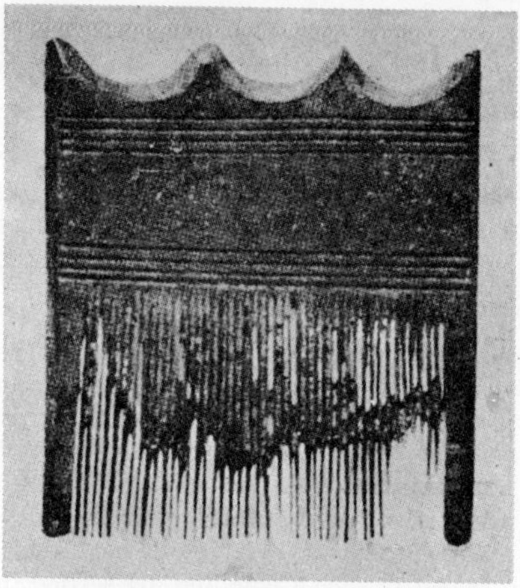

FIG. 156. ANCIENT COMB

After A. Erman and H. Ranke, *Aegypten und aegyptisches Leben im Altertum*, Pl. 19, 1.

The painting of the eyes with *koḥl* was practised as much in ancient times as it is at the present day (p. 59), and by both men and women. In a satirical papyrus dating from the later New Kingdom, and now preserved in the Turin Museum, there is a caricature of a woman looking into a hand-mirror and 'making up.'[5] The constant references to perfumes in the ancient religious and literary texts[6] make it evident that the modern love of scent (p. 59) is not a recently acquired taste.

[1] H. E. Winlock, "The Egyptian Expedition, 1922–1923," Part II of *The Bulletin of the Metropolitan Museum of Art, New York*, December, 1923, pp. 22, 26, 28.

[2] A. Erman, *op. cit.*, pp. 153, 248; G. Elliot Smith and Warren R. Dawson, *Egyptian Mummies* (London, 1924), p. 117, Fig. 33.

[3] A. Erman and H. Ranke, *op. cit.*, p. 243.

[4] W. M. F. Petrie, *Abydos*, Part I (London, 1902), Pl. IV, Fig. 7.

[5] A. Erman and H. Ranke, *op. cit.*, p. 258.

[6] *E.g.* A. Erman, *op cit.*, pp. 28, 33, 61, 133, 209, 244, 247, 249, 252.

The men's custom of cutting the hair short or shaving their heads entirely (p. 57) is very ancient. Paintings of barbers shaving or cropping men's heads occur in two tomb-chapels of the Middle [1] and in one of the New Kingdom.[2] In the New Kingdom painting (Fig. 157) the barbers are quite clearly plying their trade out of doors, as they so often do at the present day. The well-known *Instruction of Duauf* speaks of the barber shaving " late into the evening, . . . he betaketh himself from street to street in order to seek him whom he may shave." [3]

FIG. 157. ANCIENT EGYPTIAN BARBERS AT WORK
After W. Wreszinski, *Atlas zur altaegyptischen Kulturgeschichte*, Pl. 44.

The custom of shaving off the body hair (p. 57) is certainly ancient. Herodotus,[4] it is true, speaks of it only in connexion with the priests, but there is some evidence that it was practised by both sexes, as at the present day.[5] Herodotus [6] tells us that " the Egyptians, on occasions of death, let the hair grow both on the head and on the face, though till then wont to shave." This custom still obtains, as can be seen from my statements on p. 58.

Two articles of clothing, the veil for women and the *gallabīyeh*, may be quite ancient. There is possibly a reference to the former

[1] See L. Klebs, *Die Reliefs und Malereien des mittleren Reiches* (Heidelberg, 1922), p. 41 ; *cf.* also A. Erman, *op. cit.*, p. 28.
[2] A. Erman and H. Ranke, *op. cit.*, Pl. 20, Fig. 1 ; W. Wreszinski, *op. cit.*, Pl. 44.
[3] A. Erman, *op. cit.*, p. 69.
[4] ii, 37.
[5] See A. M. Blackman, " Purification (Egyptian)," in Hastings, *op. cit.*, vol. x, pp. 477, 481 ; *Journal of Egyptian Archæology*, vol. x, p. 200.
[6] ii, 36.

in an inscription of Ramesses III at Medīnet Habu,[1] and the Egyptian peasants seem to have been wearing a garment very like the latter, only sleeveless, by the early Ptolemaic period, judging from the reliefs in the tomb of Petosiris at Derweh ; [2] but the *gallabīyeh* may date back even to the Sixth Dynasty.[3] It should be observed that women wearing veils on their heads like those worn by the modern peasant women in many parts of Egypt occur several times in those reliefs in the tomb of Petosiris that are executed in Greek style.[4]

It might here be mentioned that blue was the colour for mourning in ancient Egypt,[5] and that dark blue as well as black is still the mourning colour in modern Egypt (see pp. 50, 111, 264, 295).

I have not, as I should, referred in the previous chapters to the custom of washing before and after a meal and before private and public prayers. This is a very old custom and is often referred to in the ancient Egyptian literary and religious texts.[6]

It was evidently considered as important to have a large family in ancient as it is in modern Egypt (see p. 97). The sage Anii advises his son to "take a wife when thou art a youth, that she may give thee a son. Thou shouldst beget him for thee whilst thou art yet young, and shouldst live to see him become a man [?]. Happy is the man who hath much people, and he is respected because of his children." [7]

Several of the ceremonies connected with birth can be shown to be of ancient origin. Apart from the reference in the Old Testament,[8] the existence of professional midwives in ancient Egypt is suggested by the account of the birth of the divinely begotten triplets of Red-djedet in the tales of *King Kheops and the Magicians*, which dates from the time of the Twelfth Dynasty (2000–1788 B.C.).[9] In earliest times the Egyptian women squatted to

[1] J. H. Breasted, *Ancient Records*, vol. iv (Chicago, 1906), § 47.
[2] M. G. Lefebvre, *Tombeau de Petosiris*, vol. iii (Cairo, 1924), Pls. XII–XV.
[3] See W. M. F. Petrie, *Deshasheh* (London, 1898), pp. 31 f.
[4] M. G. Lefebvre, *op. cit.*, Pls. XIX, XX, XLXVI.
[5] A. H. Gardiner, *Zeitschrift für ägyptische Sprache*, vol. xlvii, pp. 162 f.
[6] For a number of interesting references see A. M. Blackman, "Purification (Egyptian)," in Hastings, *op. cit.*, vol. x, pp. 477, 480 f., *Luxor and its Temples*, p. 7, *Journal of Egyptian Archæology*, vol. v, pp. 153, 154 and note 5.
[7] A. Erman, *op. cit.*, p. 235.
[8] Exodus i, 16.
[9] A. Erman, *op. cit.*, pp. 44 ff.

give birth, with either foot planted on a brick.[1] From these two bricks was developed a structure resembling in outline the modern confinement chair (p. 63), but, so Professor Spiegelberg supposes, made of brick. A confinement chair of this kind was already in use in the Old Kingdom (2900–2475 B.C.).[2] It would be interesting to know at what date the wooden confinement chair replaced the brick structure. It may have done so at quite an early period, and " the brick," which is the designation of the bearing-stool even in a Nineteenth-Dynasty text, may be simply an archaism.

The midwife or female attendant in ancient times cut the umbilical cord [3] as she does to-day (p. 63). But unfortunately it is no longer the custom to wash the child immediately after birth.[4] This performance is now put off till the seventh day after that, and even then the child is only partly washed (p. 76).

Importance was evidently attached to the placenta (see pp. 63 ff.) in ancient times ; there seems to have been a priest of the royal placenta.[4] The umbilical cord seems also to have been preserved as it is to-day (pp. 64, 79), for in the Myth of Horus we are told how that god set out to obtain the umbilical cord of his father Osiris, which had fallen into the hands of Sēth, Osiris' murderer, and how, having won it from Sēth, Horus buried it in the place sacred to Osiris in Herakleopolis Magna.[5]

It is to be observed that the sieve played a part in ancient as in modern birth ceremonies (pp. 63, 79), for Anubis is shown trundling one in the scene in the temple of Ḥatshepsut at Deir el-Baḥri which represents the gods determining the duration of the new-born royal infant's life.[6] This determining of the duration of the royal child's life may be compared, perhaps, with the modern naming ceremony on the seventh day after birth (pp. 78 ff.). In ancient Egypt, however, a child's name seems to have been given it at birth,[7] and, anyhow in the case of a princely family, to have been also registered.[8] On the other hand, it is to be noted that

[1] W. Spiegelberg, *Aegyptologisches Randglossar zum Alten Testament* (Strassburg, 1904), pp. 19 ff.
[2] As can be seen from the determinative of the word in K. Sethe, *Die altägyptischen Pyramidentexte*, § 1180.
[3] A. Erman, *op. cit.*, p. 45.
[4] A. Erman, *ibid.*
[5] A. M. Blackman, *Journal of Egyptian Archæology*, vol. iii, pp. 243 ff.
[6] *Ibid.*, p. 204.
[7] A. M. Blackman, *Luxor and its Temples*, pp. 168 ff.
[8] A. Erman, *op. cit.*, p. 45.
[9] F. Ll. Griffith, *Stories of the High Priests of Memphis* (Oxford, 1900), p. 19.

festivities connected with the birth of a child took place in ancient Egypt, certainly during the Middle Kingdom, fourteen days after birth, a mother being accounted unclean until she had purified herself with a fourteen days' purification.[1]

FIG. 158. KHNUM MODELLING THE ROYAL CHILD AND ITS KA
After A. Gayet, *Le temple de Louxor*, Pl. LXIII.

I have stated on pp. 67, 99, 100 (see also p. 63) that a belief in reincarnation exists among the *fellāḥīn*. It seems also to have existed among the ancient Egyptians, anyhow in the late New Kingdom, judging from certain episodes in the *Tale of the Two Brothers*.[2]

The statements on pp. 69 ff. about the *ḳarīn* and *ḳarīneh* recall the ancient Egyptian belief about the *ka*. The modern idea that the *ḳarīn* is born at the same time as its human counterpart calls to mind the reliefs in the temples of Luxor and Deir el-Baḥri [3] depicting the god Khnum modelling

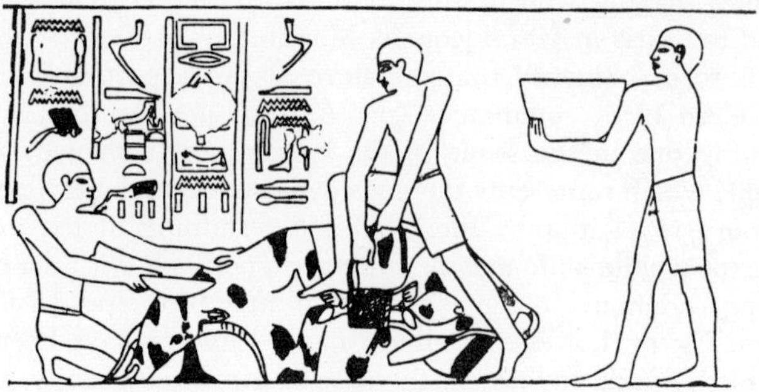

FIG. 159. MAN HOLDING A BASIN AT THE SLAUGHTER OF A VICTIM
After A. M. Blackman, *The Rock Tombs of Meir*, Part I, Pl. XI.

the royal child and its *ka* (see Fig. 158) and their simultaneous birth.

In modern Egypt a child is suckled for two years (p. 81); in

[1] A. Erman, *op. cit.*, p. 46.
[2] A. Erman, *ibid.*, pp. 158 ff.; see also Herodotus, ii, 123; W. Spiegelberg, *The Credibility of Herodotus' Account of Egypt*, p. 32.
[3] A. M. Blackman, *Luxor and its Temples*, p. 165.

ancient Egypt, according to the passage in the *Wisdom of Anii* quoted on p. 283, it was not weaned till it was three years old.

On p. 82, in describing the slaughter of a victim at a festival held on behalf of a child, I stated that the animal was placed on its back and its throat cut, and that a quantity of the blood was preserved in a bowl. Victims were slain exactly in this manner at ancient Egyptian festivals. In almost every decorated tombs chapel they are depicted extended on their backs with the butchers cutting their throats. Occasionally in these scenes an assistant is

FIG. 160. ANCIENT HARPER AND VOCALIST
After A. M. Blackman, *The Rock Tombs of Meir*, Part II, Pl. III.

shown holding a large bowl,[1] evidently to catch the blood (Fig. 159). Did the practice of smearing the door with blood exist in Egypt as far back as the Old Kingdom ? The blood was evidently required for some ceremonial purpose, otherwise what need would there have been for the basin ?

To sing or recite with one hand laid against a side of the face and the other hand extended (p. 82) is a very ancient practice (Fig. 160), and so, too, is the throwing of one's clothes about as a sign of admiration and rejoicing (p. 83). Thus in one of the *Pyramid Texts*,[2] dating from about 2600 B.C., we read how the dead king, having reached the celestial realm of the sun-god,

[1] A. M. Blackman, *The Rock Tombs of Meir*, Part I (London, 1914), Pl. XI ; *cf.* also Part IV (London, 1924), p. 27 ; P. Montet, *Les scènes de la vie privée dans les tombeaux égyptiens de l'ancien empire* (Strassburg, 1925), p. 165.

[2] K. Sethe, *Die altägyptischen Pyramidentexte*, Spruch 518.

"found the gods waiting, wrapped in their garments, their white sandals on their feet. Then cast they their sandals to the ground, then threw they off their garments. 'Our heart was not glad until thou camest,' said they."

The custom of shaving, in performance of a vow, a boy's head save for a number of tufts, which are dedicated to one or more Muslim or Coptic saints, and of ceremonially cutting off the tufts when they have grown to a certain length (pp. 84 ff.), is evidently very ancient. Clay balls containing infantile hair, such as are

FIG. 161. ANCIENT CLAY BALLS FROM EL-'AMARNEH, ONE BROKEN AND SHOWING INFANTILE HAIR INSIDE

described on p. 86, have been found both at el-'Amarneh (Fig. 161) and in a Twentieth-Dynasty tomb at el-Lāhūn.[1] Herodotus[2] seems to be referring to this or some very similar custom when he says:

> All the inhabitants of the cities perform their vows to the keepers [of the sacred animals] in the following manner. Having made a vow to the god to whom the animal belongs, they shave either the whole heads of their children, or a half, or a third of the head, and then weigh the hair in a scale against silver, and whatever the weight may be, they give to the keeper of the animals; and she in return cuts up some fish, and gives it as food to the animals. Such is the usual mode of feeding them.

Circumcision (pp. 87 f.) seems to have been practised universally in ancient times (as it is in modern Egypt) until the reign of the Emperor Hadrian, when it was restricted to candidates for the

[1] W. S. Blackman, *Man*, vol. xxv, pp. 65 ff.
[2] ii, 65.

priesthood.[1] A relief in an Old Kingdom tomb-chapel at Saḳḳāreh[2] depicts the circumcision of two boys, the operation being performed, anyhow in one case, by a funerary priest (*ḥm-kȝ*, "servant of the *ka*"). I mention on p. 88 that, when the barber is about to cut off the foreskin, the boy is taken hold of and told not to be afraid. In the above-mentioned relief one of the operators is represented as saying: "Hold him, do not let him move about [?]," to which the assistant replies: "I will do your bidding."

I refer on pp. 43, 47, and 90 to the early age at which modern Egyptian girls of the peasant class are often married. In Roman times we know that boys of fifteen married girls of twelve and thirteen.[3]

Charms to win love (pp. 90 ff., 224), and also to separate a man from his wife (*cf.* pp. 190 ff.), were employed in ancient Egypt, and examples of such are preserved in magical papyri dating from the Roman age.[4]

We possess a number of ancient Egyptian marriage contracts (*cf.* p. 92). The two earliest date from the reign of Takelōthis I or II, of the Twenty-second Dynasty (895–874 or 860–834 B.C.),[5] the rest mostly from Ptolemaic times.[6] A perfectly preserved marriage contract dating from the reign of the last native Egyptian Pharaoh, Nektanebos, was published a few years ago by Dr Junker.[7] As it is quite complete and as no English translation of it has ever appeared, I think the following may perhaps interest my readers:

> Year 15, second month of the season of Inundation, of Pharaoh Nektanebos (may he live, prosper, and be happy!): The *msḥ* [8] of Edfu, who belongeth to the Wall of Nektanebos,[9] Usir'an, son of Eskhons, whose mother is Tentmeḥet, saith to the lady Taubasti, daughter of Eskhons, whose mother is Tamunis: I have made thee my wife, I have given thee $\frac{5}{10}$ of a *deben* of silver, making $2\frac{1}{2}$ staters, making again $\frac{5}{10}$ of a *deben* of silver, as thy woman's gift.[10] If I abandon thee as wife [*i.e.*,

[1] See Herodotus, ii, 36 f., 104; G. Elliot Smith and Warren R. Dawson, *Egyptian Mummies*, p. 93; A. M. Blackman, "Priest, Priesthood (Egyptian)" in Hastings, *op. cit.*, vol. x, pp. 299 f.

[2] J. Capart, *Une rue de tombeaux*, Pl. LXVI.

[3] A. Erman and H. Ranke, *Aegypten und aegyptisches Leben im Altertum*, p. 180.

[4] F. Lexa, *La magie dans l'Egypte antique* (Paris, 1925), vol. ii, pp. 139 ff.

[5] G. Möller, *Zwei ägyptische Eheverträge aus vorsaïtische Zeit* (Berlin, 1918).

[6] See F. Ll. Griffith, *Catalogue of the Demotic Papyri in the John Rylands Library* (Manchester, 1909), vol. iii, pp. 114 ff., 139 ff.

[7] H. Junker, *Papyrus Lonsdorfer I* (Vienna, 1921).

[8] Unknown title.

[9] Either a fort built by Nektanebos or a quarter of the town newly founded by him.

[10] See F. Ll. Griffith, *op. cit.*, p. 114, note 8.

divorce thee] and hate thee and take me another wife beside thee, then will I give thee $\frac{5}{10}$ of a *deben* of silver, making $2\frac{1}{2}$ staters, making again $\frac{5}{10}$ of a *deben* of silver, apart from that $\frac{5}{10}$ of a *deben* of silver entered above, which I have given thee as thy woman's gift, so amounting in all to 1 *deben* of silver, making 5 staters, making again 1 *deben* of silver.

And I give thee $\frac{1}{3}$ of all the goods and all the possessions that I shall acquire, I together with thee.

The children whom thou shalt bear me are the owners of all the goods and all the possessions that I possess and that I shall acquire.

Herewith the list of the possessions which thou hast brought with thee into the house :

1 *hrḳ*, woven, which is 2 cubits long and $3\frac{1}{3}$ cubits wide, worth $\frac{3}{10}$ *deben* of silver.

1 *ḥmdt*, woven, which is 2 cubits long and $3\frac{1}{3}$ cubits wide, worth $2\frac{1}{2}$/10 *deben* of silver.

1 *inšn* of byssus, which is $5\frac{1}{2}$ cubits long, worth $1\frac{1}{2}$/10 *deben* of silver.

A woman's robe, worth $\frac{1}{10}$ *deben* of silver.

A chased [?] bronze mirror, worth $\frac{1}{10}$ *deben* of silver.

A woman's *msḥ*-garment, worth $\frac{1}{10}$ *deben* of silver.

A *hrḳ*-case, which is a bronze receptacle, worth $\frac{2}{10}$ *deben* of silver.

A silver ring, worth $\frac{1}{10}$ *deben* of silver.

The value of thy metal goods and thy woven goods which thou hast brought with thee into mine house amounteth in money value to $1\frac{4}{10}$ *deben* of silver, making 7 staters, making again $1\frac{4}{10}$ *deben* of silver.

While thou art within, they are within with thee. While thou art without, they are without with thee.[1] But if thou departest and desertest me thine husband, I will give thee $2\frac{1}{2}$/10 *deben* of silver, making $1\frac{1}{4}$ staters, making again $2\frac{1}{2}$/10 *deben* of silver, of those $\frac{5}{10}$ *deben* of silver entered above, which I have given thee as thy woman's gift.

Written by Harmakhoros son of Eskhons.

There then follows a list of witnesses.

As stated on p. 92, the bride is usually taken to her husband's house in the evening. Such, too, was the custom in ancient Egypt, certainly at the time when the *First Tale of Khamuas* was written, for in the account of the marriage of Ahure [2] we read how Pharaoh said to his steward : " Let Ahure be taken to the house of Neneferkaptaḥ to-night, and let all beautiful things be taken with her." We are also told that Pharaoh likewise had a present of silver and gold taken to Ahure, and that " all the household of Pharaoh caused themselves to be brought unto me [Ahure is speaking] ; and Neneferkaptaḥ made merry with me, and he

1 Meaning that the wife has absolute right of possession over the property which she has brought with her.

2 F. Ll. Griffith, *Stories of the High Priests* (Oxford, 1900), p. 18.

entertained all the household of Pharaoh." This account suggests that in ancient as in modern times the bride's furniture was conveyed with some ceremony from her parents' house to that of her husband (p. 93); we also see that the ancient like the modern bridegroom used to entertain his male friends on the night of his marriage (p. 93).

It is stated on p. 95 that a sum of money is sometimes paid by the party who applies for a divorce to the other party. That, as can be seen from the ancient marriage-contract translated above, and from those published by Professor Griffith,[1] was the prevailing custom in late Pharaonic and Ptolemaic Egypt. Ancient bills of divorcement are still extant, the earliest dating from the time of Darius, and some of them have been published and translated by Professor Griffith.[2]

It is interesting to observe, in connexion with the modern practice (p. 107) of a mother's attaching a small piece of fox-skin to the head of her last-born living child to ensure her bearing again, that the sign 𓄟 (*ms*), used in writing the verb *msy* (give birth) and its derivatives, consists in well-formed examples of three fox-skins tied together.[3] This suggests that there may have been some association of foxes with fertility in ancient Egypt.

The water used for washing a dead Muslim is brought either from a mosque or from some sacred well or pool connected with a sheikh (p. 109). Similarly, in ancient times the formulæ pronounced while the washing of the corpse took place state that the water has issued from Elephantine, and so is the exudation of Osiris, or that it has been drawn from some sacred pool connected with the sun-cult, or that it is the efflux of the sun-god or the womb of the sky-goddess out of which the god emerged.[4]

That the washer of the corpse may be a *fiḳīh* (p. 109) shows that this performance still possesses some, though probably quite vague, religious significance.

The utterly uncontrolled grief displayed by the women when

[1] See p. 291, footnote 6.

[2] *Catalogue of the Demotic Papyri in the John Rylands Library*, vol. iii, p. 117.

[3] See A. M. Blackman, *Man*, vol. ix, pp. 9 f.; L. Borchardt, *Zeitschrift für ägyptische Sprache*, vol. xliv, pp. 75 f.; A. Erman, *Zeitschrift für ägyptische Sprache*, vol. xlv, p. 92.

[4] See A. M. Blackman, *Recueil de travaux relatifs à la philologie et l'archéologie égyptiennes*, vol. xxxix, pp. 44 ff.; *Proceedings of the Society of Biblical Archæology*, vol. xl, pp. 57–66, 86–91; *Journal of Egyptian Archæology*, vol. v, pp. 117 ff., 157 ff.

a death occurs (pp. 111 f., 122 ff.) is still admirably illustrated by a relief in an Old Kingdom tomb-chapel at Saḳḳāreh.[1] The widow is depicted as having collapsed in a faint on hearing of her husband's sudden death, and then, after having been restored to consciousness and dragged to her feet, as tottering along supported by two friends. The various attitudes of grief of the women surrounding the widow are characteristic of modern female mourners. It is interesting to observe, too, that one of the attendants holds the widow's necklace, which has been taken off on receipt of the news of her husband's death (*cf.* p. 50). Further proof that the modern Egpytian peasant women display their grief before and at a funeral by exactly the same gestures and conduct as did their ancestors—by dishevelling the hair, tearing the clothes, exposing the breasts, gathering up mud and with it plastering the head, breasts, and arms, and by wildly waving the arms and beating the head and breasts—is to be found in numbers of ancient paintings and reliefs.[2] An admirable example is the photograph

FIG. 162. WAILING WOMEN
After W. Wreszinski, *Atlas zur altaegyptischen Kulturgeschichte*, Pl. 8.

[1] J. Capart, *Une rue de tombeaux*, Pls. LXXXI f.

[2] See W. Spiegelberg, *The Credibility of Herodotus' Account of Egypt*, Fig. 5 on p. 33; W. Wreszinski, *Atlas zur altaegyptischen Kulturgeschichte*, Pls. 120, 166, 167, 209, 210; Norman de Garis Davies, *The Tomb of Two Sculptors at Thebes* (New York, 1925), Pls. XIX ff. (Pl. XXI shows a woman placing mud or dust on her head); Nina de Garis Davies and A. H. Gardiner, *The Tomb of Amenemhēt* (London, 1915), Pl. XXIV; G. Roeder, *Die Denkmäler des Pelizaeus Museums zu Hildesheim* (Berlin, 1921), pp. 111 f.

(Fig. 162) of a painting in the tomb-chapel of Reʿmōse at Thebes.

The attitude of the wailing mother in Fig. 50, p. 110, and Fig. 137, p. 236, finds an exact parallel in the wailing women depicted in a painting in the tomb-chapel of Amenemḥēt at Thebes.[1]

The modern custom of smearing the hands, arms, and face with blue dye (pp. 111, 122, 264) may also be ancient, in view of blue having been the ancient mourning colour (p. 286); but, so far as my brother is aware, the ancient artists have not shown this in the pictures of wailing women.

FIG. 163. FUNERARY DANCE PERFORMED BY FEMALE MOURNERS
After W. Wreszinski, *op. cit.*, Pl. 419.

The perambulation of the town or village by the female relatives and friends immediately after a death has taken place (p. 109) is described by Herodotus [2] in the following words:

> When a member of any distinction dies in an household, all the female members of that family besmear their heads and faces with mud, and then, leaving the corpse in the house, they parade the town, and smite themselves, having their garments girt up and their breasts exposed; and all their female kin accompany them.

The pre- and post-burial dance performed by the mourning women, described on pp. 114, 123, 263, finds close parallel in a relief from a New Kingdom tomb-chapel at Saḳḳāreh, now in the Cairo Museum (Fig. 163). As in the funerary dance described on p. 114, the women are dancing to the beating of single-membrane

[1] Nina de Garis Davies and A. H. Gardiner, *ibid.*, bottom register, left.
[2] ii, 85.

drums. The attitude and motions of the wailing sister who advanced toward me with arms extended and swaying from side to side (p. 122) may perhaps be compared with those of the female dancers (musician-priestesses of Ḥatḥor) who are depicted performing at the funeral of Senet in that lady's tomb-chapel at Thebes.[1]

The viewing of the corpse by visitors and relatives, as it lies

FIG. 164. BRICK SUPERSTRUCTURE ABOVE A MIDDLE-KINGDOM GRAVE
After D. Randall-MacIver and C. L. Woolley, *Buhen*, Pl. 81.

extended on a bed, was evidently an ancient practice, for in a relief at el-ʿAmarneh [2] King Akhenaten and his wife Nefertiti are depicted taking a farewell look at the corpse of one of their daughters, which lies on a bed. Near at hand the women are wailing, as I have described them as doing in similar circumstances on p. 122.

Palm-branches were carried in ancient, as they are in modern, funeral processions (p. 116), as can be seen from the picture of

[1] Norman de Garis Davies, *The Tomb of Antefoḳer* (London, 1920), Pl. XXIII.
[2] A. Erman and H. Ranke, *Aegypten und aegyptisches Leben im Altertum*, p. 365, Fig. 164.

the funeral procession of a Nineteenth-Dynasty priest named Kynebu in his tomb-chapel at Sheikh ʿAbd-el-Ḳurneh.[1] The custom of slaughtering an animal at the graveside on the occasion of a funeral (p. 110) is, of course, exceedingly ancient, and is referred to in the *Story of Sinuhe*: "slaughtering is made at the door of thy façade-stela."[2] Was the false door, one wonders, sprinkled with the victim's blood?

With the statement on pp. 113 f.,[3] that on returning from the funeral "the men seat themselves outside the doorway, where they are joined by friends," is to be compared a passage in a letter written to his dead wife by an official of the late New Kingdom: "I bewailed thee exceedingly along with my household in front of my dwelling."[4]

FIG. 165. SHADOW AND BAI OUTSIDE THE DOOR OF A TOMB

After E. Naville, *Das aegyptische Todtenbuch der XVIII bis XX Dynastie*, vol. i, Pl. CIV.

The rectangular brick superstructure of a modern grave, with its vaulted roof and door-like recess at one end (p. 116), closely resembles the superstructure of the ordinary middle-class grave of all periods (see, for example, Fig. 164).[5] Ancient examples of the large burial chamber with vaulted roof described on p. 116 are also to be found.[6]

The idea that a man's shadow is a separate entity (p. 113) also prevailed in ancient Egypt. A vignette in an Eighteenth-Dynasty copy of *The Book of the Dead* depicts a man's shadow

[1] J. G. Wilkinson, *The Ancient Egyptians* (London, 1878), vol. iii, Pl. LXIX.

[2] A. Erman, *The Literature of the Ancient Egyptians*, p. 24; A. M. Blackman, *Journal of Egyptian Archæology*, vol. x, p. 199.

[3] *Cf.* also pp. 121 f.

[4] A. M. Blackman, *Luxor and its Temples*, p. 25.

[5] *E.g.*, W. M. F. Petrie, *Tarkhan* (London, 1914). Part II, Pl. XV; D. Randall-MacIver and C. L. Woolley, *Buhen* (Philadelphia, 1911), Pls 77–82.

[6] D. Randall-MacIver and C. L. Woolley, *op. cit.*, Pl. 84; H. Schaefer and W. Andrae, *Die Kunst des alten Orients*, p. 266, Fig. 2.

and his *bai* (soul, or manifestation [1]) outside the door of his tomb [2] (Fig. 165).

The weekly visit to the cemetery, the *Ṭalaʿ*, described on pp. 117 ff., and the performances there during the Muslim festivals of *el-ʿĪd eṣ-Ṣughaiyar* and *el-ʿĪd el-Kibīr* (pp. 259 ff.), and on the Coptic festival of *Yōm el-Ghiṭās*, are all undoubtedly survivals from the past. From the earliest times it was the custom to honour the memory of the dead at certain definite periods by celebrating the funerary liturgy in the tomb-chapel or at the graveside. This liturgy consisted mainly in presenting the deceased with numerous articles of food and drink, which at an early date acquired a mystical significance. But through the whole of Egyptian history the idea persisted that the dead must somehow or other be adequately supplied with food. The name given to this ancient rite was *prt*, meaning 'the coming forth' or 'going up,' and the word *Ṭalaʿ* means exactly the same. From the same root is derived *ṭulūʿ*, used in the combination *ṭulūʿ esh-shems*, 'sunrise.' *Prt* has also this meaning in Egyptian. Both the Egyptian *pry* and the Arabic *ṭalaʿ* are the ordinary verbs used, with the meaning 'to rise,' of the sun.

In ancient Egyptian *prt* (Arabic *ṭalaʿ*), in its technical sense of 'ascent,' 'going up to,' or 'procession to' the necropolis, nearly always appears in the combination *prt-r-ḫrw*, a 'coming forth,' or a 'going up at the voice'—*i.e.*, with offerings to the cemetery, the 'voice' being originally that of the living king (Horus),[3] bidding the offerers draw nigh to the grave of his predecessor, the dead king (Osiris). Later, of course, the 'voice' was the voice of the funerary priest who replaced the king, Horus, at the funerals of his subjects, or who acted as the king's deputy at the royal tombs.

In the tomb-chapel of Methen, who lived at the end of the Third Dynasty, the following formula occurs:

> Grace granted by Anubis who presides in the necropolis, a coming-forth-unto-the-voice there by all his [*i.e.*, the deceased Methen's] villages [that formed his funerary endowment] on the *wag*-festival, . . . the first day of the month, the first day of the half-month, the first day of every week.[4]

---

[1] A. H. Gardiner, *Proceedings of the Society of Biblical Archæology*, vol. xxxvii, p. 258.

[2] E. Naville, *Das aegyptische Todtenbuch der XVIII bis XX Dynastie*, vol. i (Berlin, 1886), Pl. CIV; S. Birch, *Transactions of the Society of Biblical Archæology*, vol. viii, pp. 386 ff.

[3] Nina de Garis Davies and A. H. Gardiner, *The Tomb of Amenemhēt*, p. 85.

[4] A. M. Blackman, *Journal of Egyptian Archæology*, vol. iii, p. 32.

Immediately below this text, and intimately connected with it, four women are to be seen, each carrying a basket of bread on her head and holding a vessel containing water in her right hand.[1] Such representations of men and women going in procession to the cemetery loaded with provisions are very common in tomb-chapels, especially in those of the Old and Middle Kingdoms. Very conspicuous in these scenes are the baskets containing articles of food, generally borne on the heads of women as they are at a modern *Ṭalaʿ*, and of exactly the same shape as those used for that purpose to-day. A similar text to that just quoted, and dating probably from the Sixth Dynasty, reads as follows : " A coming-forth-unto-the-voice for him in his tomb-chapel at the monthly and half-monthly festival, on the firsts of the seasons, the firsts of the months, and the firsts of the weeks." [2] In later times this weekly offering seems often to have degenerated into a mere pouring out of water, accompanied by the recitation of formulæ, a custom still surviving in Lower Nubia and parts of Upper Egypt.[3] With regard to this weekly graveside ceremony, it might be pointed out that Isis of Philæ was supposed to perform it at the ' Holy Place ' on the island of Bīgeh, the burial-place of Osiris, doubtless in the capacity of a wife visiting the grave of her dead husband.[4]

Prt occasionally occurs in its funerary significance without the following *r-ḫrw*, and then it seems generally to be accompanied by the attribute *ʿ3t*, ' great '—*i.e.*, ' the great going forth,' or, to use the modern equivalent, ' Great *Ṭalaʿ*.' [5] For example, a man prays that on the day in which he departs this life there may be " a great going forth of my fellow-townsfolk." [6] The same expression is used in *The Decree of Canopus*, where it is employed to denote the annual commemoration of the death of the deified Berenike.[7] In the Greek version of this last-mentioned inscription *prt ʿ3t* is rendered μέγα πένθος, ' great lamentation,' an indication that those taking part in this ' going forth ' wailed at the graveside, and probably also on their way there and back, as is the custom in modern times.

[1] C. R. Lepsius, *Denkmaeler aus Aegypten und Aethiopien* (Berlin, 1849–58), vol. ii, Pl. 5.
[2] A. M. Blackman, *loc. cit.*
[3] *Ibid.*
[4] *Ibid.*, with note 4 and the following pages.
[5] Used without the attribute *ʿ3t* when denoting the 'procession' of Upwawet in the Osirian mysteries ; see H. Schäfer, *Die Mysterien des Osiris in Abydos* (Leipzig, 1904), p. 21.
[6] H. Schäfer, *op. cit.*, p. 25.
[7] *Ibid.*

In view of the evidence obtained from the meaning of the names given to both the ancient and the modern rite, together with many similarities in the funerary ritual of the ancient and modern Egyptians, as well as the interesting fact that 'the going up' was in both instances to the desert, we have distinct justification for supposing that the modern ceremonies are in origin pre-Christian and pre-Islamic, and are direct ritualistic survivals from the earliest period of Egyptian history. One realizes this all the more fully when one reads Professor Breasted's or Dr Reisner's vivid account of the observances in the cemetery at Asyūṭ during an annual festival in the time of the Middle Kingdom.[1] In the modern as in the ancient festivals quantities of loaves of bread are brought to the tomb, incense is burned (see p. 266), and victims are slain (p. 260). The burning of incense was, of course, a most important and prominent feature of the ancient funerary ceremonial, and the dead were supposed to take a special delight in smelling it,[2] and also to derive benefit therefrom.[3]

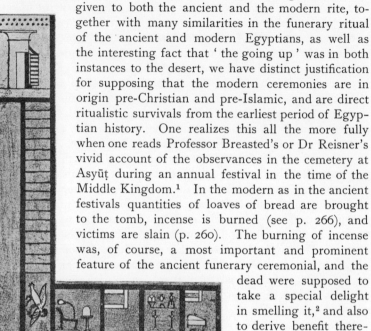

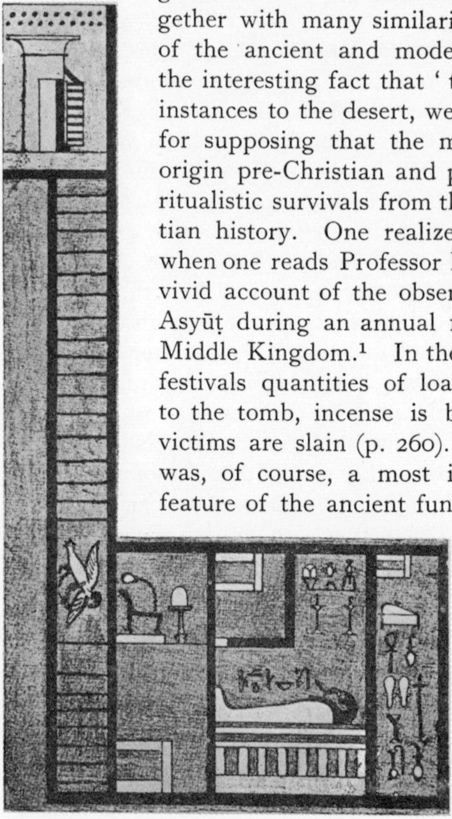

FIG. 166. THE SOUL DESCENDING THE BURIAL-SHAFT
After G. Maspero, *The Dawn of Civilization* (London, 1894), p. 198.

The modern conception that the soul visits the body on the day of the *Ṭalaʿ* (pp. 117, 120) finds an excellent parallel in a well-known vignette in *The Book of the Dead* depicting the soul (*bai*) in the form of a bird, descending the shaft admit-

[1] J. H. Breasted, *Development of Religion and Thought in Ancient Egypt* (London, 1912), pp. 259 ff.; G. A. Reisner, *Journal of Egyptian Archæology*, vol. v, p. 92. Dr Reisner, speaking of the jars of beer, loaves of bread, and the roast meat presented to Djefaiḥap's statue on the great New Year's festival, says: "All these offerings were, of course, distributed to the poor or to such scribes as came to repeat the offering formula before the statue. In modern practice, the scribe reads or recites a chapter from the Korân, repeating it over and over according to what he receives."

[2] See, *e.g.*, A. M. Blackman, *Rock Tombs of Meir* (London, 1924), Part IV, p. 22.

[3] A. M. Blackman, *Zeitschrift für ägyptische Sprache*, vol. l, pp. 69 ff.

ting to the burial-chamber in order to unite with the mummy which rests there (Fig. 166). The idea that the dead resided

FIG. 167. WIDOW BEWAILING HER DEAD HUSBAND
After W. Wreszinski, *op. cit.*, Pl. 417.

in their tombs as well as in the realm of Osiris or in heaven with the sun-god is to be found in Egyptian religious texts of all periods.[1]

An ancient painting (Fig. 167) depicting a widow bewailing her husband at one of her weekly or less frequent periodical visits

FIG. 168. ANCIENT POTTERS
After F. Cailliaud, *Recherches sur les arts et les métiers* (Paris, 1831), Pl. 16.[2]

FIG. 169. ANCIENT POTTERS
After F. Cailliaud, *ibid.*[2]

to his tomb may be compared with one of my photographs (Fig. 150) of a modern widow similarly engaged.

[1] *E.g.*, A. Erman, *Handbook of Egyptian Religion* (London, 1907), pp. 106 ff.; see, too, F. Ll. Griffith, *Stories of the High Priests*, pp. 15, 38.
[2] See also P. E. Newberry, *Beni Hasan*, Part II, Pl. 7.

The accounts of the two inter-village fights given on pp. 129 ff. bear striking resemblances to the account given by Juvenal, in his famous Fifteenth Satire, of the fight between the inhabitants of Ombos and Dendereh. That fight and one of those that I witnessed occurred at the celebration of a local religious festival, and, moreover, it and the fight described by me on p. 130 began with stone-throwing.

FIG. 170. ANCIENT AND MODERN POTSHERDS, SHOWING CORD-MARKINGS, THE LOWER ANCIENT, THE TWO ABOVE MODERN

Though the pots used in a modern Egyptian village differ greatly in shape from those used in ancient times, the modern potter seems to employ much the same methods as did his ancestors in the manufacture of his vessels (Figs. 168, 169).

As can be seen from the photograph of the Eighteenth-Dynasty sherd (Fig. 170) picked up by me at el-ʿAmarneh, the ancient like the modern potter used cord to strengthen the large pots before they were baked (see pp. 138, 150 f.); he likewise separated the newly turned vessel from the mass of clay beneath it by cutting it off with a string (Fig. 171, and see p. 152).

FIG. 171. CUTTING THE NEWLY MADE VESSEL FROM THE CLAY BENEATH IT
After F. Ll. Griffith, *Beni Hasan*, Part IV, Pl. XX.

The ancient kilns closely resembled the modern ones in shape, and like them were evidently roofless, for a painting in a tomb-chapel at Beni Ḥasan (Fig. 168) shows the flames issuing from the top (*cf.* p. 148 and p. 141, Fig. 65). This painting also shows (Fig. 169) two men preparing the clay by kneading it with their feet (*cf.* pp. 135, 151).

The resemblance of the ancient to the modern clay granaries

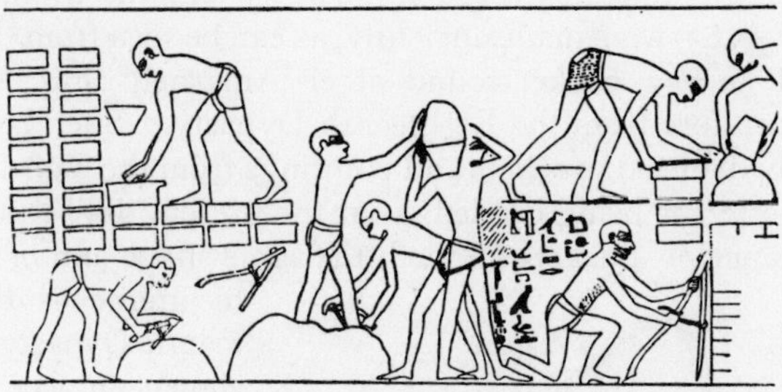

FIG. 172. ANCIENT BRICK-MAKERS
After P. E. Newberry, *The Life of Rekhmara* (London, 1900), Pl. XXI.

has already been pointed out (p. 280). Tall granaries standing on the ground, such as I saw at el-Kāb (p. 153), were of course exceedingly common in ancient Egypt.[1]

The ancient and modern methods of brick-making (p. 154) are identical, as can be seen from Fig. 172. The Twelfth-Dynasty brick-mould found by Professor Petrie at el-Lāhūn (Fig. 173) is exactly like that used at the present day (see p. 154, Fig. 81).[2]

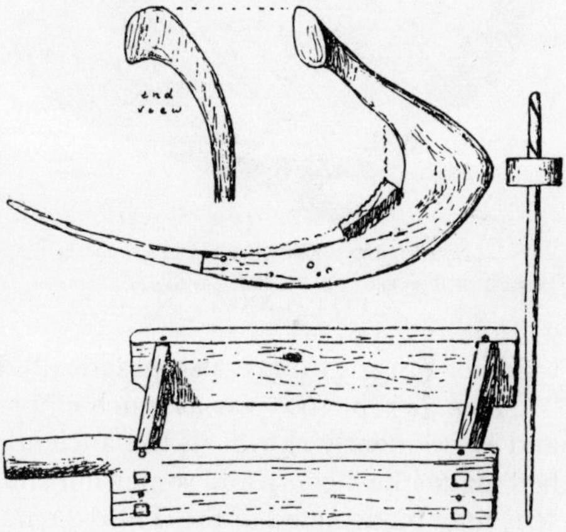

FIG. 173. TWELFTH-DYNASTY SICKLE, SPINDLE, AND BRICK-MOULD
After W. M. F. Petrie, *Kahun, Gurob, and Hawara*, Pl. IX.

Sheep-dung, which is still commonly used as fuel in Egypt, was similarly employed anciently, certainly during the Eighteenth Dynasty,[3] and so, too, probably was cow-dung. Herodotus

[1] See, *e.g.*, W. Wreszinski, *Atlas zur altaegyptischen Kulturgeschichte*, Pls. 60*a*, 63; A. Wiedemann, *Das alte Ägypten*, p. 173, Fig. 31; Erman and Ranke, *op. cit.*, p. 520.

[2] See also W. Wreszinski, *Bericht über die photograph. Expedition* (Halle a. S., 1927), Pl. 13, B.

[3] See T. E. Peet and C. L. Woolley, *The City of Akhenaten*, Part I, p. 64.

may have been referring to the way in which cow-dung is made into cakes for fuel (p. 154) when he says:[1] " They take up dung with their hands."

Baskets of the same shape and same technique as the *maḳṭaf* (p. 156, Fig. 83) were made anciently, as can be seen from the photograph of such a basket found at el-ʿAmarneh (Fig. 174), and dating therefore from the Eighteenth Dynasty. Such baskets are constantly depicted in reliefs and paintings from the Third Dynasty onward, often as being carried, as at the present day, on the heads of the women.[2] Baskets of much the same shape and of the same technique as the Eighteenth-Dynasty baskets shown in Fig. 175 are woven at the present day (p. 159)—*i.e.*, they are made of palm-leaf with a foundation of split midribs and built up spirally with over-sewing.[3] In el-ʿAmarneh was found a basket tray[4] that is almost an exact replica of that depicted in Fig. 89, p. 161, while the two baskets, the one ancient and the other modern, shown together (Fig. 176) are also practically identical.

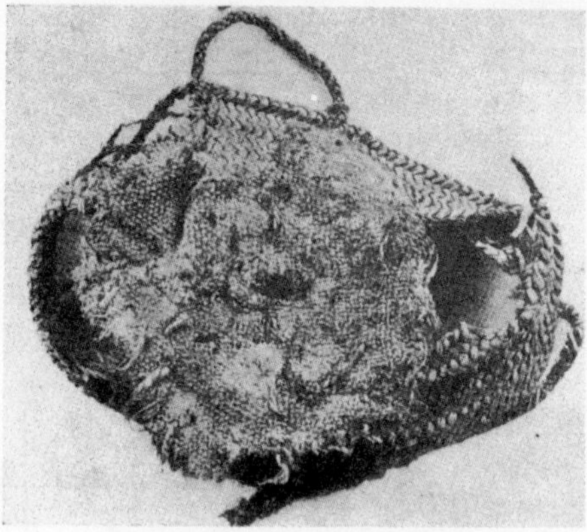

FIG. 174. ANCIENT MAḲṬAF
After T. E. Peet and C. L. Woolley, *The City of Akhenaten*, Part I, Pl. XXI, 4.

The *ḳafaṣ* (p. 160) was as much employed anciently as it is now, and is frequently shown in the ancient reliefs and paintings.[5] A bed made like a *ḳafaṣ*, and somewhat similar to that mentioned on p. 161, may be depicted in the Third-Dynasty tomb-chapel of Ḥesy.[6]

Palm-fibre rope like that in use at the present day (see p. 161 and Frontispiece) has been found in tombs of all periods.[7]

[1] ii, 36.
[2] See above, p. 299, and *cf.* p. 37, Fig. 14, p. 80, Fig. 38.
[3] See also W. M. F. Petrie, *Tarkhan*, Part I, Pl. X, 1.
[4] T. E. Peet and C. L. Woolley, *op. cit.*, Pl. XXI, 3.
[5] *E.g.*, P. E. Newberry, *El-Bersheh* (London, 1893), Part I, Pl. XXII.
[6] W. E. Quibell, *Excavations at Saqqara, 1911–12: The Tomb of Hesy* (Cairo, 1913), p. 29 and Pl. XIX.
[7] See, *e.g.*, W. M. F. Petrie, *Deshasheh* (London, 1898), p. 33 and Pl. XXXIV.

Looms like those used by modern Arab women (p. 162 and Fig. 93) are depicted in Twelfth-Dynasty paintings at Beni Ḥasan and elsewhere[1] (Fig. 177). The modern and ancient (Fig. 173) spindles are hardly to be distinguished from one another.[2]

On p. 163 I speak of loaves being put to rise in the sun before

FIG. 175. EIGHTEENTH-DYNASTY BASKETS
After W. M. F. Petrie, *Sedment*, Part II, Pl. LV.

being baked. This seems also to have been done in ancient Egypt.[3]

The open-air market (pp. 164 ff.) was evidently as distinctive a feature of ancient as it is of modern Egyptian life.[4] The part played by saleswomen in the markets was noticed by Herodotus,[5] and, it would seem, somewhat exaggerated.

The breaking up of the fields into small squares separated from each other by ridges of earth and narrow trenches (p. 169) is an ancient practice, as we learn both from reliefs and paintings[6]

[1] See L. Klebs, *Reliefs und Malereien des Mittleren Reichs*, pp. 126 ff.; see also H. E. Winlock, "Heddle-Jacks of Looms" in *Ancient Egypt* (1922), pp. 71 ff.
[2] L. Klebs, *op. cit.*, p. 126.
[3] T. E. Peet and C. L. Woolley, *The City of Akhenaten*, Part I, p. 64.
[4] A. Erman and H. Ranke, *op. cit.*, pp. 508 f.
[5] ii, 35.
[6] See, *e.g.*, P. E. Newberry, *El-Bersheh*, Part I, Pl. XXVI.

and from the excavations of the Deutsche Orient-Gesellschaft at el-ʿAmarneh.[1] The shifting of the boundary-stone (pp. 169f.) is condemned in *The Teaching of Amenōphis, the Son of Kanakht.*[2]

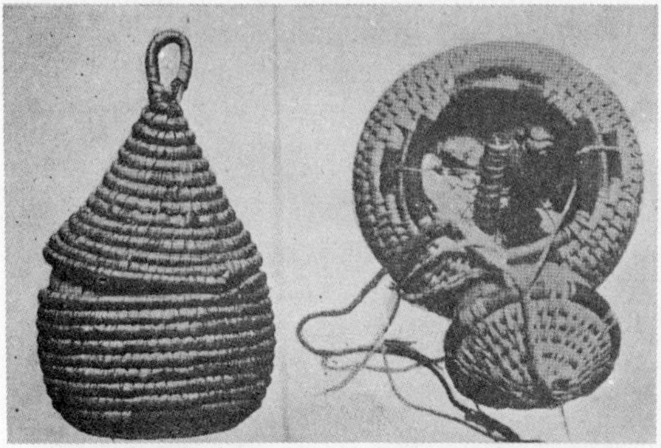

FIG. 176. A MODERN (LEFT) AND ANCIENT (RIGHT) BASKET
The latter after H. E. Winlock, *Bulletin of the Metropolitan Museum of Art, New York*, Part II (December, 1922), p. 35, Fig. 24.

The modern plough (p. 170 and Fig. 97) is almost exactly like the ancient one (see Fig. 178).[3] For a drawing of an ancient plough reconstructed from still surviving portions see Fig. 179. Dr Borchardt thinks that the ancient like the modern plough was furnished with a metal share. Accordingly the wooden share in Fig. 179 is represented as sheathed in metal. Dr B. P. Grenfell told my brother that the blade of the *ṭūriyeh* (hoe) had acquired its present shape, and was already made of iron, by Roman times, for he had found such blades in rubbish mounds of the Roman period.

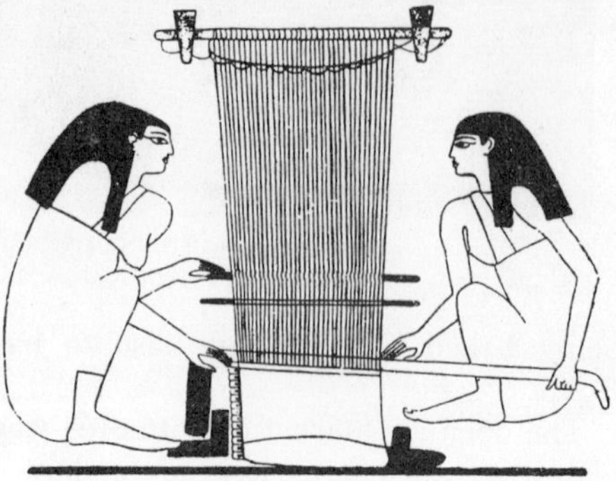

FIG. 177. TWO WOMEN WEAVING ON A HORIZONTAL LOOM
After F. Cailliaud, *Recherches sur les arts et les métiers*, Pl. 17A.

The modern *shādūf* (pp. 170 f.) finds its exact counterpart in

[1] *Mitteilungen der Deutschen Orient-Gesellschaft zu Berlin*, vol. l, p. 17. For a photograph showing a modern cultivated patch of ground so divided, see G. Steindorff, *Die Blütezeit des Pharaonenreichs* (Leipzig, 1926), Fig. 54.

[2] F. Ll. Griffith, *Journal of Egyptian Archæology*, vol. xii, p. 204.

[3] A. Erman and H. Ranke, *op. cit.*, Pl. 35; A. Erman, *Life in Ancient Egypt*, translated by H. M. Tirard (London, 1894), p. 426; J. G. Wilkinson, *The Ancient Egyptians*, vol. i, p. 281; L. Borchardt, *Priestergräber . . . vom Totentempel des*

paintings dating from the New Kingdom (Fig. 180). Wooden *shādūf*-hooks, the hooks from which the leather buckets are hung,

FIG. 178. AN ANCIENT PLOUGH
After Norman de Garis Davies, *The Tomb of Nakht at Thebes*, Pl. XVIII.

have been found in graves of the Second to Third Dynasties (*c.* 3000 B.C.).[1]

The object now known as *'arūset el-ḳamḥ*, 'the bride of the corn,' is depicted in several Theban tomb-chapels of the Eighteenth Dynasty,[2] and can possibly be traced back to the Old Kingdom in a different form.[3] It is stated on p. 172 that "in some parts of Egypt 'the bride of the corn' is temporarily placed on the heaps of grain

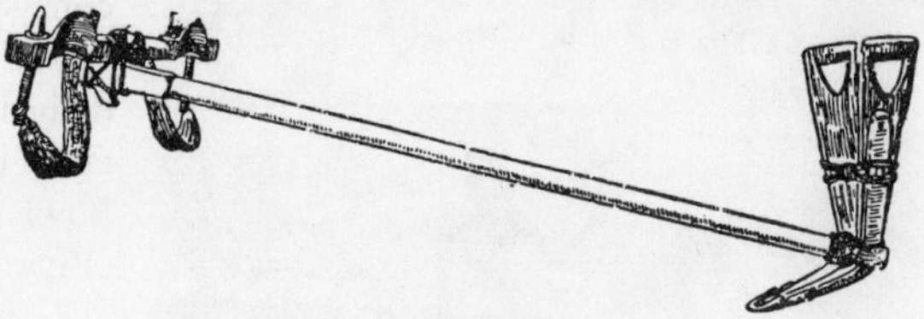

FIG. 179. AN ANCIENT EGYPTIAN PLOUGH IN THE BERLIN MUSEUM
After L. Borchardt, *Priestergräber . . . vom Totentempel des Ne-user-rê*, p. 116.

Ne-user-rê (Leipzig, 1908), pp. 165 ff.; A. Wiedemann, *Das alte Ägypten*, p. 24 and note 3.

[1] W. M. F. Petrie, *Tarkhan*, Part I, Pl. X, 6.

[2] W. S. Blackman, *Journal of Egyptian Archæology*, vol. viii, pp. 235 ff. and Pls. XXVI–XXIX.

[3] J. Capart, *La mise à mort du dieu en Égypte* (Paris, 1927).

after the winnowing is completed, as a charm to secure a good

FIG. 180. ANCIENT SHAWĀDĪF
After A. Erman and H. Ranke, *op. cit.*, Pl. 35, Fig. 1.

harvest the following year." According to several ancient representations of winnowing this object was placed on the winnowing-floor while the winnowers were at work (Fig. 181), and an offering was laid before it consisting either of a vessel of water and dishes containing cakes, etc. (Fig. 182), or of a bowl of water only (Figs. 181 and 183).

FIG 181. ABOVE: 'BRIDE OF THE CORN' ON THE EDGE OF THE WINNOWING-FLOOR. BELOW: SUPPLIES OF FOOD BESIDE THE THRESHING-FLOOR
After W. Wreszinski, *op. cit.*, Pl. 177.

I mention (p. 172) that gifts of the first-fruits are bestowed on the *mueddin* of the village mosque, the *zummāreh* - player, the barber, and the *fuḳahā*, besides the deserving poor. This custom finds a parallel in ancient Egypt. In the second of the famous contracts of Djefaiḥap engraved on the walls of his tomb-chapel at Asyūṭ the following passage occurs :

That which he [Djefaiḥap] gave to them [the priesthood of the temple of Upwawet of Asyūṭ] in return [*i.e.*, for bread presented to his statue]

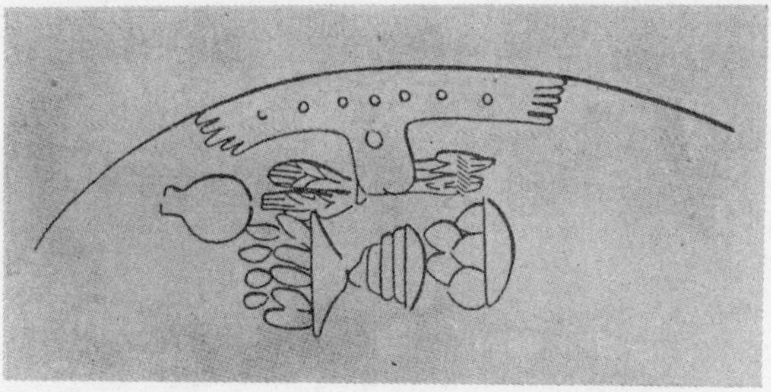

FIG. 182. AN ANCIENT 'BRIDE OF THE CORN'
After Norman de Garis Davies, *The Tomb of Nakht at Thebes*, p. 63.

was one *ḥeḳat* measure of northern barley for every field of the endowment [*pr-ḏt*], from the firstfruits of the harvest of the nomarch's estate, just as [or in the measure which] every commoner of Asyūṭ gives of the firstfruits of his harvest, for he was the first to cause every one of his peasants to give it to this temple from the firstfruits of his field.[1]

The offering of the firstfruits to the *mueddin* and the *fuḳahā* is perhaps a survival of the custom referred to in the above quotation, the *mueddin*, the *fuḳahā*, and the mosque taking the place of the priests and the temple. The *fiḳīh* in his funerary functions corresponds exactly to the ancient 'lector' (*ẖry-ḥb*).

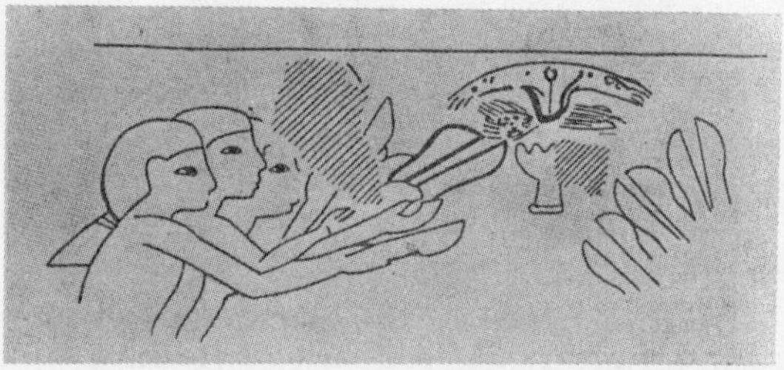

FIG. 183. AN ANCIENT 'BRIDE OF THE CORN'
After Norman de Garis Davies, *ibid.*

The custom of putting loaves of bread in the heaps of wheat (p. 173) may be a survival of the offerings originally made to the

[1] G. A. Reisner, *Journal of Egyptian Archæology*, vol. v, p. 83 ; J. H. Breasted, *Ancient Records*, vol. i, § 546.

corn *ʿarūseh*, of which mention has been made above. Or both this custom and that of bringing food to the threshing-floor and, after distributing it among friends, placing what is left in the heaps of *dura* to satisfy the *ʿafārīt* (pp. 176 f.) may be a survival of the presentation of offerings to the harvest-goddess Ernūtet. Such offerings to Ernūtet are often depicted in tomb-chapels of the New Kingdom. Thus Zeserkereʿsenb is shown making food-offerings

FIG. 184. MAKING OFFERING TO ERNŪTET
After W. Wreszinski, *op. cit.*, Pl. 143.

to that goddess "on the day in which the barley is measured, Pharmuthi 27th" (Fig. 184).[1]

In the tomb-chapels of Khaʿemḥēt[2] and Nakht (Fig. 181) victuals of various sorts are represented as lying close to the threshing-floor, evidently an offering to the harvest-goddess, but at the same time reminding us at once of the custom still observed in connexion with the threshing of the *dura* (pp. 175 f.).

The paying of the harvesters and ferryman in kind (pp. 173 f., 180) finds many a parallel in ancient Egyptian records.[3] It is to

[1] See also J. G. Wilkinson, *The Ancient Egyptians*, vol. i, pp. 348, 385; A. Erman and H. Ranke, *op. cit.*, p. 520.

[2] W. Wreszinski, *Atlas zur altaegyptischen Kulturgeschichte*, Pls. 189, 194.

[3] A. Erman and H. Ranke, *op. cit.*, p. 591 ; T. E. Peet, *Annals of Archæology and Anthropology*, vol. vii, p. 82.

be noted in this connexion that the determinatives of the ancient Egyptian word *hmt*, the 'fee' paid to a ferryman, are those regularly affixed to words signifying foodstuffs—*i.e.*, an oval roll of bread above the three plural strokes, or a conical loaf and a jar of beer above a circular loaf.[1]

The wooden fork used nowadays on the threshing-floor and for winnowing (p. 173 and Fig. 105) is exactly like the ancient one (Fig. 185). Also much the same sort of iron sickle as the modern one (p. 173, Fig. 101) was already in use in the Roman period

FIG. 185. ANCIENT HARVESTING-FORKS
After W. Wreszinski, *op. cit.*, Pl. 234.

(Fig. 186). At an earlier date the sickle consisted of a wooden body, in shape closely resembling the lower jawbone of an ox, in which flint teeth were inserted (Fig. 173).[2]

It is only necessary to read that part of chapter xiv in A. Erman and H. Ranke's *Aegypten und aegyptisches Leben im Altertum*[3] which deals with medical knowledge to see how nearly ancient and modern prescriptions and magico-medical cures are alike. Appended comments such as "Tried and true" (p. 207) find close parallels in the famous *Papyrus Ebers*.[4] In ancient as in modern times the 'physician' wrote out spells commanding a disease to depart,[5] and both adults and children were cured of sickness, or protected against both it and ghostly malice, by means of written charms

[1] See A. H. Gardiner, *Egyptian Grammar* (Oxford, 1927), pp. 515 f.
[2] See W. M. F. Petrie, *Kahun, Gurob, and Hawara* (London, 1890), p. 29; *Illahun, Kahun, and Gurob* (London, 1891), pp. 53 ff.
[3] Pp. 409 ff.; see also A. Erman, *Life in Ancient Egypt*, pp. 357 ff.
[4] A. Erman, *op. cit.*, p. 359.
[5] *Ibid.*, p. 356.

or other amulets hung round the neck.[1] The collection of charms used by mothers to protect or cure their infants, referred to in note 1 below under the title of *Zaubersprüche für Mutter und Kind* (*Spells for Mother and Child*), dates probably from the Hyksōs period (1788–1580 B.C.); it is preserved in the Berlin Museum. The object of one of the charms in this ancient collection [2] was to protect a child from a spirit of the female sex (possibly, according to Professor Erman, a dead woman), which was trying to take it from its mother. With this idea may be compared, perhaps, the modern one that a child's falling ill is due to the mother's *ḳarīneh* wishing to draw it away from her (p. 72). The spell in question reads as follows:

FIG. 186. IRON SICKLE OF ROMAN PERIOD

After *A Guide to the Third and Fourth Egyptian Rooms in the British Museum* (London, 1904), p. 41.

> Run out, thou [fem.] that comest in the darkness, that slinkest [?] in with nose behind thee and face averted, that failest in that for which thou hast come.
>
> Hast thou come to kiss this child? I will not suffer thee to kiss him.
>
> Hast thou come to kill him? I will not suffer thee to kill him.
>
> Hast thou come to harm him? I will not suffer thee to harm him.
>
> Hast thou come to take him away? I will not suffer thee to take him from me.
>
> I have made his protection against thee with *'fꜣy*-herbs which make . . . [?], with onions which harm thee, with honey which is sweet for mankind and bitter for the dead, with the . . . [?] of the *ꜣbḏw*-fish, with the jaw-bone of the . . . [?], with the back of the perch.

My accounts of the eye-specialists on pp. 201 ff. and 211 f. may be compared with Herodotus' statement on the subject of Egyptian medicine [3]: "Each physician treats a single disorder, and no more. All places abound in physicians; some physicians are for the eyes, others for the head. . . ."

The professions of magician and physician were no less closely

[1] A. Erman and H. Ranke, *op. cit.*, p. 408; A. Erman, *Zaubersprüche für Mutter und Kind* (Berlin, 1901), pp. 30, 32, 35, etc., and *The Literature of the Ancient Egyptians*, p. 218 and note 6.

[2] A. Erman, *Zaubersprüche für Mutter und Kind*, pp. 11 f.

[3] ii, 84.

associated in ancient than they are in modern Egypt, as is evident from Dr A. H. Gardiner's illuminating article, " Professional Magicians in Ancient Egypt." [1] It is interesting to note also that the two titles *swnw*, 'physician,' and *sȝw*, 'amulet-man'—*i.e.*, 'maker' or 'purveyor of amulets'—are borne more than once by the same person.[2]

The necessity for a magician's being clean (p. 186) is strongly emphasized in ancient Egyptian magical texts.[3]

The modern belief that a person can be possessed by an *ʿafrīt* (pp. 231 f.) or a sheikh (pp. 187, 197 ff.) finds an ancient parallel in the tale of *The Daughter of the Prince of Bakhtan and the Possessing Spirit*.[4] The peacemaking feast held by people who have appeased the possessing sheikh (pp. 186, 199 f.) is likewise parallelled in the same story, where we are told [5] that the spirit, while agreeing to leave the princess, demanded that a feast-day be celebrated with him and with the chief of Bakhtan, a demand that was carried out.

The magical ceremony described on p. 188 began with the sweeping of the ground and the sprinkling of water.[6] In ancient Egypt the priest, before beginning the toilet episodes of the temple liturgy, swept the floor of the sanctuary with a cloth.[7] As the king (the high-priest *par excellence*) is shown in a relief in the temple of Derr [8] holding a ewer as well as the cloth used for sweeping the floor, it is highly probable that the priest often sprinkled the floor as well as swept it. It was certainly the custom to sprinkle water while the floor of a house was being swept, as we learn from a wall-painting found by Professor Petrie at el-ʿAmarneh.[9] With regard to the lighting of a fire and the burning of a hoopoo's feathers (p. 188), it should be pointed out that the ancient magicians also burned various strange substances while pronouncing their spells.[10]

[1] *Proceedings of the Society of Biblical Archæology*, vol. xxxix (1917), pp. 31 ff.
[2] *Op. cit.*, p. 33.
[3] A. M. Blackman, " Purification (Egyptian)," in Hastings, *op. cit.*, vol. x, p. 482.
[4] G. Maspero, *Popular Stories of Ancient Egypt* (London, 1915), pp. 172 ff.; J. H. Breasted, *Ancient Records*, vol. iii, pp. 188 ff.
[5] J. H. Breasted, *op. cit.*, § 444.
[6] *Cf.* A. M. Blackman, " Purification (Egyptian)," in Hastings, *op. cit.*, vol. x, p. 482.
[7] A. M. Blackman, " Worship (Egyptian)," in Hastings, *op. cit.*, vol. xii, p. 778.
[8] A. M. Blackman, *The Temple of Derr* (Cairo, 1913), Pl. LXIV, left.
[9] W. M. F. Petrie, *Tell el Amarna* (London, 1894), Pl. V.
[10] F. Ll. Griffith and H. Thompson, *The Demotic Magical Papyrus of London and Leiden* (London, 1904), pp. 37 ff.

On pp. 189 f., 193 ff., 198, 229, 232, and 237 I speak of incense being burned, and of water being sometimes simultaneously poured out as well (p. 229), during the recitation of spells by a magician. As we learn from existing copies of the ancient Egyptian funerary liturgy and from the reliefs and paintings depicting its performance, incense was burned and water poured out at stated intervals during the recitation by the lector of the formulæ appropriate to the various episodes of which this liturgy was composed.[1]

On pp. 192 ff. I describe how a magician brought a woman from a distant village to the room in which he recited the spell summoning her. Similarly, we read in *The Second Tale of Khamuas* that an Ethiopian sorcerer brought the Egyptian Pharaoh from Egypt to Ethiopia and back again to Egypt, all in the space of six hours, and that an Egyptian magician retaliated by bringing the viceroy of Ethiopia to Egypt and back again to Ethiopia in the same space of time.[2]

Wax figures such as those mentioned on p. 197 were also used for sinister purposes in ancient Egypt.[3]

Superstitions about the evil eye evidently existed in ancient Egypt, but references to them are very rare in the literature, as has been pointed out by Dr A. H. Gardiner.[4] However, in the library of the temple of Horus at Edfu there was a book containing "spells for driving away the evil eye," and in a well-known hymn to Thōth dating from the New Kingdom occur the words: "O Thōth, if thou wilt be to me a champion, I will not fear the eye."[5]

In connexion with the statement on p. 224 that horns of sheep and other animals are hung over doors as a charm against the evil eye, a passage in the *Pyramid Texts* might be quoted which describes how the door admitting to the royal pyramid precincts was adorned with bucrania and "sealed with two evil eyes, that Osiris may come not in this his evil coming."[6]

On p. 236 I speak of the slaying of a victim on the threshold

[1] See, *e.g.*, A. M. Blackman, *The Rock Tombs of Meir*, Part I, Pl. X; Part II, Pl. X, p. 20; Part III, Pls. XXI ff., pp. 29 ff.

[2] F. Ll. Griffith, *Stories of the High Priests*, pp. 55 ff.

[3] A. Erman and H. Ranke, *op. cit.*, p. 407; see also J. H. Breasted, *Ancient Records*, vol. iv, p. 209, §§ 454 f.; *A History of Egypt* (London, 1906), p. 498.

[4] *Proceedings of the Society of Biblical Archæology*, vol. xxxviii, p. 128.

[5] A. Erman, *The Literature of the Ancient Egyptians*, p. 306.

[6] J. H. Breasted, *Development of Religion and Thought in Ancient Egypt*, p. 26; K. Sethe, *Die altägyptischen Pyramidentexte*, §§ 1266 f.

of a new house and at the installation of a new engine or water-wheel. With this may be compared the slaying of victims—an ox and a goose—at the ceremony of laying the foundation of an ancient Egyptian temple.[1]

The unwillingness to save a drowning person mentioned on pp. 238 f. may be the last remains of an ancient belief that to be drowned was to "do the pleasure of Rēʿ," and that by being drowned a person was divinized, a belief to which Herodotus refers somewhat vaguely.[2] Professor Griffith wrote a very illuminating article on this subject some years ago in the *Zeitschrift für ägyptische Sprache*,[3] and my brother, Dr A. M. Blackman, has also dealt with it at some length in his *Temple of Dendûr*.[4] It is, perhaps, to be remembered in this connexion that, according to more than one account, Osiris himself met his death by drowning.[5] Possibly the water-spirit, who apparently claimed (in the end successfully ?) the foredoomed Prince,[6] is to be compared with the *ʿafrīt* that the modern *fellāḥīn* suppose to be claiming one who is drowning.

It is interesting to note that virtue was evidently attached to onions in ancient as it is in modern times (p. 261), for persons who took part in the procession round the walls of Memphis at the annual festival of Sokar, the funerary god of that city, had onions hung round their necks.[7] People also tied onions round their necks on the night preceding this festival.[8]

The love of listening to stories was certainly no less strong in the ancient Egyptians than it is in their descendants, as is shown by the number of folk-tales preserved to us from all periods. The existence of these stories points also to there having been professional story-tellers in antiquity as at the present day (pp. 268 ff.).[9]

[1] W. von Bissing and H. Kees, *Das Re-Heiligtum des Kōnigs Ne-woser-re*, vol. ii (Leipzig, 1923), Pl. I, Fig. 2.

[2] ii, 90.

[3] Vol. xlvi, pp. 132 ff.

[4] Cairo, 1911, pp. 82 f.

[5] A. Erman, "Ein Denkmal memphitischer Theologie," in *Sitzungsberichte der königl. preussischen Akademie der Wissenschaften*, vol. xliii, 1911, pp. 926 ff.; J. H. Breasted, *Development of Religion and Thought in Ancient Egypt*, pp. 25, 41.

[6] T. E. Peet, *Journal of Egyptian Archæology*, vol. xi, pp. 228 f.

[7] S. Sharpe, *Egyptian Inscriptions from the British Museum and Other Sources* (London, 1837–55), Part II, p. 78.

[8] H. Brugsch, *Hieroglyphisch-Demotisches Wörterbuch* (Leipzig, 1867–80), p. 295; *Thesaurus Inscriptionum Aegyptiacarum* (Leipzig, 1883–91), p. 1144; J. Duemichen, *Altaegyptische Kalenderinschriften* (Leipzig, 1866), Pl. XXVI.

[9] See A. Erman, *The Literature of the Ancient Egyptians*, p. xxix; W. Spiegelberg, *The Credibility of Herodotus' Account of Egypt*, pp. 30 f.

It should be observed that the story of *The Shah of Persia and his Daughter* (pp. 272 ff.) bears a certain resemblance to the tale told to Herodotus [1] about Mykerinos, his daughter, and the golden image of a cow. If there is any connexion between the two stories, that told to Herodotus may after all be a genuine native folk-tale and not, as Professor Spiegelberg has suggested,[2] a mere dragoman's explanation of a monument—unless, of course, the modern tale is simply a modification of the Herodotean, and reached the masses by way of the Hellenized Egyptians of Græco-Roman times.

[1] ii, 130 f.
[2] *The Credibility of Herodotus' Account of Egypt*, p. 15.

LIST OF ARABIC WORDS
EMPLOYED IN THE TEXT

A[1]

abb (pl. *abahāt*), father; *Yā abūi!* O my father! an exclamation of distress or pain, 119, 226
aḥsan, better; *aḥsan khāliṣ*, much better, 123
aiwa, yes, 83
akh, alas! fie!, 225 f.
akhkh (pl. *ikhwāt*, *ikhwān*[2]), brother; *Yā akhūi!* O my brother!, 123
atl, tamarisk, 205

B

baḳīyeh, el-, what remains over, 114
ballāṣ (pl. *balālīṣ*), water-pot, 142, 153
barakeh, blessing, healing virtue, good luck, 33, 65, 99 f., and *passim*
barūkeh, lucky coin, 99
bashkūr, iron rod for moving bread in the oven, 164
battaw, bread made from *dura*-flour and resembling oatcake, 65, 163
buhāḳ, fumes, 53
būṣ, dry maize-stalks, 27 f., 148, 150, 192

D

darābukkeh, pottery drum, 85, 168
dastūr, permission, 229
dikkeh (pl. *dikak*), wooden bench with back and arms, 27
duḳḳ, tattoo! (imperat. masc. sing. of *daḳḳ*, he has tattooed), 51
dura, maize, 39, 163 f., 175, 182, 192, 310

Ḍ

A strong palatal.

ḍufr, nail, claw; possibly 'horn' of a cerastes (horned viper), 66

E

ēy, what, 120

F

fakrūn, tortoise, 194, *n.* 2
farrāsh, sweeper, 248, *n.* 1, 249
Fātiheh, el-, the first chapter of the Ḳorān, 212, 252
faṭīr, sweet pastry, 175 f.
feddān, acre, 38 f.
fellāḥ (fem. *fellāḥeh*, pl. *fellāḥīn*), cultivator, peasant, *passim*
fi, in, 114
fiḳīh (pl. *fuḳahā*), person who recites the Ḳorān and who is more or less versed in the religion and law of Islām, 109, 111 f., 114 f., 117 ff., 172, 256, 259, 293, 308 f.
fiṭāmeh, act of weaning; used metaphorically of the last time of irrigating a field of *dura*, 175, 177
fulān, so and so, 118
fūweh, madder, 194

G

gallabīyeh (pl. *galālīb*), a long blouse, often made of white or blue cotton cloth, 32, 73, 88, 187, 285 f.
garūt, an implement used in pottery-making, 149 f.
gebel, mountain, 246
ginār, excellency; *ginār es-sitt*, honoured lady, 69
ginn, class of supernatural beings, 68 f., 227

GH

A very guttural r

ghiṭās, baptism by immersion; *Yōm el-Ghiṭās*, 263, 298

---

[1] For the pronunciation of modern Egyptian Arabic vowels and consonants see J. S. Willmore, *The Spoken Arabic of Egypt* (London, 1905), pp. 1 ff.
[2] *Ikhwān* means 'brethren,' 'associates.'

Ḥ

A smooth but very strong guttural aspirate.

ḥagar, stone, 203
ḥalfa, coarse kind of grass, 248
ḥamr, reddish clay used in pottery-making, 145
ḥaseneh, charity, 65, 118
ḥayāt, life; *El-baḳīyeh fi ḥayātak*, May what remains over be in your life, 114
ḥelbeh, fenugreek, 78
ḥenna, red dye made from the leaves of the shrub *Lawsonia inermis*, 57, 87 f.
ḥigāb, charm, amulet, 71
ḥirbāyeh, chameleon, 66

I

iblīz,[1] mud of the Nile left behind after the inundation, 62
ibrīḳ (pl. *ibārīḳ*), ewer with long, curved spout, 78
iddī, give!; *iddīnī*, give me, 118
ism, name; *Bismillāh er-Raḥmān er-Raḥīm*, In the name of God the Compassionate, the Merciful, 82
iswid, black, 206

K

kaḥk, cakes, 115, 118
kammūn, cumin, 206
keda, thus, 83
kenīseh, church, 106
kishk, wheat mixed with milk, made into small balls, and dried in the sun,[2] 89, 222 f.
kisweh, rug, carpet, 264, *n.* 1, 265
Kiyakh, fourth month in the Coptic year, 234
koḥl, antimony, 59, 79 f., 284
kunāfeh, fine macaroni, vermicelli, 175 f.
kurbāg, whip made of hide, 131
kūz (pl. *kīzān*), mug, 75, 167

Ḳ

Deep guttural k.

ḳāḍi, judge; one who draws up marriage contracts and who arranges divorces, 43, 92, 191 f.
ḳādūs (pl. *ḳawādīs*), special kind of pottery jar, several of which are attached by cords to the water-wheel,[3] 101
ḳafaṣ (pl. *aḳfāṣ*), basket or cage made of palm-ribs, 160 f., 165, 304
ḳamḥ, wheat, corn, 172 f.
ḳandīl (pl. *ḳanādīl*), old-fashioned saucer-lamp, 237
ḳarīn (fem. *ḳarīneh*, pl. *aḳrān*), personality born with each human being and of the same sex, pp. 54, 64 ff., 69 ff. and *passim*
ḳibleh, prayer-niche in a mosque, 250
ḳulleh (pl. *ḳulal*), earthen water-bottle, 140, 149, 151 f., 167, 231 f., 237

KH

Pronounced like ch *in Scottish* loch.

khāliṣ, much, very, exceedingly, 123
Khamasīn, the period immediately following the Coptic festival of Easter Sunday and terminating on Whit Sunday—an interval of forty-nine days,[4] 261
khubz, wheaten bread, 64 f., 163
khud, take!, 118

L

lāzimeh, obligatory gift, a special kind of charm, 199
līf, fibre from the trunk of the palm-tree, 161

M

mā, what, that which, 220 f.
mabsūṭ, pleased, 58
maḥalleh, implement on which wool is wound after it is spun, 73
maḥāreh, kind of shell, 203

---

[1] Derived from πηλός, according to E. W. Lane, *An Arabic-English Lexicon* (London, 1863–), vol. i, p. 248.
[2] See also E. W. Lane, *The Manners and Customs of the Modern Egyptians* (London, 1871), vol. ii, p. 223, n. 1.
[3] See p. 171, and E. W. Lane, *op. cit.*, vol. ii, p. 26.
[4] See E. W. Lane, *op. cit.*, vol. ii, pp. 222 f.

maktaf (pl. *makāṭif*), large basket woven from palm-leaves, 65, 155 f., 304
malāk (pl. *malāyikeh*), angel, 78
malkaf (pl. *malākif*), ventilator on roof of house, 280
mandareh, reception room, 27
maṣṭabeh (pl. *maṣāṭib*), brick bench, 32, 242, 281
mikhaleh, bottle for *kohl*, 59
mughreh, red ochre, 146
moiyeh, water; *moiyet el-malāyikeh*, water of the angels, 78
mubārakīn, blessed ones; used euphemistically of the *'afārīt*, 229
mueddin, officiant (often blind) who chants the call to prayer from the mosque, 31, 172, 308 f.
mukarraṣ, made into little cakes; descriptive of the way in which a boy's hair is cut by the barber before he undergoes circumcision, 87
mūlid (pl. *mawālid*), festival, 81, 83, 244 ff., 252 ff.; *Mūlid en-Nebi*, Festival of the Prophet—*i.e.*, the annual celebration of the Prophet's birthday, 252
mūṣ, very finely chopped straw, 149

N

nāb, double tooth, 66
nabbūt (pl. *nabābīt*), single-stick, 129, 131, 133
nadam, single-membrane drum, 265, 267
nahār, day; *Nahārak sa'īd*, Good day!, 120
nāi, kind of flute, 167
nebi, prophet, 79, 220 f.
nōrag, threshing-machine, 173
nūr, light; *Yōm Sabt en-Nūr*, the Saturday of the Light, 262

R

rashād, nasturtium, 204
rashteh, macaroni cooked in milk, 175 f.
ratl, a weight of rather more than 1 lb., 64
rōh, soul, 110 f., 118, 237

S

sabt, sabbath; *Yōm Sabt en-Nūr*, the Saturday of the Light, 262
sādif, implement used in pottery-making, 152
sa'īd, happy; *Nahārak sa'īd*, Good day!, 120
semn, clarified butter used in cooking, 167, 195
sibākh, earth from rubbish mounds used as a fertilizer, 156
sibheh, rosary, 114
sitt, lady, 69, 118

Ṣ

A very strong sibilant pronounced well back in the mouth.

ṣabī, lad, 51
ṣabr, aloes, 116, 242
ṣalla, bless!; *Ṣalla 'a 'n-Nebi*, Bless the Prophet, 79, 220 f.
ṣughaiyar, little, small, 259, 298
ṣulheh, peace-making feast held by persons who have appeased the sheikh or sheikhs by whom they were possessed, 186 f., 199 f.

SH

shā, he hath willed; *Mā shā Allāh*, What God willeth is, 220 f.
shādūf (pl. *shawādīf*), water-hoist, 170 f., 175, 306 f.
shagareh, tree; designation of special tattoo pattern, 52, 55
shahīd (pl. *shuhadā*), martyr, 121
shemm, (act of) smelling; *Shemm en-Nesīm*, the Smelling of the Zephyr, a festival celebrated in April on the first day of the *Khamasīn*,[1] 33, 261
shems, sun, 298

T

tāni, other, second, 63
ta'āla, come!, 51, 124
tibn, finely chopped straw, 149
tōb, outer garment worn by women out of doors, 105
tūtia, sulphate of zinc, 203

[1] See p. 318, note 4.

Ṭ

A strong palatal.

ṭafl, yellow clay used in pottery-making, 146, 151
ṭala', going up; visit (generally weekly) to the cemetery, 117, 263, 298 f., 300
ṭarfā, tamarisk, 188; *ḥagar eṭ-ṭarfā*, stone of the tamarisk, 203
ṭīn, earth, clay, 62
ṭulū' esh-shems, sunrise, 298

U

ukht (pl. *ikhwāt*), sister; also a personality born simultaneously with each human being, but distinct from the *ḳarīn* and *ḳarīneh*, 64, 74 ff., 186 f.

W

walad, child, boy, 63
walī, saint,[1] 244

Y

Yā, O (introducing the vocative), 119 f., 151
yōm, day; *Yōm Sabt en-Nūr*, the Saturday of the Light, 262; *Yōm el-Ghiṭās*, 263, 298

Z

zār, ceremony performed by and for persons possessed by a sheikh or sheikhs, 198 ff.
zarībeh, enclosure for sheep, goats, or cattle, 222
zēy, likeness; *Ēy-zēyak*, How are you?, 120
zikr, religious dance, 255 f., 258
zīr (pl. *ziyār* or *izyār*), large pottery jar in which the household water is stored, 75, 137 f., 149, 151, 153, 220
zummāreh, double reed-pipe with a drone, 167, 172, 308

'

A strong guttural of the same nature as ḥ, and peculiar to the Semitic languages.

'afrīt (fem. *'afrīteh*, pl. *'afārīt*), a supernatural being supposed to be made of fire and to dwell underground, *passim* and especially 69 f., 177, 223, 227 ff.; summoned by a magician, 193; ghost, 111, 225, 237
'arīf, cantor in a Coptic church, 125 ff., 234
'arūseh, bride; *'arūset el-ḳamḥ*, 'bride of the corn,' 172 f.
'īd, festival; *el-'Īd es-Ṣughaiyar*, the Little Festival, 259, 298; *el-Īd el-Kibīr*, the Great Festival, 259 f., 298
'irḳ (pl. *'urūḳ*), root; *'urūḳ el-fūweh*, roots of madder, 194
'omdeh, headman of a village, 225, 235 f., 269

[1] See also E. W. Lane, *op. cit.*, vol. i, p. 289.

INDEX OF NAMES

---

[1] Dr G. Scholem refers me to T. Canaan, *Aberglaube und Volksmedizin im Lande der Bibel* (Hamburg, 1914), p. 22, who states that "The tribes of demons are governed by princes. There are seven chief princes. . . . They are called Murrah, Maḏhab, el-Aḥmar, Barḳān, Shemhūrish, el-Abyaḍ, and el-Meimūn." See also E. Doutté, *Magie et religion dans l'Afrique du nord* (Algiers, 1909), p. 120.

[2] See note 1. Baraḳān, or Barḳān, means 'Shining One.' He appears as Barakon in an invocation addressed to him in the *Clavicula Salomonis*; see H. Gollancz, *Sepher Maphteaḥ Shelomo* (*Book of the Key of Sọlomon*), *an exact Facsimile of an original Book of Magic in Hebrew* (Oxford, 1914), pp. xii ff.

[3] For the use of his name in charms see F. Lexa, *La magie dans l'Égypte antique de l'ancien empire jusqu'à l'époque copte* (Paris, 1925), vol. i, p. 158; vol. ii, pp. 169 f., 171 f., 174 f., 178, 182.

[4] Otherwise not known. He is not included in the well-known list in note 1.

---

[1] For the use of his name in a charm see F. Lexa, *op. cit.*, vol. ii, p. 177.

[2] For a number of occurrences of his name in charms see F. Lexa, *op. cit.*, vol. i, p. 194 (index); also see F. Ll. Griffith and H. Thompson, *The Demotic Magical Papyrus of London and Leiden* (London, 1904), p. 135.

[3] Mīyemūn (or Meimūn) and Barḳān are, Dr Scholem informs me, the most popular names in North-African Arabic magic. Meimūn occurs in the Greek form Ἀμαιμον, which is found already in the *Testamentum Salomonis*.

[4] See E. W. Lane, *The Manners and Customs of the Modern Egyptians* (London, 1871), vol. i, p. 84; vol. ii, p. 265.

[5] For the occurrence of his name in charms see F. Lexa, *op. cit.*, vol. ii, pp. 165, 169, 172, 182.

[6] For other occurrences of this angel's name in charms see F. Lexa, *op. cit.*, vol. ii, pp. 165, 169, 172.

[7] This name does not occur in the list on p. 321, note 1, and is unknown to Dr Scholem. Mr E. S. Thomas, however, reminded my brother that Ṭarish is mentioned along with an associate Ṭaryūsh in a spell published by E. W. Lane, *op. cit.*, vol. i, p. 339. It is to be noted that Ṭarish (or Ṭarsh, as Lane spells the name) and Ṭaryūsh do not appear in this spell as kings, but Lane states that the magician who wrote it claimed them as his familiar spirits.

[8] This name does not occur in the list on p. 321, note 1. Dr Scholem tells me that Zoba is only known to him in the name Abu Zoba', which is mentioned in the Hebrew *Clavicula Salomonis* (see H. Gollancz, *op. cit.*, folio 36*b*) in a portion that is entirely Arabic in its origin. But there Abu Zoba is one of the three servants of Bargan (=Barḳān), not a king himself.

GEOGRAPHICAL INDEX

GENERAL INDEX

[1] My brother informs me that treasure, believed to be hidden in Kōm ed-Dīnār (an ancient rubbish mound) at Ehnāsiyeh el-Medīneh, is likewise supposed to be guarded by a cock.

GENERAL INDEX

GENERAL INDEX

Sweet-seller, 266
Sycamore leaves used in remedy for diarrhœa, 210

Table, small, made of mid-ribs of palm-branches, 161
Taboos, 42, 68, 121
Tamarisk, branch of, used in magical ceremony, 188; leaves of, 205; stone of, 203
Tambourines, 198, 245
Tattoo patterns, 51 ff.
Tattooer, 51, 168
Tattooing, 50 ff., 283 f.; as cure for toothache and other complaints, 53; as cure for spirit-possession, 54; as sign of manhood, 55; to prolong life of child, 54
Tattooing needles, 51
Teaching of Amenōphis the Son of Kanakht, The, 306
Thread, silken, used in cure of pain in stomach and in cure for fever, 210
Threshing, 173; primitive method of, 180
Threshing-floor, 173; feast at, food remaining from, placed in heaps of grain, 176
Threshing-machine (*nōrag*), 173
Tiles, 148
Tinsmith, 167
Tomb, of dead child visited by mother to ensure conception, 101; of sheikh, 31, 240 ff.; endowed with land or money, 240; model of boat hung up in, 242; perambulation of catafalque in, 242; sick animals brought to, 242; visited by childless women, the sick, etc., 99, 242; votive candles lighted in, 31, 241, 246; votive offerings hung in, 99, 241 f., 248
Town, 280
Traders, 165, 168
Train, railway, 102
Treasure, hidden, 188 ff.
Tree, sacred, of Māri Mīna el-'Agayebi, 248
Trenches, narrow, for purposes of irrigation, 169, 305
Twin, soul of, in cat, 75, 89
Two Brothers, Tale of the, 288.

Umbilical cord, 64, 79, 287
Unchastity in girls, 44 f., 283
Unfaithfulness in wives, 283
Urine of man, 195

Vault, family burial, 116
Veil, 59 f., 285 f.; ornaments of gold and silver on, 59 f.; torn off in demonstration of grief, 124
Vendors, itinerant, 29
Venereal disease, 108
Ventilator (*malḳaf*), 280
Viceroy of Ethiopia, 314
Villages, 26, 28 f., 280; dirt and squalor of, 30
Vinegar, red, 205
Vizier, 272, 275 f.

Wages in kind, 32, 173 f., 180, 310
Wailing—*see under* Cemetery, Funeral and funerary ceremonies, *and* Mourners
Washing of child on seventh day after birth, 76 ff., 287; of corpse, 109, 123
Water, fetching household, 40; for washing corpse, 102, 109, 293; holy, 263; regularly given to dying Muslim, 109; sprinkled in Coptic funerary ceremony, 127
Water-bottle (*ḳulleh*), 140, 149, 151 f., 167, 231 f., 237
Water-carrier, 168, 266, 269
Water-hoist (*shādūf*), 170 f., 306
Water-jar, 75, 137 f., 142, 149, 151, 153, 220; carried on the head, 156
Water-wheel, 171
Weaning, 81, 288 f.
Weaver, 29
Weaving, 162
Wedding, and wedding procession—*see under* Marriage, procession and ceremonies at
Wheat, 78
Wheat-flour, 163
Whip, leather, 130 f.
Wife's brother, special position of, 39, 282
Wigs, 284
Winnowing, 172 f., 180; ceremonies connected with, 172, 308 ff.
Winnowing-fork, 173, 311
Women, Egyptian, 36 ff.; emancipation of, 36; inferior position of, 36

Yeast, 163, 205

Zaubersprüche für Mutter und Kind, 312
Zephyr, smelling of the (*Shemm en-Nesīm*), 261
Zinc, sulphate of, 203